Canterbury

Foothills
Forests

Second

A Walking and Tramping Guide

Canterbury

Foothills
& Forests

Second Edition

PAT BARRETT

First edition published in 2002 by Shoal Bay Press
This edition published in 2014 by
CANTERBURY UNIVERSITY PRESS
University of Canterbury
Private Bag 4800, Christchurch
NEW ZEALAND
www.cup.canterbury.ac.nz

ISBN 978-1-927145-57-9

A catalogue record for this book is available from the National Library of New Zealand.

Cover concept by Working Ideas
Book design and layout by Quentin Wilson & Associates, Christchurch
Maps by Allan Kynaston
Typeset in Adobe Garamond Pro

Front cover: Pat Barrett on summit of Mt Grey, Ashburton Lakes Basin in background
Back cover, left to right: Dominique and Christine Barrett at Lake Coleridge lakeside; Twin Fall Stream, Arthur's Pass National Park; Nick Ashley in Terrible Gully, Steepface Hill, Rakaia Valley, Hakatere Conservation Park
Half-title page: Tops above Lake Lyndon looking to Foggy Peak, Korowai/Torlesse Tussocklands Park
Title Page: Fr Antoine Thomas climbing onto Craigieburn Range summit, Puketeraki Range in background

Printed in China through Asia Pacific Offset Limited

Contents

Preface   **9**
Introduction   **11**

Rangitata Region   **35**
Peel Forest and Mt Peel   35
Te Kahui Kaupeka Conservation Park   43
Tenehaun Conservation Area   49

Ashburton Lakes and Rakaia Valley   **51**
Hakatere Conservation Park   51
Wilberforce Valley and Lake Coleridge   96

Waimakariri Plains Region   **115**
Korowai/Torlesse Tussocklands Park   115
North Canterbury Foothills and Lees Valley   135

Waimakariri Basin and Arthur's Pass National Park   **157**
Craigieburn Conservation Park and Ranges   157
Arthur's Pass National Park   179

Lewis Pass Region   **243**
Lewis Pass – Western Side   251
Lewis Pass – Eastern Side   265
Hanmer Springs Region   285

Trip Planner   **289**
Further Reading   **294**
About the Author   **295**

List of Maps

Map 1: Peel Forest and Mt Peel   36
Map 2: Te Kahui Kaupeka Conservation Park   44
Map 3: Tenehaun Conservation Area   49
Map 4: Hakatere Conservation Park   52
Map 5: Mt Somers   55
Map 6: Mt Hutt   82
Map 7: Wilberforce Valley and Lake Coleridge   98
Map 8: Korowai/Torlesse Tussocklands Park   116
Map 9: North Canterbury Foothills and Lees Valley   136
Map 10: Oxford Forest   138
Map 11: Mt Thomas Forest   143
Map 12: Ashley Forest   151
Map 13: Craigieburn Conservation Park and Ranges   158
Map 14: Arthur's Pass National Park   184
Map 15: Arthur's Pass   186
Map 16: Lewis Pass   250
Map 17: Hanmer Springs   285

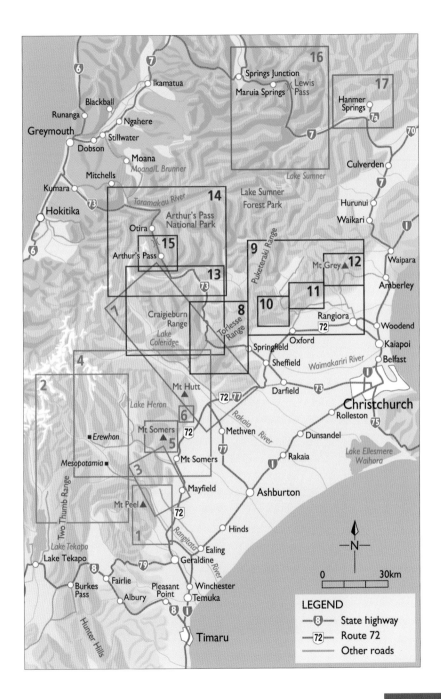

Dedication

Canterbury Foothills & Forests is dedicated to all those in our community who, for various reasons, either physical or psychological, may never get to visit the great outdoors of the region.

Pat Barrett

I had my tent in the heights, and my throne was a pillar of cloud. Alone, I have made the circuit of heavens and walked the depth of the abyss. Over the waves of the sea and over the whole earth, and over every people and nation I have held sway.

Ecclesiasticus 24:4–6

Tent camp on Foggy Peak, Korowai/Torlesse Tussock-lands Park

Preface

I have long cherished my outdoor associations with Canterbury and in particular the region's iconic high country. Though not a born and bred Cantabrian, having been raised in Wellington, I have come to love the uniqueness of the mountain landscape that broods on the back doorstep of Christchurch. It is a landscape that is difficult to ignore, be you an outdoor enthusiast or not, as the nuances of the land regularly funnel nor'west gales over the plains, southerlies plaster the alps with masses of ski-able snow each winter and in the process often curtail travel almost anywhere in the region for days at a time, while fairer weather brings an influx of holidaymakers to swim or boat at one of the numerous lakes and rivers.

Having tramped, climbed and canoed throughout the high country I can claim to know it well, yet there is always the elusive, the unknown, the unvisited corners of the alps and foothills where I have not yet trod, and perhaps never will. For no matter how many years one might invest in such pursuits one can never see it all, nor during each passing season when the colour and form of the land change by the week. It is these attributes of the landscape, and the means to reach them, that I have attempted to capture in this book and so to share my enthusiasm with those of you who may wish to follow me on some of these journeys of discovery.

This edition is much expanded from the first, having become a 'work of the years', tramping hidden corners in an effort to illustrate other works and the columns I write for various publications, or just to imbibe the perfect beauty of a cool morning atop a foothill summit when tomorrow seemed a lifetime away. That many of these excursions have taken place in the passage of one day, and in some cases just a morning, highlights the accessibility of the high country. Yet I must add a note of caution here, for though these places are accessible from Christchurch, or other parts of the plains, they come so at a price – the price of endeavour. To reach a foothill summit, or valley, at dawn, or indeed at any time, takes planning and some aptitude for the dangers and challenges that accompany such a mission.

Timing is crucial, as is season, weather, wind, snow, cloud, river levels, fitness, equipment, and of course the will to go and forsake the normal comforts of life. Companions are often lacking for this sort of commitment, though I have found a few along the way, as you will also, so some of my forays are solitary affairs, which for me heightens both the sense of endeavour and achievement and moves the heart and mind to a greater awareness of God in His creation.

The natural beauty of Canterbury is then a reflection of God, and this book a waypoint, a signpost to a greater beginning, which I pray you may find as you journey with me through the Canterbury foothills and forests.

Pat Barrett

Disclaimer

While every effort has been made to ensure that all information is accurate, the mountains of New Zealand are a dynamic region; storms and erosion are continually modifying the environment. As well as this, decisions by the Department of Conservation (DOC) and landowners continue to affect access rights and facilities. I therefore accept no responsibility or liability for any accident, injury, perceived right of access, or use, associated with this guide. Note that all routes and tracks marked on maps in this guide are approximate only. These should not be taken as an accurate indication of the route or track as it lies on the ground and/or as a right of access where the route crosses private land.

Acknowledgements

This book would not have been possible without the help and support of many people, especially Catherine Montgomery, Publisher at Canterbury University Press, for her commitment to this project, Allan Kynaston for his excellent maps, Katrina Rainey for her careful editing, Ray Prebble for his meticulous proofreading, and Quentin Wilson for his effective design. With special thanks to Michael, Ben and Nick Latty, Fr Antoine Thomas, Tim and Ben Hayward, Bryce Jenkins, Peter and Ian Umbers, Nick Ashley and Zac, my daughters, Anna-Marie, Dominique and Bernadette, and especially my wife, Christine, for enduring many a strenuous encounter with the foothills in search of elusive routes and views.

Introduction

Background to the Second Edition

Since I penned the first edition of this book in 2002 and the subsequent reprint in 2004 there have been some major changes to the accessibility of the Canterbury high country, particularly to the Crown leasehold land throughout the region and notably in the major river catchments of the Rakaia, Wilberforce and Rangitata valleys. Fortunately I am able to report that much of this tenure review process has resulted in numerous additions to the high-country recreational estate, which is now managed by the Department of Conservation (DOC). While this process of land retirement and the way in which payments have been made has not been without some controversy, and is still ongoing, the areas that have come 'on-stream' for recreationalists have been welcome additions to the breath of outdoor opportunity in the greater Canterbury area. More areas will follow in the future and this will continue to add to the incredible variety of places to visit, which are entirely free of any difficulties relating to access. It remains to be seen, however, how DOC and the increasing influence of Māori and commercial interests will govern this land for all New Zealanders in perpetuity and not be swayed by an elite cartel of big-business-minded individuals and groups. I hope that the freedom of access, in its broadest sense, to the wild lands that lie on the doorstep of both Cantabrians and all New Zealanders will remain inviolate so that future generations may enjoy and benefit from interacting with nature throughout the many places in this magnificent region.

About this Book

Canterbury Foothills & Forests draws together most of the marked tracks, huts and recognised tramping routes of the foothills region. It covers the area from Mt Peel/Rangitata River in the south to Mt Grey in the north. It also includes Korowai/Torlesse Tussocklands Park, Hakatere Conservation Park, Te Kahui Kaupeka Conservation Park, Craigieburn Conservation Park, parts of the St James Conservation Area, the Lewis Pass region road corridor, and the high-country basins and lakes of the designated region. These include the mid-reaches of the Rangitata, Rakaia, Wilberforce and Waimakariri rivers. Lees Valley and Arthur's Pass National Park have been added for completeness. Aside from the popular tramping areas in Arthur's Pass, the guide does not cover access to, or tramps/climbs in, the central Southern Alps.

Canterbury Foothills & Forests includes walks and tramps suitable for a range of fitness levels. Families and the moderately fit will enjoy the many short walks along well-marked tracks. Those who aspire to harder trips, or who simply love the spectacular nature and astonishing variety of views gained from the tops, will wish to attempt some of the higher summits, some of which are very challenging excursions. Many of these routes make good training climbs for harder peaks in the Southern Alps. All the longer walks in the guide can be completed in 2–3 days and are within the scope/ability of most averagely fit trampers.

Canterbury Foothills & Forests does not include every peak or route but does incorporate the most notable or accessible options in each area. None of this can currently be found in any one book, and in fact, many of the basins and peaks have never before been presented in a single guidebook for trampers and climbers.

The Walk Descriptions

Each walk description includes:
- The walking time involved.
- A grade for the walk (from **Easy** to **Hard+**).
- Standard access information (including phone numbers for landowners where applicable).
- Details for the best route available.
- The attractions of a particular track/peak.
- Notes on the weather, terrain and equipment you need to carry.
- A brief overview of the geography, vegetation and history of the region.

Where possible there is also a map provided in order to show routes and tracks, however it is not intended that they should be a substitute for carrying the appropriate map.

Walk Times

Assessment of walk times assumes the following criteria: average fitness and ability, fine weather, no (or minimal) snow, average river levels, summer or autumn conditions, regular rest stops for longer walks (5–10 minutes each hour), a light day-pack weight for day walks and an average pack weight (15–18kg) for overnight or multi-day walks. No allowance has been made for lunch stops. There are, of course, many variables to consider when attempting a particular trip, and therefore a grading system is always a little subjective.

The terms 'river right' and 'river left' have been used throughout the text, this denotes right and left, respectively, when facing downstream in a river or valley.

Walk Grades

Easy: Short day walks (up to 2 hours) on well-defined paths or tracks, no major river crossings. Generally a flat or easy gradient that is suitable for running shoes or light-weight boots.

Easy/Moderate: Longer walks, up to 3–4 hours, on well-defined paths or tracks. River crossings possible. Tramping boots required.

Moderate: Longer day or overnight tramps; 4–6 hours walking per day on well-defined tracks. Generally moderate gradients but some steeper climbing. Some river crossings. Boots required.

Hard: As for moderate but with over 6 hours walking per day. Steep ascents/descents with river crossings. Some untracked, though possibly poled, routes on the tops. Very strenuous. Boots required. In winter an ice axe, crampons and basic snowcraft will be required on routes above the bushline.

Hard+: 8 or more hours walking per day with very steep ascents/descents and some rock scrambling. Virtually the entire route is unmarked or untracked and requires a high level of fitness, map-reading and route-finding skills, together with weather judgement skills. An arduous trek. Boots required. In winter an ice axe, crampons and basic snowcraft are essential.

Planning a Trip

The Weather: A Warning

No matter how pleasant the day may be when you set out, it can rapidly deteriorate into very chilling exposure conditions, especially if you are above the bushline or in an open valley. Your best defence is to be prepared. Carry the right equipment (see below) and check the weather forecast before you leave home.

Northwesterly conditions and associated fronts and lows will often bring moderate to heavy rainfall to the western slopes of the Main Divide, with significant spill-over rain affecting eastern catchments up to 10km east of the Southern Alps. Unless you are attempting a short walk on marked and bridged tracks, and are prepared to get wet, you should postpone your excursion to another day. Remember that New Zealand is a coastal country and intense

Morrison footbridge, Otira River in flood, 21 December 2010

bursts of rain, together with thunderstorms and strong winds, are common. During such events rivers can rise extremely rapidly (in less than an hour), stranding the unwary and turning a pleasant outing into a survival experience.

Southeasterly patterns convey heavy rain and/or snow into the region and these conditions may last for several days. Southwesterly flows often bring wet weather right along both sides of the ranges. Both southerly flows (east and west) bring snow in winter, which can fall to very low levels. Forecasts of wind speeds over 60kph will make nearly all tops routes unviable.

If you are attempting a climb of one of the major foothill summits it is vital that you check the weather and snow forecast before you go. Be prepared to try an alternative trip in a sheltered location if bad weather is forecast. **Don't take risks with river crossings.**

If you are planning to tackle a high summit in winter you must be conversant with basic alpine techniques, including the use of ice axe and crampons. Some of the routes in this guide are true alpine summits and can present significant avalanche danger during winter and spring.

Safe travel in avalanche terrain involves the use of avalanche transceivers, snow shovels, observation of the snowpack and keeping to ridgelines. Basins and faces often present a moderate to extreme hazard and should be avoided.

Alpine safety skills are taught by local mountain clubs; however, there is no substitute for experience. Be prepared, and go with those who know the dangers and terrain.

With proper preparation your visit can be very enjoyable at any time of year.

Tell Someone Where You're Going

Make sure you let someone know exactly where you are going, what you plan to do, including alternatives, and when you will be back. Leave a written description of the track or route. You should fill out any intentions cards at track entrances and enter your name and route in hut books en route. Remember to sign out again on the way home.

A personal locator beacon (PLB) is an excellent insurance measure, especially if tramping alone. With one of these, emergency help can be summoned at any time from anywhere.

Clothing and Equipment

Minimum Required for Day Trips
Durable and waterproof rain-parka, bush shirt or thermo/polar fleece jacket, woolly hat, sun hat, polypropylene longs or tracksuit bottom (1), and tops (2), warm gloves/mittens, lunch, water bottle, first-aid kit, camera, spare socks, day pack, lightweight tramping boots, map and compass, small torch, whistle, waterproof overtrousers, gaiters, shorts, toilet paper, insect repellent, pencil and paper, sun block, matches or lighter. In winter: heavier boots, ice axe and crampons on the major climbs.

Minimum Required for Overnight Trips
As above, plus: sleeping bag, large pack, sleeping mat, cooker, billies, eating utensils and plate, cup, extra set of clothing, food, tent or fly, pack liner.

Huts
Almost all huts in the area are managed by DOC (where this is not the case, it has been noted in the text), with fees payable via the hut ticket/hut pass system. This does not apply to small 2–3-person bivvies, which are free.

Most huts are 'standard', some are 'serviced'. Standard hut: $5.00; youth rate (11–17 years): $2.50. Serviced hut: $15.00; youth rate: $7.50. One ticket per person per night. No charge for children 5–10 years. Rates correct at time of writing. Annual hut passes are also available.

Please take care with fires in and around huts. Make sure they are out on departure. Sweep and tidy the hut and replace any firewood you use. Make sure the doors and windows are closed when you leave.

Camping
Numerous river- and lakeside campsites are scattered throughout the region. These have been noted in the text where relevant. All sites are available on a first-come, first-served basis, and are paid for through a self-registering honesty system at the entrance to the area (up to $8.00 per person per night; $4.50 for children). Most have toilets, tables, and designated areas for camping, and are open all year. There are also other possibilities for free roadside and track entrance camping.

You should not leave tents and equipment unattended at any of these sites.

Tramping group at Boundary Hut, South Ashburton

Car Security

Unfortunately, both the Arthur's Pass and Lewis Pass highways have a reputation for car break-ins, even when vehicles are left unattended for very short periods of time.

Wherever you are, don't leave valuables in your car while you are away walking. The best 'security' is to park your car out of sight of the main road. Another alternative is to leave your car at a nearby settlement and use a bicycle as a 'shuttle' between the carpark and track head. (Hide the bicycle in the bush for your return.)

With a little planning, any risk can be minimised or eliminated.

Wasps

We are fortunate in New Zealand to be free of large predators or other dangerous animals in forest and mountain areas. However, the German wasp has now become well established throughout our beech forests and presents a considerable hazard to trampers, especially in late summer and autumn. You would be well advised to avoid going 'off-track' in beech forests with high wasp numbers during this period.

Planning for the Wilderness

I remember tramping, late one afternoon, many years back, into the Whataroa Valley in South Westland for an overnight stay in one of the lower valley huts. The Whataroa is extremely rugged country and covers a huge catchment from Tasman Saddle at Mt Cook all the way along the Divide to the Godley/Rangitata headwaters. Consequently, rainfall and flooding in the lower valley is, at times, catastrophic. Not being very familiar with the valley we arrived tired and hungry at the hut site on the river flats and spent a frustrating hour searching for the shelter. We did find it, or at least parts of it. The roof was thrown up in the low scrub, the stove was up-ended in sand and mud, and various sections of bunks, mattresses, utensils and iron lay scattered about the sandy flat and beach near the river. A monster flood had totally destroyed the hut and thus forced us to camp in a tent fly on the wet sand, with the mosquitoes, no fire or hot dinner and little sleep. It wasn't life threatening, but it was very uncomfortable and, as the rain continued next day, a short, unpleasant introduction to the wilds of the Whataroa.

A little extra planning and information would most probably have avoided this situation. This pre-trip planning is the number one priority for any venture into the mountains, yet often it is overlooked. There may come a time when you do face a very serious outcome and then you will chide yourself for not having put in that extra effort in pre-trip planning. Of course not all trips require the same effort in planning; not all of us are hoping to ski to the South Pole or climb K2. Major expeditions like these require years of planning. However, you can put yourself at just as much risk on a weekend tramp or climb as does an explorer on a three-month trek to the Pole. In both cases there are various facets of the trip to consider.

As a background on which to base this planning framework, assume that I am relating it to trips of 3 days' to 2 weeks' duration, in lightly tracked, or untracked terrain. However, the basic principles apply to any venture in the hills, even a day trip.

Length and Difficulty

These points, along with weather, ground conditions, experience and party size, need to be considered together when planning. The sky's the limit here with regards to time and difficulty and is only curtailed by the above factors and your imagination.

I encourage you to be bold and enthusiastic about your venture and to consider untracked wilderness areas, which in most cases will take at least 2 days to reach, possibly via an alpine pass. Planning a trip of over a week's duration is exciting and absorbing. This time frame allows you, weather permitting, to enter some remote and rugged country, where you really can begin to live the experience rather than get just the quick 'shot' of enjoyment discovered on a weekend tramp. I find that it generally takes me about 2–3 days to adjust to the pace of life, the constant pack weight on my back, and the steady exercise that goes with a long trip. Long tramps are demanding, physically and mentally, but the rewards far outweigh the effort expended.

Head of Rangitata River from Mt Guy

Weather, Ground Conditions and Season

This is the catch-all for any trip: weather and conditions. If you are going far afield, for a week or more, you can probably afford some bad weather, either immediately prior to your departure (e.g. new snow on the route or high river levels), or during the trip.

Make sure you allow for rest days, which can become bad weather stuck-in-the-hut/tent days, or just days to relax and enjoy a fantastic location that has taken a week to reach. It is probable that you may never be this way again, or at least not in such perfect conditions, so make sure you enjoy it! Bad weather may of course affect the success or completion of the route you have chosen, particularly if it is over high ground (e.g. an alpine pass, glacier, summit or high ridge traverse), so plan accordingly. Make sure you have an escape route and/or enough food to sit out bad weather. Will you be able to return over your inward route, in safety, if conditions so dictate?

All of these factors must be considered and must be carefully weighed, particularly if the area you are visiting is remote and difficult to access. Season will play a big part in choosing the route through a given area or in entering an area at all. Winter conditions, avalanche risk and cold are the obvious seasonal factors, but so are spring thaw in the major rivers you have to cross, wind on exposed tops, and even sunshine. Are you prepared for days of hot sun on the tops or on a glacier, where the heat can be extreme? Has it been a good or a poor snow year? How has this affected glacier routes and passes? Are they still negotiable? In summer, will new snow on the route present a major safety risk? This may be particularly so if you are planning to traverse steep tussock faces and gullies.

Most importantly, are the rivers crossable? Have you allowed for delays, by carrying extra food and allowing extra time, if river levels rise? Rivers are still the number one hazard for all back-country trips.

Party Size and Experience

This will dictate where and when you go. A large party (more than six) will always be slower, though probably more resilient and certainly more sociable on a long trip, where personalities can clash in a smaller group. It may be that you have one or two very experienced people and the rest are relatively inexperienced, which can work well if you are entering a challenging region, as long as all are fit.

Trampers fording the Lawrence River

If you plan to use huts en route, a smaller party is better; check hut conditions and size first!

Maps, Routes, Guides and Access

I love studying maps and route guides. You can learn a great deal from careful observation of a topographical map with regard to difficulty of the terrain to be covered, the time it will take in hours and days, hazards, new routes and, importantly, escape routes. You must be familiar with, or at least aware of, the escape routes on a glacier, ridge traverse or summit. Reading the map together with any available route guide and even aerial photos will help immeasurably in planning the trip. This of course relates to untracked wilderness where information may be hard to find. Perhaps you can refer to old Alpine Club journals or speak to someone who has done the trip before. Forewarned is forearmed.

Do not plan a potentially difficult trip using only a Park map or National Park map. There is simply not enough detail on these sheets, though they are good for overall reference and planning the number of days needed. The 1:50,000 series are indispensable for proper planning. Make sure the sheet/s you take cover all of the route and escape routes.

Check with DOC to see if there has been any recent storm damage to tracks, bridges and routes you will be using. Are all the huts and bivvies still there?

Do you need to consider boat or air access? Many trampers and climbers are now using portable GPS (global positioning systems), which can be invaluable for locating your position in difficult terrain or in cloud. However, they are not infallible and should not take the place of solid map-reading and compass skills.

Access to Private Land

Public access is allowed onto all the tracks in this guide that are on public conservation land, though in some cases DOC may restrict access due to track damage or heavy snowfalls. However, some routes cross private farmland to access the track or trip route. In these cases access is not by right but solely at the discretion of the landowner concerned. It is essential that, where this is the case, permission is sought first, before going into the area. Permission to enter may be declined during lambing season (September–November) and at other times due to farm management practices. Phone numbers for the relevant stations are supplied. It is your responsibility to obtain permission first. Be prepared to find an alternative trip.

Food and Fuel

If your trip is more than 4 days long you will wish to save as much weight as possible.

Personal preferences come to the fore here, so it is up to the individual, though you might like to consider such staples for long tramps as cabin bread, salami, dehydrated stew, rice, muesli, pasta, noodles, etc. Remember to remove all unnecessary packaging and to weigh out or measure daily requirements, and especially to allow for emergency food, at least 2–3 days' worth for a trip of a week or more. This emergency quota can be less than the amount you would normally eat (i.e. rations).

Have you considered a food drop by 4WD, jet boat or air? If you are a large party it can be cost effective and allow for some mid-trip treats! Also consider the fuel required. Will you be able to cook on hut or camp-fires en route, or will you be mostly above the bushline? If so, food that requires less cooking time will be important.

There are many different types of camp cookers (e.g. Primus) now available on the market. Choose one that is efficient, lightweight, easy to pack, and can be pressurised for faster cooking and at altitude. Most of the better brands offer multi-fuel capability.

Shelters

Even if your route includes several mountain huts, you should still carry a tent for emergency shelter and in case of full huts. Tents also allow for more flexibility and for taking advantage of spectacular campsites in fine weather. Tent size will depend on party numbers, but in general 2–3-person mountain tents are the best option. Make sure tents are lightweight (1.8–2.5kg), easy to erect, double-walled, have aluminium shock-corded poles, and are robust enough to withstand New Zealand conditions, particularly the wind. Some imported and camping tents are just not strong enough to withstand our severe mountain climate.

Equipment

All of the standard items apply (see the list under 'Clothing and equipment' above), however you may require some additional special items, such as an ice axe, crampons, rope and harness, prusik loops, snow stakes, descenders and carabiners, and all basic climbing gear for glacier travel. In addition, avalanche transceivers, and maybe a mountain radio, PLB or GPS, should be carried. I am keen on mountain radios, having used them on more than one occasion to heli-vac an injured party member to hospital. They are small, light and easy to use, and you can obtain daily weather updates, pass on messages to those at home re your progress, and make any changes to destination, pick-up times and other arrangements. You can even get a new pair of boots or extra food flown in, in an emergency. You will find a local contact near you through the phonebook, outdoor shops or Federated Mountain Clubs.

Landscape and Climate

All of the main valleys are deep and steep-sided, with the typical 'U' profile of glaciated regions, though this has been rounded out somewhat in the larger valleys by the onset of erosion, which has led to slumping of the lower valley walls.

There are large active glaciers located in the heads of all the main catchments south of the Wilberforce River, with extensive ice sheets in both the upper Rakaia and Rangitata rivers. Generally, only small glaciers exist north of the Rakaia, the notable exceptions being the White River and Crow glaciers in Arthur's Pass National Park. This is also where present-day glaciation ceases in the South Island.

Screes, rock avalanches and erosion are common landscape features, accelerated by the extremes of mountain weather, heavy snow accumulation in winter, and sudden, intense rainstorms accompanied by violent winds brought about by periods of prevailing nor'west conditions.

Several major earthquake faultlines run through the region, especially in the north and west, as well as several smaller fracture lines. These faults are a dynamic feature of the uplifting and folding of the topography of the South Island mountains contained within the greater context of the Southern Alps uplift, and have shaped, and continue to shape, the land. Much of the rock throughout the region is greywacke. Sedimentary layering and folding is widespread, giving further confirmation of the rock having been laid under immense volumes of water and later lifted and tilted while still soft. Such a scenario is completely in accord with a historical catastrophic, and worldwide, deluge, as has been postulated.

A mountain climate prevails throughout the region, with variability the governing factor. High summer temperatures and dry conditions can quickly be followed by cold, rain and even snow. The entire area is subject to gale-force westerlies, which prevail in spring and summer, though some lee catchments provide welcome respite from the wind. This is especially noticeable in the foothill forests.

Rainfall ranges from 8000mm on the Divide at Arthur's Pass to 1000mm on the eastern flats of the rivers and foothill terraces. Snowfall is erratic, with some years experiencing regular heavy falls throughout the winter, while other years have late snow and smaller falls. In general, the heaviest falls occur between June and September, when the upper valley flats can experience falls in excess of 1m, with notably more on the high tops.

Vegetation

The striking differences observed in vegetation types when travelling through the region form one of the lasting impressions of the Canterbury foothills. In little more than 20km, dry tussock grasslands merge with beech forest, hardy alpine plants, and the lush sub-tropical forests of the western slopes

Sub-alpine plants, Korowai/Torlesse Tussocklands Park

Mt Cook Lilies, Zit Creek, Toaroha Range, Westland

that extend to the Tasman Sea. It is a dramatic transition, set against the beautiful backdrop of the Southern Alps.

The riverbeds contain herbs, mat daisies, woolly moss and lichens, together with dense thickets of hardy matagouri and short tussock grasses. Mountain beech forests dominate the eastern valley fringes and walls, while closer to the Divide these forests become more complex, with understorey plants such as lancewood, threefinger, mountain tōtara, cedar, and bush lawyer vines.

Beyond the beech forests, sub-alpine shrublands prevail. Near the Divide, dense interlocking communities of shrubs form colourful patchworks on the flanks of the mountains, whilst above these, in the alpine zone, can be found waving snow tussocks and flowering herbs, which are best seen in early to mid-summer. Farther east, this zone of interlocking shrubs is entirely absent: here beech forest gives way to tussock, scattered scrub and broad talus slopes.

Big tōtara, Peel Forest

Gentians, daisies, forget-me-nots, violets, eyebrights, forsterias and many others await patient exploration. There are over 300 species of alpine plants in Arthur's Pass National Park.

The foothill forests contain much more diverse vegetation owing to their lower altitude and more sheltered aspect from the drying effect of the nor'west winds. Here large podocarp species such as rimu, mataī, miro and kahikatea are found, along with Hall's tōtara, fuchsia, tree ferns, red beech, and some broadleaf species.

Bird and Animal Life

All of the common bird species are distributed widely throughout the various habitats of the region. In the forests you may see and hear rifleman, tomtit, bellbird, fantail, grey warbler, robin, wood pigeon (kererū) and brown creeper. Also present are kākā, parakeet (kākāriki; mostly yellow-crowned) and long-tailed cuckoo, which migrate from the Pacific Islands in the summer. Riverbeds reveal paradise duck, oystercatcher, dotterel and introduced species such as Canada goose and spur-winged plover.

Kea, Arthur's Pass

There are several rare or uncommon species present: rock wren, great spotted kiwi (found on both sides of the Divide and around Arthur's Pass village), blue duck, which are found in the fast-flowing regions of the river headwaters, and yellowhead in the more remote forested valleys.

Kea are also common and are inclined to be a nuisance, especially when fed by curious tourists. These fully protected native birds are the world's only alpine parrot. Their distinctive raucous call ('keeeaaa') is one of the special, haunting sounds of the New Zealand alpine environment. They are declining in numbers.

Red deer, chamois, opossum, stoat, weasel, wild cat, hare, rabbit, goat, and occasionally pig can be found throughout the region.

1080: ENOUGH IS ENOUGH

It is becoming increasingly apparent to me that the widespread use of the broad-spectrum 1080 poison is decimating kea populations as well as populations of other common forest birds, despite claims by various government agencies to the contrary. I question whether trapping and the use of other poisons have been fully explored as options for the control of possums, rats and stoats, and fear that in using 1080 indiscriminately to control predators we risk poisoning an entire ecosystem. 1080 kills everything that metabolises oxygen. It is taken up in the food chain, and may disrupt both the endocrine system and mitochondrial DNA. Little wonder that 1080 is banned in many countries. I believe that 1080 will be shown to be, in time, just the latest environmental disaster inflicted on this nation, but I hope it will not by then be too late to reverse the damage that is currently being sown. Further information on this concerning issue can be found in the sources listed below.

Further reading

Benfield, W.F. (2011) *The Third Wave: Poisoning the Land*. Tross Publishing
Department of Conservation (2014) *Battle for our Birds: Beech Mast 2014. 1080 in New Zealand: Facts and Figures.* (www.doc.govt.nz/conservation/restoration-projects/battle-for-our-birds-beech-mast-2014/1080-in-new-zealand-facts-and-figures/)
The Graf Boys. *Poisoning Paradise – Ecocide in New Zealand* (DVD)
Murray, P. (2009) *Poison-Free New Zealand: Enuf is Enuf.* (www.enufisenuf.co.nz)
New Zealand Deerstalkers' Association submission about application number HRE05002: Reassessment of sodium fluoroacetate (1080) and substances containing 1080 (a vertebrate toxin). (www.nzdanelson.co.nz/files/Nelson%20Echo%20-%20Aug.pdf)
Scanlon, P. (2014) Oral submission for 1080 application number HRE 05002. (www.godocs.org/docs/index-247747.html)
Hon. Dr Nick Smith: Annual Speech to Rotary Club at Nelson, 29 Jan 2014. (www.beehive.govt.nz/speech/annual-speech-rotary-club-nelson)

Snow road, Hakatere Conservation Park

A Brief History of the Canterbury Foothills

The history of the foothills, like much of Canterbury, began with the early Māori moa-hunters of 500–800 years ago. These nomadic groups wandered the vast area of the plains and valleys seeking their elusive prey, as well as foraging and exploring into the valley headwaters looking for trading routes and greenstone in the large catchments that drain the alps. Many of these passes were not negotiable, as they were either icebound or too precipitous to be used as regular trading trails. Some, however, were actively used by Māori tribes, especially Browning Pass at the head of the Wilberforce River and Harper Pass from the Hurunui to the Taramakau. Arthur's Pass was undoubtedly used, but only sporadically, as its gorge was steep and difficult. Evidence of these early groups can be found at Mt Somers, where primitive drawings are still preserved in rock shelters.

The hunting method employed by early Māori in their search for moa included the widespread use of fire, both to flush the birds and remove their cover. This and the subsequent burning and felling of the remaining and still extensive forests, which once covered Canterbury, by the early European settlers reduced the native forest cover to the remnants now found among the foothills.

The settlers used the timber to construct the towns and cities of the new colony and provide the comforts of a modern industrialised society, without which the fledgling nation could not have developed. Various milling operations were established throughout Canterbury, notably at Peel Forest, Mt Hutt and Mt Oxford, where large mechanised mills were set up in the 1850s and continued running until around 1912 (Coopers Creek).

With the demise of the mills came farming and grazing, which had already been well established in the high country.

Mt Somers has an additional chapter to add to the list of extraction industries developed in Canterbury: coal mining. Coal was discovered here in 1856 and collieries were delivering coal by 1864. A railway track was constructed, using pick and shovel, and this moved coal from the mine down a very steep gradient (up which the track now winds) to where it could be transported by the Mt Somers branch railway. The mine was worked until 1954, when underground fires, some of which are still smouldering, and uneconomic returns forced their closure.

(See also sections on Arthur's Pass National Park and the Lewis Pass Region.)

The High-country Basins and Summits

These southern and central areas include the Rangitata and Rakaia watersheds, from the foothills abutting the plains in the north and west into the high lakes and basins. They contain the highest foothill summits, including Mt Taylor (2333m) in the Lake Heron Basin.

Large sparkling lakes, glacier-fed rivers, steep-sided foothill peaks and small remnant forests are some of the distinctive landscape features. The mighty Southern Alps form a dramatic backdrop, the ever-changing views of which are a commendable reason for any visit to this part of the foothills. In every sense these two large catchments define the essence of the high country, its allure and mystique. The space and light here are unimaginable until viewed, especially on a clear morning, in any season.

The Te Araroa Trail

A nationwide trail, the Te Araroa Trail (the Long Pathway), extends for 3000km from Cape Reinga, at the tip of the North Island, to Bluff, at the foot of the South Island, traversing through the Canterbury high-country region. As far as *Canterbury Foothills & Forests* is concerned, the route of the trail is as follows.

Te Araroa enters the region covered by this guide from the north down the upper Waiau Valley and onto the St James Walkway, exits the walkway at the Boyle River and follows the Tui Track around to the Hope River, which it then follows through to Lake Sumner and up the Hurunui River, over Harper Pass to the Taramakau Valley. The trail heads down this valley to the Deception River footbridge, up the Deception and over Goat Pass to the Mingha Valley, and out to SH73. This is then followed around to the Lagoon Saddle Track and over Lagoon Saddle to the Harper River and out to the head of Lake Coleridge. From here the trail follows the road through to the southeastern end of Lake Coleridge, where it joins the Lake Hill Track over private land to Lake Coleridge Power Station. The section of the trail between the northern side of the Rakaia and Glenrock Stream (leading to Turtons Saddle) is classed as a hazard zone by the Te Araroa Trust, as the Rakaia River is not fordable on foot anywhere through this section. Therefore, walkers are advised to cover this section by vehicle, or to walk via the roads through to Rakaia Gorge.

Once on the Rakaia River south bank the trail continues up Glenrock Stream to Turtons Saddle and on to Comyns Hut, then to Clent Hills Saddle and out to the Lake Heron Basin via Manuka Hut and Lake Emily. Continuing through the Lake Heron Basin, it traverses through to Paddle Hill Creek (access to South Branch Ashburton), then north of Mt Guy over to the broad faces above Lake Clearwater, and from there across to the Potts River mouth on the Hakatere–Potts Road.

The next trailhead to Te Araroa is on the south side of the Rangitata River, up Bush Stream. However, walkers are advised not to cross the Rangitata on foot: this section is classed as a hazard zone by the Te Araroa Trust as the river is usually not fordable on foot anywhere. Therefore, walkers are advised to make arrangements to travel to Bush Stream on the south bank by vehicle.

Once at Bush Stream the trail continues up the stream to Royal and Stone huts, over Stag Saddle and down Camp Stream to Coal Stream and the Round Hill skifield road. From here it continues on along the faces below the Richmond Range to the Lilybank Road and Lake Tekapo.

South of here, the Te Araroa Trail is outside the area covered by this guide.

Tramper on Turtons Saddle, Hakatere Conservation Park, and Te Araroa Trail

Emily Falls, Peel Forest

Rangitata Region

Peel Forest and Mt Peel

Peel Forest Park lies on the southwestern edge of the Canterbury Plains. Its sprawling summit ridge dominates the region and is clearly visible from the Port Hills.

The park is accessed through Peel Forest, a delightful rural village with a DOC visitor centre. At Arundel, on the south bank of the Rangitata River on Route 72, take the signposted turnoff to Peel Forest and turn onto Coopers Creek Peel Forest Road. Follow this for approximately 7–8km to Peel Forest settlement. There is a DOC information centre here, with the tracks beginning just 2–3km up the road.

The densely forested lower slopes are a remnant of the mixed podocarp–hardwood rainforest that once covered the area. There are still many fine species of kahikatea, tōtara and matai in the forest canopy. Many of the mature lowland trees were felled for milling, with subsequent burning and clearing of the land for pasture over the past 150 years reducing the forest to a 600-hectare reserve. However, the Denniston Bush and Big Tree walks will surprise the visitor, with several massive specimens of matai and tōtara that are estimated to be over 1000 years old.

There are numerous tracks throughout the park, all of which are well signposted and maintained, and an information centre staffed by DOC located on the Rangitata Gorge Road. These walks, ranging in length from 1 hour to all-day tramps, provide a great variety of opportunities to explore the park.

By far the most spectacular walk is the Deer Spur Track, which climbs steeply upwards to Little Mt Peel. En route you will notice the altitudinally changing forest, which finally becomes snow tussock as you pass a small tarn near the bush edge and complete the last steep pinch to the top, where a small day hut is perched out on the east face of Little Mt Peel, just below the summit. The view is stunning, taking in the whole breadth of the Canterbury Plains. It is possible to continue on along the 7km of undulating ridge-top that eventually leads to the summit of Mt Peel (1742m).

Emily, Rata and Ackland falls are three more highlights of a visit to the Mt Peel region, and all are linked via delightful forest walks along which you

LEGEND

1. Kahikatea Walk
2. Acland Falls
3. Fern Walk
4. Big Tree Walk
5. Allan's Track
6. Denniston Bush
7. Emily & Rata Falls
8. Kaikawaka Track
9. Deer Spur & Little Mt Peel
10. Middle & Big Mt Peel
11. Orari Gorge
12. Access Easements off Rangitata Gorge Rd

- 79 State highway
- 72 Route 72
- Other roads
- Walking track
- Route only
- Picnic area
- Public toilet
- Camping area
- Native forest

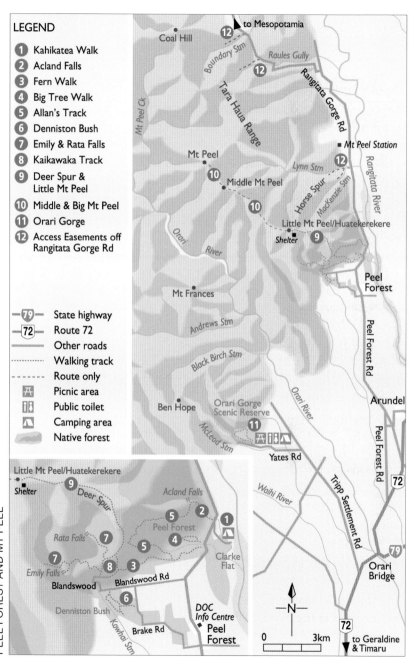

Bernadette and Christine Barrett on Big Tree Walk

may observe the more common native birds as well as the tiny rifleman as it flits from tree to tree.

Botanically, Peel Forest is significant; as well as the large podocarp varieties there are over 60 species of fern that have been identified here.

Mt Peel Forest is a place you will want to visit more than once, to cover all the walks, or perhaps to camp in the well-appointed public camping ground at Clarke Flat just 2km up the Rangitata Gorge Road. Whatever you decide, it is a wonderful mountain of walks.

1–8 Short Walks

1. Kahikatea Walk
1 hour round trip near campground. **Easy**

2. Acland Falls
1 hour round trip, up the road from campground. **Easy**

3. Fern Walk
90 minutes one way. Beautiful bush walk with big trees and numerous ferns. **Easy**

4. Big Tree Walk
30 minutes round trip to view a 1000-year-old tōtara. Suitable for wheelchairs. **Easy**

5. Allan's Track
2–3 hours round trip, climbing and traversing bush faces. It can be linked to Acland Falls Track. **Moderate**

6. Denniston Bush
90 minutes round trip. Probably the best short walk if you want to see big trees: mataī, tōtara and kahikatea. Magnificent forest. **Easy**

7. Emily and Rata Falls
1.5–2 hours round trip. Both tracks begin near Blandswood and fork to the respective falls. **Moderate**

8. Kaikawaka Track
20 minutes round trip. A loop track for a view of mountain cedar. **Easy**

9. Deer Spur and Little Mt Peel (1308m)
4–6 hours return. **Moderate**

A steep, well-formed track to an attractive bush-edge tarn at 900m for a lunch stop and onward to the summit of Little Mt Peel, the most accessible of the three summits.

For experienced walkers, the South Ridge Route can be descended by taking the main ridge behind the hut. Keep to the ridge until well down near the bush edge, where a sign indicates left, down tussock to the forest, eventually emerging in Emily Stream above the falls.

10. Middle and Big Mt Peel (1742m)
Full day. **Hard**

This is a very long, demanding ridge trip, extending for 7km beyond Little Mt Peel. It is exposed to the weather, can carry heavy snow during winter,

Morning at Little Peel Memorial Hut

and the final 1km to Mt Peel is along a narrow, loose rock ridge, which can carry snow at any time of year.

It is not a technical climb and the ridge provides fast travel, but it is suitable for experienced parties only. An ice axe and crampons should be carried if there is snow on the route. The views are outstanding.

EYES PEELED FOR DAWN – MT PEEL

Thick ice lies underfoot, freezing fog surrounds me, and darkness envelopes the frozen tussock-strewn hillocks above. I'm at the bushline on Little Mt Peel in South Canterbury, it's 7am on a winter's morning and the race is on for a short-stop summit sunrise at the peak of the mountain. The tramp up here has been easy enough despite the dark; after all there's an excellent track and some fine bush to walk through – if I could see to appreciate it. A headlamp beam doesn't quite suffice to make an impression on the gloom to reveal the vegetation, so I will have to wait for the downward leg of my sortie to experience the forest cover. Never mind, there's a task in hand and I am closing on the goal; just a few slippery boardwalks and gullies to traverse and the summit cone will be in sight. From the road at Blandswood the day before there didn't appear to be much snow on the top at all, but then 1000m lower and 4km away from the

Sunrise from trig, Little Mt Peel

top can deceive, which I am currently finding as I make my way slowly upwards. There's a hint of colour in the sky out beyond the Plains and a subtle lightening of the darkness about me, so I need to hurry before I miss the sunburst of dawn on snow and ice.

Mt Peel has three summits on the Tara Haoa Range, which runs westwards up the Rangitata Gorge to near Ben McLeod Station; they are Little Mt Peel, Middle Mt Peel, and Mt Peel, the highest at 1743m. There is close to 7km of undulating ridgeline separating the three peaks; and crossing it entails a big day out – I know as I have done it once and thoroughly enjoyed the experience.

On the upper slopes, not far from the summit trig, the ice is thicker still and encases the track surface as well as all the tussock leaves, the rocks, and flax seed heads. They make striking subjects for photography and I mark them off mentally for the descent. Some careful footwork gets me to the summit trig and then even more careful placement of my tripod and camera to avoid sending them over the south face of the mountain as the ridges begin to brighten to the northwest. The spectacle is energising, and despite this being a relatively small mountain the snow and ice cover presents a dramatic alpine scene. The ridge crest curves away toward Mt Peel, its deeply creased face providing plenty of interest for photography – that and the ice-encased trig beside me.

Fortunately, the wind is only light and I can survive comfortably enough in the dawn freeze-up to capture a good selection of images before descending to the tiny shelter resting on the steep south face of Little Mt Peel, just 50m below the trig. There's no one home, just more ice and a freezer-like interior – descent looks good.

11. Orari Gorge
90 minutes return. **Easy**

A reserve in south Canterbury, near Geraldine, with a pleasant picnic spot set in grassland and backed by a remnant forest, Orari Gorge Scenic Reserve provides a nice diversion for an afternoon and has a short walk through regenerating forest. This walk begins at the gate into the picnic area and moves up into the bush and onto a low, forested hillside. A loop track circles through the reserve from the track junction at the top of the first hill. The south side of the walk is mostly through large kānuka forest. This slowly merges with mixed native forest near the hilltop lookout at Cabbage Tree Top. Descending the other side, the track passes through scattered pockets of tōtara, matai, māhoe (the most common) and kahikatea (white pine). As the track curves away from the ridge it joins the line of the old bush tramway, which was once used to log the forest. It then intersects with the other side of the loop before dropping down the tramway incline to the picnic area.

Access is from Route 72 (signposted) just north of Geraldine, turn into Tripp Settlement Road and travel 7km before turning left into Yates Road. Follow this for 3km to the reserve.

12. Access Easements off Rangitata Gorge Road
1–2 hours from the road. These are graded as **moderate** to **hard** routes.

Several signposted and marked access ways have been provided across private farmland up the Rangitata Gorge Road en route to Mesopotamia. Please respect these easements and keep to the marked routes until inside the conservation boundary. These routes exist mostly for hunting access but some also provide routes to the open tops. They are listed here from the south.

(i) **MacKenzie Stream:** This is unnamed on topographical maps and is on the southern side of Horse Spur.

(ii) **Lynn Stream**

(iii) **Raules Gully**

(iv) **Boundary Stream:** Access is possible up this stream and spurs to the open tops.

(v) **Coal Hill:** 2–3 hours. This is the best access for Coal Hill (1617m) and open ridge-tops.

Te Kahui Kaupeka Conservation Park

The newest of the recent additions to the Canterbury high-country estate, Te Kahui Kaupeka covers a large chunk of mountainous country between the Godley–Macaulay and Rangitata valleys centred on the Two Thumb and Sibbald ranges. The southern section of the park is much easier to traverse than those parts nearer to the Main Divide, and it is also in this section that the Te Araroa Trail makes an incursion through the Bush and Camp stream catchments, two large, scenic valleys dominated by extensive tussock landscapes and backed by the rocky spine of the Two Thumb Range. There are a number of huts in the park, mostly in the Havelock feeder of the Rangitata and its tributaries, with others sited along the Te Araroa Trail and in the Macaulay. Access into this park is seldom easy, with the notable exception of the Te Araroa Trail, though even here rivers guard all access points. This is a hazard that grows as you enter further into the park, where very large rivers flow from the alps, making routes into the interior challenging propositions. Some 4WD access also exists, in good conditions, up the Havelock and Godley–Macaulay valleys.

The Two Thumb Range dominates the park, extending over a massive swathe of mountain country from Burkes Pass highway to the Main Divide near Mt D'Archiac. The southern and central portions of the range, where the terrain is of a moderate nature, facilitates numerous tramping, hunting, and mountain biking trips, along with skiing (there are two skifields) and fishing. However, north of Bush Stream, near Mesopotamia Station, the terrain changes into considerably more difficult mountain country, where high, glaciated peaks and valleys predominate. Multi-day trips are an attractive feature of this range and in many cases a necessity for those who want to complete a return option over one of the many high passes. Much of the range is open country, devoid of bush cover.

MOUNTAIN BIKING TRIPS

The southern portion of the range has the most potential for mountain biking trips, especially from near Burkes Pass along the range to Mts Burgess and Maude. Local landholders will need to be contacted for access.

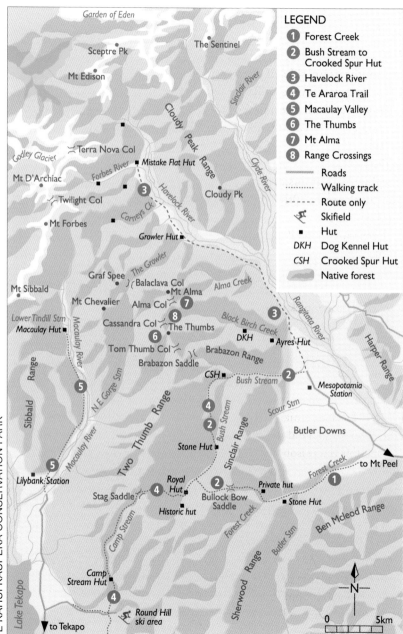

LEGEND

1. Forest Creek
2. Bush Stream to Crooked Spur Hut
3. Havelock River
4. Te Araroa Trail
5. Macaulay Valley
6. The Thumbs
7. Mt Alma
8. Range Crossings

〰〰 Roads
········ Walking track
‒ ‒ ‒ Route only
⛷ Skifield
▪ Hut
DKH Dog Kennel Hut
CSH Crooked Spur Hut
⬛ Native forest

TE KAHUI KAUPEKA CONSERVATION PARK

1. Forest Creek
4–5 hours. **Moderate**

This moderately sized catchment on the southeastern side of the range grants access to the Sinclair Range and head basin of Bush Stream over Bullock Bow Saddle via a steep 4WD trail.

The historic Stone Hut, upstream of Butler Stream on the river right, is registered as an historic place and dates to the early 20th century. It is worth visiting.

Keen mountain biking enthusiasts can also reach the saddle via this route along vehicle tracks on the valley floor.

Access is directly up the riverbed from the Forest Creek road bridge.

Historic Stone Hut, Forest Creek, Mesopotamia

2. Bush Stream to Crooked Spur Hut
3–4 hours. **Moderate**

From the river flats carpark at the mouth of Bush Stream just past Mesopotamia Station, a marked route exists up Bush Stream to Crooked Spur Hut (8 bunks), an old musterer's hut at 1000m under the Brabazon Range. Though this is a reasonable route, be aware that Bush Stream often carries a large volume of water and must be crossed several times to reach the hut – in high flow this would be a dangerous undertaking. This is spectacular country nestled beneath the high peaks of the range and there are several options for a round trip. The first option is an ascent of Brabazon Saddle (1731m) to the northwest and descent of Black Birch Creek to the Rangitata. There are two basic huts along Black Birch Creek: Dog Kennel Hut and Ayres Hut. Black Birch Creek can also be difficult to ford in high flows. This round trip could be done in a day from Crooked Spur Hut. The second option is to follow the Te Araroa Trail up Bush Stream to Stone Hut (8 bunks) or Royal Hut (8 bunks) and return to the Rangitata Gorge Road via Bullock Bow Saddle, or do a traverse of the Sinclair Range to the Scour Stream 4WD trail. Permission will be required from Mesopotamia Station to access this road (ph. 03 696 3738). This track and route will take 1–2 days.

3. Havelock River
2–3 days. **Moderate**

This is the largest watershed draining the eastern side of the Two Thumb Range and it will take at least 2 days just to reach the valley head. The river is swift, as are its tributaries, but there are numerous huts for shelter and some fine adventures to be had along the flanks of the ranges, particularly the crossings of Twilight, Balaclava or Cassandra cols to the Godley or Macaulay valleys.

4. Te Araroa Trail
2–3 days. **Moderate**

The Te Araroa Trail cuts through the central section of the range from Bush Stream into the headwater basin and over Stag Saddle to Camp Stream and the mountain faces above Lake Tekapo. This crossing takes 2–3 days and is facilitated by access to several historic musterers' huts en route.

5. Macaulay Valley
2–3 days. **Moderate**

The Macaulay is a large river system that rises in the upper Two Thumb Range and drains into the Godley River near the head of Lake Tekapo. Lower valley access is possible by 4WD to Macaulay Hut in mid-valley near Lower Tindill Stream. This 14-bunk facility is maintained by the Mackenzie Alpine Trust and is free of charge to the public. The valley has a spectacular alpine nature and is quite remote.

6. The Thumbs
2 days. **Hard+**

With the exception of Mt D'Archiac, a difficult alpine summit near the Main Divide, the twin-summitted Thumbs is one of the range's more accessible and highest peaks, though it still requires basic alpine skills and possibly a rope.

At 2500m it commands views over a huge portion of the range and valleys. The more southerly Thumb is the higher of the two at 2546m and can be reached via Black Birch Creek.

7. Mt Alma
2 days. **Hard+**

A neighbouring 2500m summit is Mt Alma, gained from the Havelock Valley and Alma Creek to Alma Col. Though not a difficult summit, a rope may be required.

8. Range Crossings
3–4 days. **Hard+**

Alma Col, Tom Thumb Col and Cassandra Col are key to providing a circumnavigation of the central portion of the range, though in reality there are numerous other unnamed passes that could also be used to access the upper Macaulay from the Havelock tributaries. Terra Nova Col and the extreme head of the range is a difficult alpine crossing to the upper Godley, requiring sound glacier skills.

HISTORIC HEADINGS

Keen to sample a little of the Te Kahui Kaupeka Conservation Park bordering western Mesopotamia Station in the Rangitata Valley, I set out one weekend with a tramping mate, Tim Hayward, to explore some of the high basins of Bush Stream.

Taking mountain bikes to speed our progress up Forest Creek, our accessway to the park, we covered the first 10km in good time before parking them in the riverbed and continuing on foot towards Bullock Bow Saddle. Forest Creek has a large catchment up in the peaks of the Two Thumbs and could prove to be problematic during or after heavy rain. Beyond the river the route ascends a steep vehicle trail to the saddle, passing through magnificent high-country terrain where golden tussocks, interspersed with the odd patch of snow, predominate.

The cloud cover from the previous evening began to lift as we approached the pass, treating us to a grand panorama over the head of Bush Stream into the dramatic post-glacial cirques of the Two Thumb Range. Yet even here we felt a little cheated of the best of the view, so we elected to head higher, onto a small summit on the southern end of the Sinclair Range. At just over 2000m this unnamed peak offered us the view we had been seeking, of the high alps with Mt Cook resplendent among her lower but no less beautiful sister summits. A sharp wind on the ridge crest hastened us into the lee of some rocks, where we could survey the Rangitata Valley and far-off Banks Peninsula. It was a spectacle worth the hard 20km slog we had put in since dawn. Beyond the summit the ridge top was easily traversable, even with the soft snow cover we encountered, so we headed north to a neighbouring peak and began our descent from there into Bush Stream.

At the 1600m contour on the descent we spotted four thar observing us from 30m away. In a flash of silver and brown they were off, vanishing among the bluffs and grasses below. The valley floor was not far off now and once gained we negotiated a few small creeks before fording Bush Stream to access the main valley track.

This track is part of the Te Araroa Trail and cuts through the central section of the Two Thumb Range between the Rangitata Valley and Lake Tekapo. Royal Hut was our destination for the night. It sounds grand but the reality was a disappointment – dirt floor, rough bunks, un-insulated, draughty, and worst of all no firewood. The hut name is derived from the fact that Prince Charles and Princess Anne visited here in 1971. 'I bet they had plenty of firewood here then', I grumbled to Tim as I shrugged into my sleeping bag to ward off the all-pervading chill of night in the mountains.

Next day brought with it a freshening wind from the south and cloud cover. This was our day to head back, and though chased by the southerly we felt pleased with our discoveries, especially the historic Stone Hut in Forest Creek, sited on a lonely terrace above the river where it has stood for over 100 years – silent watchdog to the passing endeavours of high-country adventurers.

Tenehaun Conservation Area

Mt Tripp from Hinds Gorge Access Easement
6–8 hours. **Hard**

This region covers access to the Moorehouse Range and Mt Tripp (1368m) on the northern side of the Rangitata River. There are no marked tracks, only access easements into the conservation area. The route to Mt Tripp is long, 10km approximately one way, covers some moderately rough terrain and is best done as a 2-day trip.

Access is off the Main South Road (Route 72) at Ealing, and follow Ealing Montalto Road for 19.5km. At the 'T' junction, turn left onto Hinds Gorge Road and then right onto Chapmans Road. The public access easement starts at the end of this road.

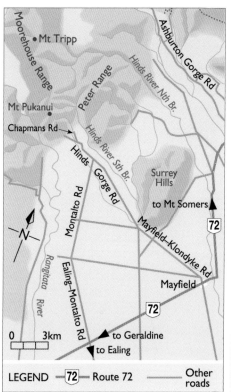

Boundary Hut, South Ashburton

Ashburton Lakes and Rakaia Valley

Hakatere Conservation Park

This park is unusual as it is not one continuous region but a series of largely unconnected conservation areas that in total make up Hakatere Conservation Park. It is possible that in future additional areas will be added to the park to link up some of the sections. For now, however, the park is contained between the Rakaia River to the north and east and the Rangitata River to the west. Within this rough boundary lie a large number of lakes, wetlands, high-country valleys, and river headwaters, which combined form the 50,000 hectares of the park.

Hakatere contains extremely diverse environments: from the slopes of Mt Hutt skifield, to the mixed podocarp forests of Mt Somers, to the high-country wetlands around Lake Heron and Mt Harper, through the remote tussock-filled valleys of the Cameron and South Ashburton, to the rugged headwater catchments of the Lyell, Clyde and Lawrence valleys. Hakatere has something to offer everyone, and in addition has excellent road access around most of the park. Day-trip and overnight excursions abound, many facilitated by huts and tracks, along with unmarked routes onto the innumerable high foothill summits in the Rakaia and Ashburton catchments, as well as mountain biking opportunities galore. Much of the eastern portion of the park is easily accessed by road and can make a great bolt-hole for a tramping trip when nor'west conditions render the western section of the park inaccessible due to flooded rivers. The landscape that the park covers is truly representative of Canterbury high country and a delight to explore. The Ashburton Lakes region, which is within the greater orbit of Hakatere Conservation Park, contains 12 lakes, which, together with their associated wetlands, make up one the best intact inter-montane wetland systems, as well as being home to a variety of wildlife, with over 30 species of birds regularly present here. The lakes also comprise a nationally significant fishery.

LEGEND

1. Mt Somers Walkway
2. South Face Route
3. Woolshed Ck Short Walks
4. Sharplin Falls
5. Mt Somers Ascent
6. Mt Winterslow
7. Mt Alford Scenic Reserve
8. Mt Barossa
9. Mt Harper, Erewhon
10. Mt Guy & Lake Clearwater Tracks
11. Lake Camp to Lake Emma
12. Mt Potts, Erewhon
13. Potts River and Hut
14. Te Araroa Trail
15. Mt Sunday
16. Lawrence & Clyde Valleys
17. Mt Taylor
18. Mt Catherine, Lake Heron Basin
19. Cameron Valley, Arrowsmith Range
20. South Branch Ashburton
21. Lake Heron Walks
22. Mt Hutt Forest & Awa Awa Rata Reserve
23. Pudding Hill Stm & Scott's Saddle
24. Pudding Hill Range
25. Rakaia Gorge Walkway
26. Mt Hutt Summit
27. Steepface Hill
28. Redcliff Saddle & Tribb Hut
29. Turtons Saddle
30. Double Hill
31. Palmer Range & Godley Peak
32. Banfield Hut, Rakaia River

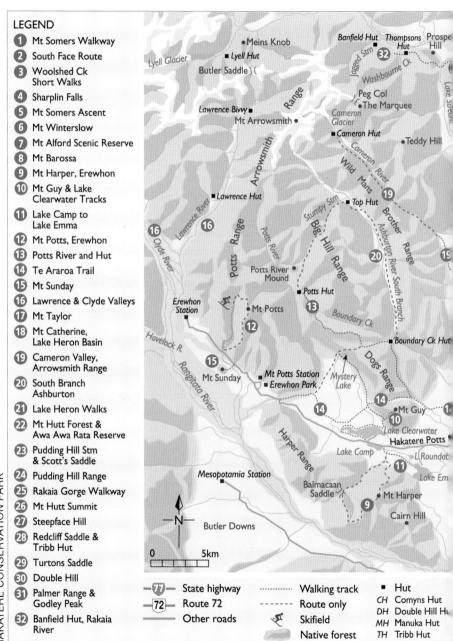

State highway	Walking track	Hut
Route 72	Route only	CH Comyns Hut
Other roads	Skifield	DH Double Hill Hut
	Native forest	MH Manuka Hut
		TH Tribb Hut

HAKATERE CONSERVATION PARK

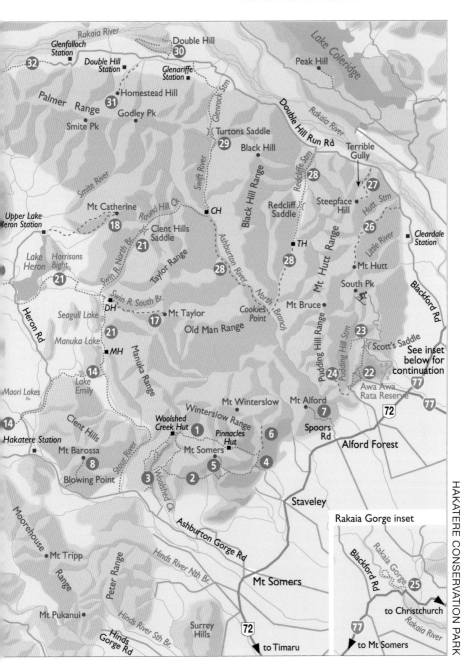

Rakaia River

Glenfalloch Station

Double Hill

Lake Coleridge

32

Double Hill Station

30

Peak Hill

Glenariffe Station

Palmer Range

31 Homestead Hill

Godley Pk

Smite Pk

Glenrock Stm

Rakaia River

Double Hill Run Rd

Turtons Saddle

29

Black Hill

Terrible Gully

27

Swift River

Smite River

Black Hill Range

Redcliff Stm

28

Steepface Hill

Hutt Stm

Upper Lake Heron Station

Mt Catherine

Round Hill Ck

CH

18

Clent Hills Saddle

21

Redcliff Saddle

26

Cleardale Station

Lake Heron

Harrisons Bight

Swin R. North Br.

Taylor Range

Ashburton River

TH

28

Mt Hutt Range

Mt Hutt

South Pk

Blackford Rd

21

28

Heron Rd

Seagull Lake

DH

Swin R. South Br.

17 Mt Taylor

Old Man Range

North Branch

Cookies Point

Mt Bruce

Pudding Hill Range

23

Scott's Saddle

See inset below for continuation

21

Manuka Lake

MH

Manuka Range

Pudding Hill Stm

77

14

Lake Emily

24

22

Maori Lakes

Awa Awa Rata Reserve

77

14

Clent Hills

Stour River

Mt Winterslow

Winterslow Range

Mt Alford

Mt Somers

7

72

Hakatere Station

Woolshed Creek Hut

1

Pinnacles Hut

6

Spoors Rd

Alford Forest

Mt Barossa

8

2

5

4

Blowing Point

3

Woolshed Ck

Staveley

Moorehouse Range

Mt Tripp

Peter Range

Ashburton Gorge Rd

Hinds River Nth Br.

Rakaia Gorge inset

Blackford Rd

Rakaia Gorge

Mt Pukanui

Mt Somers

25

to Christchurch

Rakaia River

Hinds River Sth Br.

Surrey Hills

72

77

to Mt Somers

Hinds Gorge Rd

to Timaru

53

1. Mt Somers Walkway

Woolshed Creek Hut from carpark: 2–3 hours. **Moderate/Hard**
Woolshed Creek Hut to Pinnacles Hut via saddle. 3–4 hours.
Woolshed Creek Hut to Sharplin Falls via South Face. 6–8 hours.
Pinnacles Hut to Sharplin Falls. 3–4 hours.

It is possible to walk this track in either direction but the most popular starting point is the Woolshed Creek picnic area. The track follows a gentle slope through some attractive beech forest beside Woolshed Creek to the lower mine site, before commencing a steep uphill grind over the incline of the old 'jig' railway, down which coal trucks would thunder from the Blackburn Mine. One such coal wagon, mangled and rusted, can be seen here at the base of the climb where it ran off the tracks. At the Blackburn Mine, near the bush edge in an open area, numerous old relics discarded by the miners can be found rusting in the soil. There are also some old coal seams here. Beyond the mine the track continues to climb and contour around the hillside far above the creek until the Trig R side-track is reached. Here a 15-minute detour grants a fine panorama of inland Canterbury and the distant Arrowsmith

MT SOMERS WALKWAY AND SUMMIT

Mt Somers is an ancient volcano set on the edge of the Canterbury Plains, offering walkers a huge variety of trails, climbs, scenic walks and picnic spots. Walks range from just an hour or so up to a 2–3-day tramp. The 17km Mt Somers Walkway is the major focus for the area and it also links two attractive picnic spots: Woolshed Creek and Sharplin Falls. These picnic spots are the starting point for several of the short walks for which the area is renowned.

To reach Woolshed Creek drive through Mt Somers township and follow Ashburton Gorge Road for 10.5km, turning right onto the signposted road for 3.5km to the Woolshed Creek picnic area. There is an information panel, tables, toilets and camping here.

To reach Sharplin Falls from Staveley, a tiny hamlet 19km south of Methven on Route 72, take the road between the shop and the hall and then turn right into Flynns Road, just past the bridge. Follow signposts to the carpark, shelter and picnic area on the banks of Bowyers Stream.

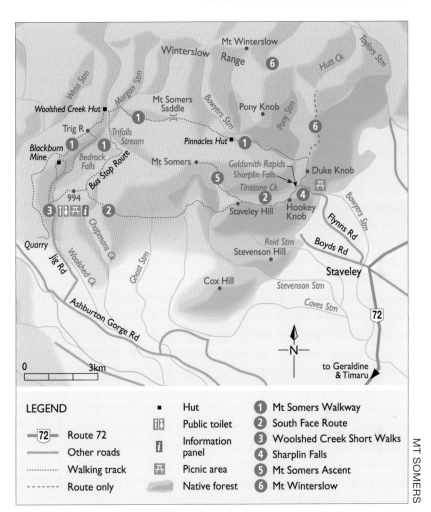

LEGEND

- Hut
- Public toilet
- 72 Route 72
- Other roads
- Walking track
- Route only
- i Information panel
- Picnic area
- Native forest

1. Mt Somers Walkway
2. South Face Route
3. Woolshed Creek Short Walks
4. Sharplin Falls
5. Mt Somers Ascent
6. Mt Winterslow

MT SOMERS

Ranges. From Trig R the track descends gradually to the hut (26 bunks), located beside the stream on a small terrace. A short detour just before the hut will introduce you to some of the delights of upper Woolshed Creek. Here a marked route drops into the shallow canyon where waterfalls, rock shutes, the 'Spa Pool' and 'Emerald Pool' will hold you enthralled at their enchanting beauty and the diversity of the region. A delightful afternoon can be spent here exploring the hidden twists and turns of the canyon.

If you are returning to Woolshed Creek carpark, two variations on the route are possible; both are more suitable for experienced trampers.

(i) **The Bus Stop Route**
3–4 hours. **Moderate**

Beginning below the hut, take the poled route for 5 minutes, cross the stream and climb over a spur before passing through Trifalls Stream. The route then traverses a series of ladders and rock ledges before crossing the junction with the Hydroslide Loop Track. Then climbs steeply to an open ridge at 1100m altitude before descending over Point 994m, down an open spur, a stream and gully to the carpark. A bus stop sign placed on this route has bestowed its identity and a long wait for a bus!

(ii) **The Bedrock Falls and Canyon Route**
2–3 hours from Trig R. **Moderate**

This can also be used as a variation on the inward journey. It begins at Trig R and descends steeply into Woolshed Creek, where it follows the stream, with numerous river crossings, back to the picnic area.

Continuing on along the walkway above Woolshed Creek Hut, the track follows an old 4WD track up and over a small saddle to Morgan Stream, where a side-track indicates a detour to view a series of caves carved out by the stream in the rhyolite rock. From here a steady climb up the 4WD track takes walkers to Mt Somers Saddle (1170m). Here are some of the best views on the walkway: to the east the Canterbury Plains, while to the west and north the Southern Alps and peaks of the Taylor and Winterslow ranges. Down from the saddle the trail contours through beautiful patches of snow tussock, where it is not uncommon to find snow during winter. This is a spectacular part of the walk, especially as it approaches the huge rock buttresses of Mt Somers, where more unusual rock formations and pools will be encountered. Beyond, the bush is entered and the well-sited Pinnacles Hut is reached (19 bunks). Pinnacles Hut is named after the unusual rock formations on the north face of Mt Somers. These were produced by cooling lava and are a magnet for rock climbers. A comfortable night can be spent at the hut watching the lights of Christchurch glittering in the distance. The final part of the walk continues to hug the steep bush face above Bowyers Stream. This part of the walk can be quite demanding, especially if wet and muddy. Later the track descends to and crosses the stream several times before climbing out of the final gorge and over Duke Knob to the carpark and the Sharplin Falls tracks.

Note: The track and stream route from Pinnacles Hut to Sharplin Falls can become impassable after heavy rain.

2. South Face Route
6–8 hours. **Hard**

This extension of the walkway links the Woolshed Creek area with Sharplin Falls carpark via the Hookey Knob Track to the summit of Mt Somers. It branches off the Bus Stop route on the high plateau at around 950m elevation and descends into and traverses the gullies and flanks of the South Face. It is a demanding tramp.

3. Woolshed Creek Short Walks

(i) **Nature Trail**
30 minutes return. **Easy**

This walk crosses the creek and climbs up the valley into a patch of montane vegetation before heading back to the river and up though an area of old coal tailings to reach the walkway.

(ii) **Sidewinder Track**
2 hours return. **Moderate**

Upriver from the carpark on the Bedrock Falls route, this track climbs steeply from the river to the Blackburn Mine, where a reconstructed mine entrance has been built. It passes through the Ancient Forest, which is thought to be the only patch of original forest cover that escaped the fires ravaging the area in pre-European times. Return via the Miners Track down the incline.

(iii) **Rocky Lookout and Black Beech Tracks**
30–40 minutes return. **Easy**

Two short walks from the carpark, which can be combined to give a brief overview of both the watershed and vegetation of lower Woolshed Creek.

(iv) **Lime Kiln and Stone Cottage**
Two historic sites signposted on the access road to Woolshed Creek with excellent information panels.

4. Sharplin Falls
90 minutes return. **Easy**

This beautiful walk is probably the best and most scenic short walk in the reserve. It begins across the large swingbridge over Bowyers Stream and traverses the first part of the walkway, through ferns and mature forest, before climbing to a junction where it is possible to descend to the river again and walk upstream to the Goldsmith Rapids, formed after a major landslip into the valley. From the rapids a steel gantry, which traverses the bluff upriver, is easily reached. A track then descends to the falls. The twin falls drop 7m over the Mt Somers Southern Fault into two large pools, which make ideal swimming holes on a hot day. A high-level route can be taken from near the eastern end of the gantry to return to the lower section of Bowyers Stream; this is useful if the stream is high.

5. Mt Somers Ascent
Sharplin Falls carpark to summit: 3–4 hours. **Moderate/Hard**

The volcanic cone of Mt Somers (1687m) dominates the southern central region of the Canterbury Plains and is an exciting objective for a winter day excursion from Christchurch. It is reached via the track over Hookey Knob, which is part of the South Face route for the Mt Somers Walkway. Although the route traverses a marked track to the bush edge, there are no markers above the bushline and cloud on the face and ridge can make route finding hazardous. It is not a difficult climb, though it is steep and an ice axe and crampons will be required in winter. Alternative unmarked routes are possible on the peak from Woolshed Creek Hut and saddle.

Warning: The area is subject to sudden weather changes and storms.

6. Mt Winterslow

8–10 hours. **Hard+**

An ice axe may be required if snow is on the tops.

A broad ridge carpeted in luxuriant snow tussock curves in a gentle arc toward the distant summit dome of Mt Winterslow (1700m), the highest peak on this mountain range, which lies immediately north of Mt Somers (1687m) and directly south of Mt Hutt, on the edge of the Canterbury Plains. Mt Winterslow is a long, demanding trip for a day excursion and is not recommended for inexperienced parties.

From the Sharplin Falls carpark tramp up to Duke Knob and descend the walkway track (westward) for about 3 minutes. Keep a sharp lookout on the right, on a level section of track, for two trees spray-painted blue and the rough beginnings of the old track through the bush to the Winterslow Range. This track keeps to the ridgeline in the forest and is generally easy to follow. It climbs steadily north, to exit the bush on the south side of Trig U (1320m). An unmarked route then heads northwest along the open ridge to the top. From the summit head west to Point 1625m and descend a southeast spur from there. An initially steep descent on snow and scree grants access to a tussock spur and later the stream and a climb to gain the walkway track and Pinnacles Hut. (See notes for 'Mt Somers Walkway' for the route out from here.)

Mt Winterslow is not in Hakatere Conservation Park and permission is required to access the summit and ridges from Winterslow Station.

7. Mt Alford Scenic Reserve

2–3 hours. **Moderate**

This small, untracked reserve south of Mt Hutt contains good stands of beech forest and has a steep 4WD road up to 900m elevation, where repeater equipment is located.

The road provides good access and grand views of the plains, especially if you are feeling like a workout without any obstacles. It would also provide a good route to the top after heavy snow in winter, when other ridges may be too difficult to follow.

A rough route (unmarked) is possible onto the top of Mt Alford (1171m) through patchy sub-alpine scrub.

Access at Mt Alford Forest settlement on Route 72, 7.5km south of the Mt Hutt skifield turnoff, turn right into Spoors Road and drive up this to the base of the hill and the marked DOC carpark and access easement.

8. Mt Barossa

2.5 hours from road. **Moderate**

Standing near the southern limit of the Clent Hills Range, Mt Barossa (1364m) is a relatively new addition to Hakatere Conservation Park and is accessed most easily from the Ashburton Gorge road at Blowing Point, 9km west of the Woolshed Creek access road. A small carpark and signpost indicate the poled route. The route up follows a steepening watercourse and then onto a narrow ridgeline to reach the open tussock fields around 1000m and then northwards to the summit. The entire route has wonderful views, which broaden as you approach the summit.

View from Mt Barossa

From the top there are incredible views of the Ashburton Lakes Basin, with Lake Clearwater and Lake Emma in view, behind which is the upper Rangitata and the great peaks of the Southern Alps. Closer to hand are impressive peaks of the upper South Ashburton – the Arrowsmiths, as well as the Cameron Valley, Lake Heron and distant peaks of the Rakaia Valley. Directly east lie Mt Somers, Mt Winterslow and the Canterbury Plains – this summit view is one to savour!

The summit region of Mt Barossa is dominated by a series of rocky tors, which provide great photographic subjects and welcome relief to the rolling hills, and if the wind is up, some very handy shelter. A through trip could be made north and west along the ridge to reach Lake Emily. This would be a full-day trip.

9. Mt Harper, Erewhon
Summit from lake: 2–3 hours. **Moderate/Hard**
Balmacaan Saddle from summit: 2 hours.
Lake from Balmacaan Saddle: 1–2 hours.

Mt Harper (1829m), a modest summit with grand views of the upper Rangitata headwaters, offers an easier and shorter option for viewing and trekking on the tops in the Erewhon region. The route is not marked.

From the Lake Camp camping area, near Lake Clearwater, cross open flat paddocks for 2km to the foot of the mountain, which rises ahead as a massive block of spurs leading to a relatively flat top. Various steep spurs lead up the northern face and with some careful selection you should be able to locate one that is free of scrub and small bluffs. The recommended route is immediately east (i.e. on the left side when looking at Mt Harper) of a small stream draining the face. This stream runs down into a large gravel fan and is directly opposite the south end of Lake Camp. From the foot of the spur a steady 600m ascent, with little respite, will bring you up to a broad, flat ridgeline at around 1400m. This ridge is very easy to traverse, west, to a high point at 1506m and then south, at a slightly increased gradient, though still moderate, to the summit plateau. There are good specimens of alpine tussock here, especially just off the ridge to the east. If snow lies on the ridge it may prove to be a tiring ascent, however.

The Rangitata River sweeps past on the southern flanks of Mt Harper, beyond which stand the farmed terraces of Mesopotamia Station beneath the weathered Sinclair and Ben Mcleod ranges. Up valley the glaciated watersheds of the Havelock and Clyde lure the eye onto hidden snowfields and along the ragged spine of the alps. If a nor'wester is blowing off the Divide your stay might be cut short by its icy blast, ripping over these exposed tops. But spare a moment for the view to the north, which encompasses the Lake Heron Basin and craggy Arrowsmith Range.

A good round trip is possible for the descent route. It traverses the broad, open tops to the south and west, descending to a high saddle and crossing over two minor highpoints, 1644m and 1658m, before dropping sharply to Balmacaan Saddle (1150m) and Stream.

The ridge provides very easy travel and is interspersed with tussock, scree and some alpine herbs. It also grants walkers a wonderful changing perspective of the Rangitata River headwaters. Once down in the stream follow the 4WD track out to the open fans and paddocks near Lake Camp, taking care to avoid the matagouri thickets, and back to your vehicle.

Access is from Mt Somers township. Follow the Ashburton Gorge Road and the Hakatere Potts Road to Lake Camp. Leave the road at the eastern end of Lake Camp and drive along vehicle tracks beside the lake to a fenceline. Beyond this fenceline a short strip of farmland (private) is crossed for about 300m to enter the reserve.

10. Mt Guy and Lake Clearwater Tracks
Around the lake: 2–3 hours. **Easy**
Mt Guy: 3–4 hours return. **Moderate**
Mystery Lake: 5–6 hours. **Moderate**

Lake Clearwater lies beneath Mt Harper and Dogs Range and is a popular haunt for day-trippers and bach owners due to the large cluster of weathered dwellings mid-way along the lake's southern shoreline. The lake itself has a picnic and camping area also associated with the baches and makes an agreeable destination for an easy day out in fine weather.

There are several walking and mountain biking trails that can be accessed here. The most popular is the Round-the-Lake combined walking and mountain biking trail that completes a full circumnavigation via the lake-shore and provides some stunning views of the mountain country beyond the lake.

There are numerous places to cast a line here in season, and for mountain biking enthusiasts it provides a good leg stretch before tackling some tougher trails elsewhere.

Mt Guy (1319m) is the large, steep mound at the lake's northeastern end. It is readily accessible from the Round-the-Lake trail and has a marked and signposted route right to the summit. The upper section is steep and loose, but not difficult. From the summit there are excellent views of the Rangitata, Southern Alps, Taylor Range, Lake Heron Basin, and Lake Clearwater. A descent can be made over Point 1274m and down via a western spur to link up with the Mystery Lake Track. This route down is quite steep and rough near the bottom; care is required.

Mystery Lake is set on a post-glacial trench north and west of Mt Guy at an elevation of 1100m, making it a reasonably strenuous 400m climb from the shores of Lake Clearwater. The lake cannot be seen from below and it is necessary to climb right up into the hollow containing Mystery Lake to view it. The knolls south of the lake command extensive views over the upper Rangitata Plain. This route can be linked to the South Ashburton to Potts River track by climbing onto the large tableland north of the lake and picking up the 4WD trail about 1km away to the east.

11. Lake Camp to Lake Emma
2.5 hours. **Easy**

An easy walking and biking trail exists around the back of Lake Camp and then continues on over undulating terraces to nearby Lake Emma, about 3km away. Lake Emma can also be walked or biked around, then either return or go out to the Hakatere Potts Road, past Lake Roundabout. This is a great track for the whole family and has easy walking throughout. It passes through some interesting high-country landscapes and environments. Emma Hut, on the south shore of the lake, is an historic building, but there is no accommodation here.

Access is either from Lake Camp or Lake Roundabout.

LAKE CLEARWATER PADDLE

Tucked in among the foothills and valleys of the Ashburton Lakes is the often-windswept body of Lake Clearwater, a large post-glacial basin west of Mt Somers in Canterbury. At almost 4km long and just over 1km wide it is one of the largest of the string of lakes and lakelets hidden away in the tawny ranges that shut the region off from the Canterbury Plains. Lake Clearwater stands at 680m elevation, so it is often cold enough to freeze in its entirety during the winter months, transforming it into an ice skater's dream. At other seasons it presents a more benign face, yet one often tinged with danger as the winds that can howl over the surface of this mountain sea are not to be trifled with. Autumn is possibly the best season to visit, when the lake-shore is tinged with golden willows and peace reigns supreme over the waters. It's an ideal time to launch the canoe and skim the surface, heading toward the distant Potts Range and the great rumpled uplift of the Southern Alps.

On a family visit to the lake I load into the canoe two of my daughters and we set off on a mission of discovery over the glassy sheen of the lake, its crystal clear waters adequately endorsing its name. We have the perfect autumn day – no wind, warm sunshine, clear skies, deep russet hues staining the landscape, and not another watercraft to be seen. The lake is ours and we set out to claim her beauties wherever we may find them. At the lake's northern end is a large island, which almost touches the shoreline at this point, yet with a little care the shallows can be navigated to make a circuit, to land, which we do, and to cruise on. Coming around the eastern shore of the island we are greeted with a fine view of the Clearwater baches and the great rounded shoulders of Mt Harper (1829m) rising directly behind them. A little farther on and we can strike out for the western head of the lake some 2.5km away. I'm not sure my two crew members are up to the distance, even with the promise of a few treats along the way, but hey who's counting the paddle strokes, it's just fantastic to be out here on such a sublime day.

Nor'west sunrise across Lake Clearwater

My fibreglass Canadian cuts a pretty straight course when up to its full cruising speed of about 7kph and will peel off the distance to any set point with ease, so it's not long before we have ranged in on the head and can slacken the pace as we pass though some small bays along the shore. The best thing about our paddle is that there's not a sound, and the views of the omnipresent mountains are enough to stir the heart and quicken the pulse – adventure it seems is but a breath away.

With the lakehead under our belts we can return to the village cluster of baches at a more sedate pace, the thought of BBQ sausages spurring us onward.

12. Mt Potts, Erewhon
Allow a full day. **Hard+**

Mt Potts (2184m) stands near the confluence of the Clyde and Havelock rivers above Erewhon Park skifield in the central Southern Alps. It is a physically demanding climb, though not difficult, and for those with sufficient skills and equipment would make a fine winter ascent.

The climb begins at the toe of the southwest ridge on the skifield access road, which has a locked gate. This road begins almost directly opposite Mt Sunday, a small *roche moutonnée* (post-glacial riverbed feature) on the bank of the Rangitata River where a significant part of the filming for the *Lord of the Rings* motion picture was carried out. A fort was constructed on the summit of this hill, now removed, providing an unequalled visual backdrop for the film.

From the gate a small, incised creek draining the skifield basin must first be crossed by traversing north, along the west bank through forest, for 200m until the canyon eases and allows direct access to the far side. Exiting the bush and stream on the east, open tussock leads up onto the broad-stepped southwest ridge. It is some 3km and almost 1500m of ascent from here to the summit plateau and Mt Potts' three peaks. If the day is fine and calm, the ridge provides a rewarding climb to the peak as it ascends in a series of moderately angled steps interspersed with broad, almost flat, sections where the walking is easy and the views outstanding. At your back lies the great arc of the Rangitata, here over 4km across, with Mt Sunday vanishing into insignificance against the massive uplift of the mighty Southern Alps crowned with the jagged tooth of D'Archiac (2875m) above the Havelock River. There is ample time and opportunity to observe the scene unfolding below and around you as the ridge steadily gains altitude with a final short, sharp 200m scramble, taking you onto the lowest and most southerly of Mt Potts' summits. Here an undulating summit plateau, where it would be possible to camp in good weather, allows for an easy wander, perhaps on snow, across to the high peak, and of course the finest views of the climb.

Being a foothill, yet still close to the Divide, Mt Potts yields one of the best alpine views of any summit in Canterbury. If the day is clear, especially to the west, you will be treated to intimate views of some of the wildest and most inaccessible parts of the Main Divide. Beginning with Mts Cook and

Tasman to the south, the scene increases in detail and complexity as the eye roves over D'Archiac, the Garden of Eden Snowfield, Malcolm Peak, Mt Whitcombe, the Bracken Snowfield, Louper Peak and finally the Arrowsmith Range. With map and compass, an hour or more could be spent surveying summits and passes amid the welter of valleys and glaciers. This is real Erewhon country and the magnitude of it is quite overwhelming.

Descent routes from the summit will vary with time available, experience and weather conditions. The easiest option is to return either via the southwest ridge, or continue northwards, along the ridgeline from Mt Potts, over a minor summit at 2003m, and descend an easy gully, traversing right at the bottom to reach the skifield and access road and then return to the gate. For more adventurous parties an interesting scramble is possible, beyond Point 2003m, traversing Points 2054m, 2045m, 2068m and 2140m, and thus completing a circumnavigation of the skifield basin, with outstanding views in all directions. It is possible to exit this traverse at several points along the way and also to descend to a small, though very attractive, meltwater tarn beneath Point 2140m. This traverse typifies the Canterbury high country at

Tramping party at Potts Hut

its best. From the meltwater tarn descend via easy gullies to the 4WD road and follow this out to the faces above the Rangitata, where an easy spur allows a direct descent back to the gate rather than following the road as it zigzags away to the west.

So ends a magnificent high-country trek.

Access is from over the Potts River on the concrete bridge (Mt Potts and ridge are clearly visible to the northwest from here). Follow on past Mt Potts Station and Erewhon Park for approximately 3km. The skifield road joins the main road at a bend on the right-hand side just past a sharp corner in the road and over a small stream. There is a marked access easement here.

13. Potts River and Hut

Road to Potts Hut: 5–6 hours. **Moderate**
Potts Hut to South Ashburton via Stumpy Saddle: 5–6 hours. **Moderate**
Potts Hut to South Ashburton via 1755m pass: 6–8 hours. **Moderate/Hard**

Potts River is a large catchment draining the Big Hill and Potts ranges and extending northwards from the Rangitata up into the Arrowsmiths bordering the upper South Ashburton. The valley is mostly open, though a steep, rough gorge exists in the mid-section below Potts Hut (10 bunks). A marked and poled route extends from the Hakatere Potts Road, by the Potts River bridge, onto the large terrace bordering the eastern bank of the river and from there onto the Dogs Range, via Mystery Lake, to link up with the 4WD trail coming over from the South Ashburton. Parts of this route are also part of the Te Araroa Trail. The hut is an old musterer's abode, like many in these catchments, and makes a fine base for exploring the valley or as a waypoint en route to the South Ashburton. Above the hut is some attractive tussock and mountain country and relatively easy river travel, though this does involve climbing back and forth between high river terraces.

There are two high routes out of the Potts to the South Ashburton:

(i) **Stumpy Saddle (1685m):** Head northeast of the hut via high terraces, and east of Potts River mound (1319m) into the upper valley and pass to descend Stumpy Stream to the South Ashburton Hut. This is a straightforward route in good weather but is very exposed to the elements.

(ii) **Pass 1755m** lies at the very head of the Potts and can be reached by following the main valley northeast to the head forks at around 1360m. The eastern feeder stream leads to the pass, from where a tributary descends to the South Ashburton.

14. Te Araroa Trail
3–4 hours. **Moderate**

The trail passes through this region from Double Hut via Manuka Hut or the Hakatere Heron Road and into the South Ashburton access route and Dogs Range to Potts River.

SAMUEL BUTLER AND *EREWHON*

Erewhon Station was named after the musings of Samuel Butler in his book *Erewhon*, in which he described his experiences and exploration of the new colony. Samuel Butler was a young Englishman who arrived at Lyttelton in 1860, at the age of 22, determined to seek his fortune amid the grandeur of the alps. His ability and aptitude for exploration led him into the Rangitata Valley, where he built a small hut and farmed the hills and plains of Mesopotamia on the south bank of the Rangitata. Yet Butler's heart was always set on greater things: fame and fortune through discovery of gems, gold or prospecting routes into unknown and untracked Westland. So it was with a companion, John Holland Baker, and their horses that he traversed the watersheds of the Rangitata, Rakaia, Wilberforce and Waimakariri rivers, seeking a snow-free route to the west.

Though he sighted present-day Arthur's Pass and Whitcombe Pass, both of which are snow free, he and his companion did not press their advantage to become the first across; the gorges and dense forests they viewed beyond were sufficient deterrent.

Butler's best-known sorties were based around the Rangitata catchment, including those into the upper Havelock and Clyde rivers. Though spectacular journeys of discovery, they proved unsuccessful in forging a route to the west as all the cols were either heavily glaciated

Climbing to Butler Saddle, upper Lawrence Valley

or guarded by precipitous cliffs. They did, however, force a route onto a pass at the head of the Lawrence branch of the Clyde River, now named Butler Saddle, only to find that it led back to the Rakaia. But a pass to the west of the Rakaia caught their attention; it was the Whitcombe Pass. They rode around to this point but did not cross it, leaving it to the epic and tragic first crossing made by Lauper and Whitcombe in 1863. Butler later returned to England a wealthy man and with a developing writing career, yet his legacy *Erewhon* forever captured the enthusiasm, dreams and vision of the explorer.

> *The great range itself. What was beyond it? Ah! Who could say?*
> *There was no one in the world who had the smallest idea ....*
> *Could I hope to cross it ... might I find gold, or diamonds, or*
> *copper, or silver?*
>
> Samuel Butler, *Erewhon*

15. Mt Sunday
45 minutes. **Easy**

This post-glacial feature, a *roche moutonnée*, located in the middle of the Rangitata riverbed has both historical and contemporary importance. In days gone by it was the meeting place for musterers working the high country for weeks at a time. Their families would come here to meet them for Sunday lunch atop this spectacularly sited rocky mound – hence the name. In more recent years one of the movies in the *Lord of the Rings* trilogy was shot here and featured Mt Sunday as the setting for Edoras, capital of Rohan. While the movies have captured the imagination of a generation, the view from Mt Sunday will catch your breath – a 360-degree panorama of stunning proportions. The walk over to the mount from the road is through tussock and matagouri flats to reach the base of the hill, from where a steep route leads to the rocky summit.

Access is marked off the Hakatere Potts Road near Mt Potts.

16. Lawrence and Clyde Valleys
Erewhon Homestead to Lawrence Hut: 3–4 hours. **Moderate**
Lawrence Hut to Lawrence Bivvy: 3–4 hours. **Moderate**
Butler Saddle route to Rakaia Valley: 8–10 hours. **Hard+**

The Lawrence Valley, west of the Arrowsmiths, provides a long, though rewarding, high-country experience. In the valley are two small huts and the opportunity to view the main range and other parts of the Southern Alps from a secluded watershed. Near the valley head Butler Saddle (1870m), discovered by Samuel Butler when looking for a route to Westland, provides access to the Lyell River feeder of the Rakaia, and Lyell Hut.

In general, access is via the open riverbeds of first the Clyde and then the Lawrence rivers, but beware: the Clyde is a large and often boisterous mountain torrent draining a huge section of the Southern Alps and will, at times, be impassable, as may the Lawrence. There are no swingbridges in these catchments.

Butler Saddle, at the head of the Lawrence, is a steep, moderately difficult trans-alpine crossing to the upper Rakaia, which requires good fitness and judgement, and an ice axe and crampons all year round. The Rakaia

Lawrence Bivvy

side involves a short climb and traverse, west, to reach a high ridge, which descends to Meins Knob.

The upper Clyde Valley is beyond the scope of this guide.

Access is from Erewhon Station at the very end of the Hakatere Potts Road, about 5km northwest of Mt Sunday. Permission is required to enter the valley from Erewhon Station (ph. 03 303 9739).

17. Mt Taylor

Double Hut from Lake Heron: 3–4 hours. **Hard+**

Summit from Double Hut via forks and west ridge: 5–6 hours, depending on snow conditions, less in summer.

Descent to forks: 2–3 hours.

Within the capabilities of very fit tramping groups.

If snow is on the route, suitable for experienced parties only, equipped with ice axe and crampons.

Mt Taylor, at 2331m, has the distinction of being the highest peak in the Canterbury foothills. In fact it is much more than a foothill, yet because it and the surrounding Taylor and Mt Hutt ranges are not linked to the Southern Alps, it is still regarded as a mere foothill. Approaches onto the peak are long and are generally made from Lake Heron via wide, open station country over 4WD tracks. The climb can be completed in one long day. However, in winter or as an easier option, an overnight trip is to be preferred.

The Swin River, which drains into the eastern side of Lake Heron, provides the key to climbs from the lake. The upper part of this river, where it flows from steep-sided gullies in the Taylor Range, is reached after several hours' undulating walking over flats to Double Hill Hut (Clent Hills Station), where there is good camping. From the hut continue into the Swin River South Branch gorge, which is readily traversed for 2km to a major fork at 1160m. The steep spur dropping from near the summit of Mt Taylor directly into this fork is the best and most direct route. It is a very taxing climb of over 1400m from the hut, passing over Points 1766m and 2062m,

Taylor Range

heading almost due east until the Taylor Range crest is reached at 2240m. A short walk and scramble to the southeast from here lead to the summit. The view is extraordinary.

Access is via the south shore of Lake Heron to Swin River and Double Hut.

Descent routes from the summit are possible via the Mt Somers Range and a northwest spur over Points 2016m, 1761m, 1664m and 1212m to the Swin River, or via Peak 2281m north along the Taylor Range. These are long routes, especially in winter.

Alternatively, retrace your steps to the Swin River forks.

18. Mt Catherine, Lake Heron Basin

Terraces to summit via ridge: 4–5 hours. **Hard+**
Summit to terraces via Home Creek: 2–3 hours.
Ice axe and crampons essential during winter.

Deep in the central Canterbury foothills lies the high, rugged Taylor Range, with summits averaging 2000m and reaching 2333m at Mt Taylor. The western aspect of this range is bordered by Lake Heron, a large, shallow, high-country lake, resting at 700m within an amphitheatre created by the peaks. At the northern end of the range Mt Catherine (2085m) guards the approaches to the Smite River and hinterland beyond the ranges.

For road access see 'Cameron Valley, Arrowsmith Range'. From the gravel pit continue on to the northern end of Lake Heron and through Upper Lake Heron Station (ph. 03 303 9014 for permission). Cross the high terraces up behind the farm to the southwest flanks of the peak.

19. Cameron Valley, Arrowsmith Range

5–6 hours to Cameron Hut. **Moderate**

Peaks reminiscent of the Italian Dolomites, the beauty and clarity of the high country and a comfortable mountain hut are the attractions of this remote valley set in the Lake Heron Basin. The Cameron Valley offers a long and sometimes tiring approach to the eastern aspect of the jagged Arrowsmith Range, which rises to 2781m at Mt Arrowsmith. This, together with a cluster of six other major summits over 2500m and numerous minor peaks reaching

Taylor Range from Lake Spider

2300–2400m, provides a dramatic wall of alpine grandeur isolating the valley from the Main Divide farther to the northwest. It has long been a mecca for serious alpinists, with numerous steep, exposed face routes possible on the peaks, as well as opportunity for some challenging winter ice routes. A relatively large glacier, the Cameron, lies in a shaded basin at around 2000m between the main range and an outlier, granting climbers easy access onto the peaks. For trampers, however, the valley offers mostly a return trip, albeit amid spectacular surroundings.

From the vehicle track at the mouth of the Cameron River, where vehicles can be left, a 4WD trail leads into the valley alongside a bulldozed flood protection wall. As the valley narrows, the trail is left behind and flats interspersed with sections of rough track, penetrating the more dense matagouri thickets, are the tramper's fare for some hours upstream, until the remains of the old Highland homestead is passed on the far bank.

From here the valley widens to include shingle flats and easier going, until

Cameron Hut and the Arrowsmith Range

the short upper gorge is reached. This is readily traversed and leads again to more open going, still on the south bank, or river right. At the top of the upper gorge your first unobstructed view of the Arrowsmiths is gained; earlier glimpses have been just enough to spur your pace to reach the valley head. At any season the black and white wall of peaks is an astonishing spectacle, and if this is a first visit, it is quite unexpected in its bold and rugged profile.

Above the top flats a moderate climb begins on a cairned track up a shallow gully over old moraines. This starts on the river right beside the valley wall and climbs for almost 200m before curving around and descending slightly to reach the hut, sited in mid-valley on a large gravel and tussock flat beside the upper river. The hut has nine bunks and is maintained by the Canterbury Mountaineering Club, to whom fees are payable. There is also a mountain radio in the hut that broadcasts weather information at 7.30pm each day as well as maintaining a listening watch for any search and rescue emergencies.

Climbing to Peg Col

Here you are nestled beneath several very big mountains, with East Horn's sharp arêtes and sheer bluffs rising almost 1300m directly above the hut. The lower portion of the Cameron Glacier is visible from here and parties wishing to get a closer view can continue up the 'carriageway', an obvious lateral trench running up the south side of the valley above the hut.

A second night at the hut would allow for more exploration, or perhaps even an ascent of the glacier for those with glacier experience, rope, ice axe and crampons. Remember, this is no place for the inexperienced. Numerous climbs are possible from the hut but these are outside the scope of this guide. One that may be possible for experienced groups is The Marquee (2421m), northeast of the hut.

Return is via the inward route.

More competent parties, equipped with ice axe and crampons, could try Peg Col (2004m), visible to the northwest from the hut. This leads to Jagged Stream in the Rakaia Valley, returning to Lake Heron via Lake Stream, and will take 2 days of steady tramping. Permission is required from Lake Heron Station (ph. 03 303 9014).

Access is from Mt Somers township. Follow the Ashburton Gorge Road to the junction with the Hakatere Heron Road. Follow this to Lake Heron and continue along the lake-shore to the gravel pit marked on the map. Here an indistinct vehicle track leads off to the left toward the Cameron Valley, which will be seen exiting the rounded hills through a cutting. It is about 1.5km along this track to a carpark and signage, where cars are left.

Cameron Hut fees are $5.00 per person per night, payable to the Canterbury Mountaineering Club, PO Box 2415, Christchurch.

20. South Branch Ashburton
Road to Boundary Creek Hut: 2–3 hours. **Easy**
Boundary Hut to Top Hut: 2–3 hours. **Easy**
Top Hut to Cameron Hut via Wild Mans Brother Range passes: 5–6 hours. **Moderate**
Top Hut to Potts Hut via Stumpy Saddle: 5–6 hours. **Moderate**

The upper South Branch of the Ashburton River is a large, empty valley draining the southern flanks of Mt Arrowsmith. This long valley has great appeal for those who love wide, empty space amid spectacular mountains, and it has easy access. A 4WD trail heads into the mid-reaches of this valley

Tramping party in Top Hut, South Ashburton

from the Hakatere Heron Road and grants good all-weather access to Boundary Creek Hut (8 bunks), a large ex-musterer's hut located above the junction of Boundary Creek with the South Ashburton. From the hut there are two possible routes:
(i) Up the hill behind the hut, via the 4WD trail, onto Dogs Range and

Bryce Jenkins crossing Wild Mans Brother Range

over to the Potts River Hut through the head of Boundary Creek. This is a spectacular high route, with sweeping views of the Rangitata Plain and headwaters and the possibility of climbing summits on the Big Hill Range. (ii) Continue up the South Ashburton, again on a 4WD trail, through easy terrain, to reach Top Hut (10 bunks). For routes to the Potts, see notes for 'Potts River and Hut'.

The Cameron Hut can be reached via a variety of range crossings from Top Hut, over the Wild Mans Brother Range, through either a pass directly opposite the hut at Point 1432m or father northwest along the range to another unnamed pass east of Points 1722m and 1686m to reach the head of Spean Stream, which is traversed at around 1600m to a small col, west of Point 1616m, and then descend directly to the Cameron.

Access is off the Hakatere Heron Road about 2km north of the old Hakatere homestead. A marked route and signage indicate the way.

21. Lake Heron Walks

Harrisons Bight from Lake Heron carpark: 1 hour. **Easy**
Lake Heron to Double Hut: 2–3 hours. **Easy**
Double Hut to Manuka Hut: 1.5 hours. **Easy**
Manuka Hut to Hakatere Heron Road via Lake Emily: 2–3 hours. **Easy**
Manuka Hut to Ashburton Gorge Road via Stour River: 5 hours.
Moderate
Double Hut to Clent Hills Saddle and Comyns Hut (North Ashburton): 8 hours. **Hard**
(See notes for 'Rakaia Valley' for routes out from here.)

Lake Heron is the largest of the Ashburton Lakes and is an important fishery and wildlife refuge. In addition, like Lake Clearwater, no power boating is allowed here in an effort to protect the lake environment. A small public camping area is located at the south end of the lake, and from here an access road heads along the south shore to a series of walking routes heading into the Swin River and Taylor Range.

The shortest of these tracks is the delightful and easy lakeside walk to beautiful Harrisons Bight, a 2km long arm of the lake on its eastern shoreline. This is a renowned fishing area and a great location for a family picnic amid dramatic scenery.

Branching off the Harrisons Bight Track is another trail heading over undulating tussock flats and climbing gently to reach the South Branch of the Swin River and Double Hut (6 bunks). This old musterer's abode makes a great location for an overnight stop and is nicely situated under the Taylor Range and beside a small creek. This section of the track is part of the Te Araroa Trail, which comes down the North Swin Branch from Clent Hills Saddle. This is a moderately challenging route over river terraces to Clent Hills Saddle (1485m) and river valleys to reach Comyns Hut (8 bunks) in the North Branch of the Ashburton. The route is poled.

South of Double Hut lie several small lakes – Seagull, Manuka and Emily, and a beautiful, albeit sometimes stark, high-country landscape. Manuka Hut is also located just 5km south of Double Hut, near Manuka Lake, and a through trip could be made via this hut to Lake Emily and out again to the Haketere Potts Road. A car shuttle or pick-up arrangements will be needed to get back to Lake Heron, however.

The Stour River bridge on the Ashburton Gorge Road can also be reached by mountain bike or on foot from the Manuka Hut/Lake Emily area via the Stour River West Branch and Stour River, passing through some remote country between the Manuka Range and Clent Hills.

22. Mt Hutt Forest and Awa Awa Rata Reserve

Awa Awa Reserve Loop Track: 90 minutes. **Easy**
Ridge Track continuation of Awa Awa Loop: 30 minutes. **Easy**
Alder Track: 45 minutes. **Easy**
Scott's Saddle Track extension to skifield road: 2.5 hours one way. **Moderate**

Of the thousands of visitors who travel to Canterbury's best-known skifield every season, few would be aware of the delightful forest and picnic area nestled below the access road on the southeast side of the mountain. The Mt Hutt Forest, together with its two adjoining reserves, Pudding Hill and Awa Awa, is a remnant of the forests that once extended over much of the plains and were almost continuous along the foothills. Covering an area of 4441 hectares, the forest encompasses the catchments of Dry Stream and Pudding Hill Stream, the latter falling from the south summit of Mt Hutt at 2189m.

Mountain beech is the predominant species throughout the forest, with Hall's tōtara, fuchsia, kōhūhū and pōkākā present, together with the ubiquitous bush lawyer and ground ferns. Above the bushline, snow tussocks and alpine herbs are found. From a modest altitude of 1000m on the Scott's Saddle Track, which joins with the Mt Hutt skifield road, a sparkling view of the plains all the way to the Port Hills is obtained. Various tussock knobs en route provide vantage points and well-earned rest spots.

Returning from Scott's Saddle you gain an appreciation of the beauty of this small reserve tucked into the foothills and abutting the cultivated plains, criss-crossed by roads and fences.

The Awa Awa Loop and Ridge tracks provide an alternative route back around the low, undulating ridgeline immediately above the picnic area. The easy rolling track gives ample opportunity to enjoy the views of the plains once again through 'windows' in the bush, and to observe the forest, together with its abundant birdlife. This includes bellbird, tomtit, rifleman, wood pigeon (kererū), grey warbler, and kea above the bushline.

Continuing along the Ridge Track brings you to an area of exotic forest

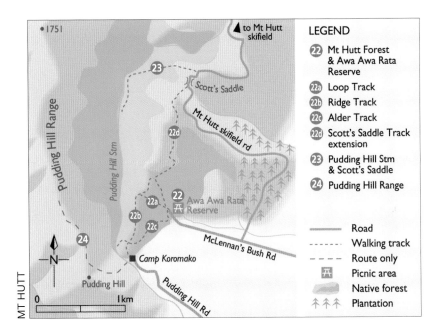

where larch has been planted. The transition from native forest is sudden, yet the larch plantation has its own beauty, as the track, now covered in needles, winds along the ridge crest and drops steeply to Pudding Hill Stream. From here an unmarked route continues up the streambed, eventually linking with another track to Scott's Saddle. This would be an interesting tramp for the experienced on a fine day. From the junction with Pudding Hill Stream, the Alder Track will return you to the picnic area.

The setting of the picnic area, complete with barbecue areas and a shelter, is secluded and peaceful beneath the flanks of Mt Hutt. Some exotics have been introduced here as well, in the form of rhododendrons, which, I am reliably informed, flower magnificently during spring. Southern rātā, a botanical rarity in this part of Canterbury, is present in the Awa Awa Rata Reserve and also in Scott's Creek. The forest can be surprisingly sheltered from the nor'westers, which rage over the summit of Mt Hutt, most frequently during spring.

The history of the original reserve dates back to 1889, when it was gazetted as state forest.

23. Pudding Hill Stream Track and Scott's Saddle to Alder Track
Via stream: 3–4 hours. **Moderate**

The entrance to this track is off the skifield road 100m above Scott's Saddle. It follows an open ridge before dropping steeply into Pudding Hill Stream. The valley is followed downstream to link with the Alder and Ridge tracks. These descend steeply, on the river left, onto a small flat just before the final hillock on the toe of the Mt Hutt Range.

Note: There are multiple crossings required of the stream and the route is not marked, but crossing is easy in all but flood conditions, when it should not be attempted.

Access is off Route 72 onto McLennan's Bush Road, which is the same road that gives access to the Mt Hutt skifield. The reserve entrance is approximately 2km past the skifield turnoff.

24. Pudding Hill Range
Camp Koromako to Point 1751m: 3–4 hours. **Moderate/Hard**
Return via ridge: 2–3 hours
Ice axe required in winter.

Access onto this easy-angled ridge, which provides enjoyable tramping for several kilometres, is at first difficult to find from an approach out of Pudding Hill Stream. However, a short, unmarked scramble up a steep forested spur (on the river right), about 800m up Pudding Hill Stream, gives way to easy, open tussock slopes and a brief section of 4WD road before the ridge proper begins. The top, open section of this spur can be glimpsed from near Camp Koromako. Here short tussock knobs, changing to a rocky crest and small scree peaks, lead you along the ridge, high above the plains and valleys.

Beyond the stream the grid pattern of the Canterbury Plains spreads away toward the distant sea. West of the ridge crest lies the steep dissected Taylor and Alford ranges, a huge tract of mountain country lying between the Rakaia and Ashburton rivers, where few tramping parties venture, perhaps because of its arid nature and steep terrain. The ridge offers a good view out over the lower summits to the great wall of the Taylor Range, which reaches 2300m.

Finally, at 1751m, a small sharp peak provides a turnaround point. Or you could continue on to Mt Bruce (1829m). A full range traverse, which continues on for some kilometres to the north peak of Mt Hutt, will take several more hours.

Note: Beware of dropping into Pudding Hill Stream from the ridge; the bush is very thick, wasps are a major problem in summer/autumn, and the final descent into the stream is gorged and badly bluffed.

For access follow the Alder Track through the reserve to the stream, or drive around to Camp Koromako (Seventh Day Adventist Camp) via Pudding Hill Road off Route 72, 4km south of Mt Hutt skifield road, and into Mt Hutt Forest and Pudding Hill Scenic Reserve. Access is also via Pudding Hill Recreation Farm direct onto the ridge via a 4WD track on the south side of Pudding Hill Stream.

25. Rakaia Gorge Walkway
3–4 hours return. **Easy**

The Rakaia Gorge Walkway offers an easy return walk passing through a number of unique features. The foremost of these is the spectacular clifftop traverse of the Rakaia Gorge, which the track follows for most of its 5km length. This major geological and glacial landmark of the eastern South Island provides a stunning landscape, through which the walkway meanders.

There are several regenerating forest and scrub communities encountered along the track, with the more common trees being kōwhai, makomako (wineberry), mountain beech, putaputawētā, cabbage tree, as well as flaxes and various ferns.

Other features of the walkway are the site of the old ferryman's cottage, from which travellers would call the ferryman, John Bryan, from the south bank, where he owned and operated the Windwhistle Accommodation House from 1851 to 1869. The 'ferry' consisted of a flat-bottomed punt, which was hauled across by a rope. Also at this location was the Home Guard fortification site built during World War II as part of the war-time defences for the highway bridge that was constructed in 1882, in two parts, between the small island that divides the river at this point. The northern bridge is original and is one of only two in the world constructed using the Bollman Truss design. The southern wooden bridge was replaced with the present concrete bridge in 1945.

Near the western end of the walkway are the remains of the Snowdon coal

Rakaia Gorge Walkway

mines, where the entrances to several mine shafts can be inspected. Julius von Haast reported coal seams here around 1871, and within a few years George Gerard, owner of the 16,800ha Snowdon pastoral run, had driven 30m shafts into the hillside to work the 3m seam. The mines closed in 1904.

Aside from the historical and geological interest of the walkway, the scenic attractions are outstanding. From a number of viewpoints along the clifftop, dramatic perspectives of the mighty blue Rakaia are gained as it swirls past the steep eroded bluffs, broad shingle banks, and patterned farm terraces. Above the river cliffs looms Mt Hutt, perhaps plastered with snow if your visit is during winter. At the upper gorge lookout point, tantalising views of the distant Southern Alps are possible, from which the ubiquitous westerly gales funnel through the gorge to the plains. There are numerous sheltered spots along the track at which to rest and enjoy the view. Water is not always easily obtainable, despite the proximity to the Rakaia River, so a waterbottle is necessary.

This is a special rural walk that provides an insight into the wilds of this huge river and the mountains and valleys of Canterbury, as well as a slice of early history.

It is also possible to walk the track one way by accessing the upper end of the walkway with a jet boat. These leave the highway bridge carpark regularly for scenic and fishing trips on the river. The Rakaia Gorge is a noted trout and salmon fishing locale.

The walkway is 75km from Christchurch on Route 72, accessed on the north side of the Rakaia Gorge highway bridge, and is 10km return.

26. Mt Hutt Summit
South bank road to summit: 5–7 hours. **Hard+**
Summit to road via Little River: 3–4 hours.
If attempted in winter, ice axe and crampons will be necessary and be aware of avalanche risk. The ridges should be kept to during winter. Beware of the wind.

For most visitors to Mt Hutt, which is Canterbury's best-known skifield, the South Peak (2075m) is easily attained via the road and ski tows. However, approximately 2km north of here, along the Mt Hutt Range, stands Mt Hutt at 2185m. It is possible to traverse the range from the South Peak and

Canterbury Plains and dawn light from Mt Hutt summit

some ski tourers do this each season. However, a far more interesting and, it must be emphasised, strenuous, alternative is to ascend one of the long, high, northeastern ridges from the Rakaia River south bank road to the high peak. As a day excursion it is an arduous climb involving over 1800m of vertical ascent from the road over a distance of 6km. Yet once above the steep, grassy, lower faces and onto the mountain proper it becomes a very interesting route with a grand spectacle encompassing the Canterbury Plains, all the way to Christchurch and the Port Hills, as well as extensive views of the major summits of the Southern Alps including Mt Cook, D'Archiac and Arrowsmith.

The summit and ridge route are both major landmarks from Christchurch, out to the southwest, and thus attractive objectives for a day trip.

Descent is via an eastern spur, approximately 500m south of the summit at 2100m to around 1300m, before dropping into Little River, where a small waterfall is easily negotiated on the river left, and then to the road. Alternatively, follow the ridge out over Points 1307m and 1186m. The lower part of this route (from the road to 700m altitude) is on private land and permission is required from Cleardale Station (ph. 03 302 8233).

27. Steepface Hill

Terrible Gully to summit via Point 1488m: 3–5 hours. **Hard+**
Redcliffe Stream to Hutt Stream via road: 90 minutes. **Hard+**

Just north of Mt Hutt stands Steepface Hill (1876m), its approach spur reducing the mighty Rakaia Valley to barely 500m width; it is mostly 3–4km wide above the gorge. This peak commands a view along the length of the Rakaia River, unobstructed by other ranges, and it is readily climbed from the Rakaia south bank. But be warned – Steepface Hill is aptly named.

Approaches are many and straightforward but unrelentingly steep until mid-way Point 1488m, on the northeast ridge, where the angle eases at a broad saddle. Above here the ridge runs up to the summit with a short scramble to the top. The southern aspects of Steepface Hill slope away into a gentle basin, which can carry deep snow during winter and well into spring.

A traverse of the summit ridge, west, over Point 1874m and then northwest down to Points 1498m and 1245m, toward Redcliffe Stream and Saddle in the Redcliffe Conservation Area, offers an interesting descent route.

Access is via the Terrible Gully easement from Double Hill Run Road (this is marked and poled into the stream only), and then south up steep slopes to Point 1488m. Alternatively, as for Mt Hutt north peak via Hutt Stream, climb onto the flat terrace on the east bank of Hutt Stream, descend to and cross the stream in the mouth of the gully and head up a very steep, fenced spur that drops northeast from Point 1488m.

The Hutt Stream route is on private land. Phone Redcliffe Station (03 318 5874) for permission.

REDCLIFFE CONSERVATION AREA

Redcliffe Conservation Area is contained within the greater Hakatere Conservation Park and includes an attractive scenic reserve in the canyon, which contains the stream. An access track climbs through this reserve on the river right (east bank) to reach Redcliff Saddle.

28. Redcliff Saddle and Tribb Hut

Road to Tribb Hut: 3 hours. **Moderate**

Tribb Hut to Cookies Point: 2 hours. **Moderate**

Cookies Point to Comyns Hut: 4–5 hours. **Moderate**

The marked track up Redcliffe Stream passes through regenerating native forest and some mature forest that has largely escaped the ravages of pastoral clearance, and as such is an important reserve for native plants and animals. Once at Redcliff Saddle, the landscape opens up into a spectacular high-country scene of rolling tussocks and high, bare, often snow-covered hills.

Below Snowy Stream, 3km south of the saddle, is Tribb Hut (6 bunks), a small, rustic building providing Spartan comfort, which seems entirely apt for the wide, barren spaces that surround it. Continuing on down Swift River, which may require care to cross during snowmelt and after heavy rain, Cookies Hut (private) is reached and a little while later Cookies Point. This latter landmark is where the North Branch of the Ashburton River enters, which can be followed back, northwest, to Comyns Hut and Turtons Saddle. A low to average river flow will be needed for this route, as there are many river crossings. It is best as a summer route.

Redcliff Saddle, Rakaia River

29. Turtons Saddle

Road to saddle: 3 hours. **Moderate**
Saddle to A-Frame Hut: 30 minutes. **Easy**
A-Frame Hut to Comyns Hut: 2 hours. **Moderate**
Comyns Hut to Cookies Point: 4–5 hours. **Moderate**
Comyns Hut to Double Hut via Clent Hills Saddle: 8 hours. **Moderate/Hard**

A broad saddle at the very head of the North Branch of the Ashburton River, Turtons Saddle (1130m) makes a great day trip in itself or as part of a longer trip into the Black and Taylor ranges. It is a pleasant tramp up Glenrock Stream to the last steep zigzags leading to the saddle, and once up, the view of the lower valley, Rakaia River and Mt Oakden are memorable. From the saddle an easy vehicle trail is followed south into the North Branch and down to A-Frame Hut (4 bunks), a neat little hut sited on a terrace near Comyns Stream. The hut has a great view and would make an excellent base for climbs onto the nearby Black Range and Black Hill (2067m). Beyond the hut the streambed is followed, with a short section of 4WD trail over a gorge, to reach Comyns Hut (8 bunks), located on a terrace beside its predecessor. This hut also has a grand setting, being ensconced in a deep canyon below 2000m peaks. From here you can return via the same route or, if time and river conditions allow (i.e. a low to average river flow), a through trip could be made downriver to Cookies Point.

Comyns Hut is also on the route for the Te Araroa Trail, which traverses the Round Hill Creek catchment, through Clent Hills Saddle, and down the Swin River North Branch to Double Hut. This route is poled.

HUT HOPPING IN THE HIGH COUNTRY

Huts have a great attraction for trampers and recreationalists of all types who, although they may journey to the outdoors for widely varying reasons, appreciate the ambience, security and heritage that huts in New Zealand have to offer. So whenever a new one comes to my attention I have a desire to visit it and check it out, record it on camera, and file it away for later reference. Comyns Hut in the North Branch of the Ashburton River is one such hut, though it's hardly new, being an old musterer's refuge now incorporated into the conservation estate of Hakatere Conservation Park up in the Rakaia River catchment. The hut, along with some others nearby, is also now part of the Te Araroa Trail, stretching from Cape Reinga to Bluff, so if you head off to the hut you may even meet some intrepid hikers out for 3–6 months walking this unique route.

For me, though, it was strictly a day trip, beginning on the south bank of the Rakaia at a marked easement that heads, gently at first, into Glenrock Stream. A poled route then travels up the long river fan, now dotted with pockets of scrub, and farther up enters a small gorge,

A-frame hut, Turtons Stream

Comyns Hut, Turtons Stream

where a 4WD trail continues more steeply to the summit of Turtons Saddle at around 1100m. This high-point of the journey is worth the steady uphill grind as it has a grand view and a spacious location among tussock-covered ridges. Now for the hut. Actually there are two up here and the first one is not far below the saddle on the Ashburton side. It's a small A-frame set beside a stream running off the Black Hill Range and makes a great lunch stop. The landscape is unrelentingly empty; a good point to keep in mind should you come in windy or cold conditions is that, save the two small huts, there is no shelter. It's a further 6km onto Comyns from the A-frame, mostly on the 4WD trail but with some indistinct sections through the riverbed where there are also several easy fords. However, as the trail closes on the hut a small gorge is encountered and the river is constricted. Climbing over the last shoulder above the gorge I spied Comyns sitting on a nice grassy terrace on the far side of the river – just 1km away. A ford of the Ashburton is necessary to reach the hut, and although I had little difficulty with it, in high flows, especially during the spring thaw, it may well prove impassable. Finally, I could stride over the terrace to reach the rustic shelter and push on inside for lunch amid the cool, dark surroundings.

Comyns Hut was built in 1957 as a replacement for the original hut constructed circa 1890; this much older and now derelict structure is nearby. The whole ambience of the hut and location are remarkable, especially the depth of the valley when seen from outside the hut – a full 1200m altitude lies between the valley floor and the high summits to the east, and that in just 2km. Finishing my lunch in the dusty interior, I headed outside, secured my pack and headed back up the lonely, windswept valley of the Ashburton, planning on a rest stop at the A-frame on my hut-hopping mission.

30. Double Hill
1–2 hours. **Moderate**

Double Hill is a massive, twin-summitted moraine mound, a *roche moutonnée*, standing in the middle of the upper Rakaia Valley, and is a legacy of the once-enormous glacial tongues that coursed through these valleys and carved out the great trenches that the rivers now occupy. Both summits can be reached reasonably easily via the conservation areas surrounding them for a fascinating view out over the Rakaia/Mathias confluence and the peaks and passes of these valleys.

Double Hill is approximately 40km upvalley from the SH77 turnoff and is instantly recognisable as the twin-summitted hill in mid-valley on extensive flats. The southern summit (closest to road), Double Hill D (682m), is contained within a fenced and marked conservation area where walking, mountain biking, and horse treks are permitted. The best route to the summit is to head northwest along the base of the hill to its far western end, where a route will be found up to the summit plateau. The northern summit (699m) is reached by following a rough vehicle trail (poled) north, over flats from near the rock quarry for 1.3km to a poled route heading west to the conservation area on the southern flanks of the summit. Once inside the protected area, fencelines can be followed to the summit ridge.

31. Palmer Range and Godley Peak
Double Hill access to range crest: 4–5 hours. **Hard+**
Range crest to Godley Peak: 2–3 hours. **Hard+**

This is an unrelentingly steep route onto the Palmer Range via a public access easement onto Homestead Hill, which is poled and marked from the carpark on the farm flats below the ridgeline. Please keep to the marked route. A broad face is then followed, later through bush, to a narrowing spur and then a series of steps on the ridgeline to the range crest around 1800m. From here a traverse can be made to Godley Peak (2087m), the highest point on the range, with a stunning view of the Rakaia watershed and the Southern Alps. It also bears the distinction of having a coldwater spring, Mother Millers Spring, on its northern ridge at around 2020m altitude. These springs may not always be visible, for example under heavy snow cover or in dry conditions. By continuing along the range to the east you can eventually reach Turtons Saddle. This would be a big day.

Mike Latty on Homestead Hill, upper Rakaia

If you have permission from Glenfalloch Station (see notes for 'Banfield Hut'), you can also traverse the range west to reach Smite Peak (2003m).

32. Banfield Hut, Rakaia River

Glenfalloch haybarn to Banfield Hut: 3–4 hours. **Moderate**

At the end of the access road up the south bank of the Rakaia River, the uniform patterns of high-country farms recede before the overwhelming majesty of the Arrowsmith Range and upper Rakaia peaks. It is worth the long drive from the plains just to see and experience the magnificent emptiness of the back-country. Banfield Hut (6 bunks) is the first public hut located up the Rakaia Valley and can be reached in half a day's walk from the road.

The first part of the tramp is delightfully easy, but unfortunately does not remain so. The unmarked trail follows a 4WD track along the base of the hills, passing through some swampy sections and gravel flats before descending down a shallow gully to Lake Stream. This stream is normally easy to cross, even after moderate northwest conditions, as it does not drain from the Main Divide. However, if heavy rain from the northeast or southeast has preceded your visit it can be very difficult to cross, and unless you are very experienced at river crossings do not attempt it. The best fords are to be found farther upriver.

The best route from here is to tramp upstream for 1.5km, heading toward the southeastern end of Prospect Hill (888m), where a fenceline drops from the hill to Lake Stream. Take care crossing Lake Stream here. Once onto the foot of the hill, walk up the fenceline and over to the low saddle south of Prospect Hill, where a 4WD track will be picked up. This cannot be followed all the way to the Rakaia River due to some bad washouts. Instead, cross the undulating plateau at around the 800m contour and drop down into Washbourne Creek and Thompsons Hut (Glenfalloch Station). From Thompsons Hut the 4WD track continues along grass and matagouri flats to Jagged Stream, where careful attention is required to avoid deep thickets of scrub.

Banfield Hut stands on the southeast bank of Jagged Stream, about 500m upstream from where the 4WD track first crosses the stream. It is not visible until very close and stands on a narrow terrace on the bush edge above the creek. This rustic little hut has a special wilderness feel to it, with the roar of the stream your constant companion and wonderful views from the terrace of the glaciers on the Arrowsmith Range. Blue duck are sometimes seen in the stream near the hut.

Return via the same route unless you are planning a multi-day tramp into the Rakaia headwaters, where there are several more huts.

Access is as for Double Hill but continue on up Double Hill Run Road to Glenfalloch Station and onto the hay barn, through the gate on the river flats.

Phone Glenfalloch Station (03 318 5843) for permission and river conditions.

Banfield Hut fees are $5.00 per person per night, payable to the Canterbury Mountaineering Club, PO Box 2415, Christchurch.

Wilberforce Valley and Lake Coleridge

One of the most dramatic regions of the Canterbury high country is the Lake Coleridge Basin and Wilberforce Valley. This region, dominated by the great blue slash of the lake, has incredible views, particularly from the peaks around the lake-shore (see notes for 'Mt Oakden' and 'Peak Hill'), and several accessible walks into remote valleys, which seldom see many visitors, making them an excellent choice to find solitude amid grand landscapes. This section of the back country is also one of the closest to Christchurch. For access to this region, take the Coleridge Road, off SH77 near Windwhistle, and then on to Homestead and Harper roads for the head of Lake Coleridge and Harper Diversion, or Homestead and Algidus roads for Peak Hill and the south side of Mt Oakden.

1. Dry Acheron Stream Access to Big Ben
Carpark to Clay Gully: 1 hour. **Easy**
Clay Gully (junction) to Big Ben junction: 1 hour. **Easy**
Big Ben junction to Conical Knoll: 30 minutes. **Easy**
Big Ben junction to Big Ben: 2 hours. **Moderate**

A marked and poled easement off the Coleridge Road grants access to the attractive little Dry Acheron Stream, two covenanted areas (Clay Gully and Conical Knoll) of natural significance, and a southern approach to Big Ben (1416m) and the Big Ben Range in Korowai/Torlesse Tussocklands Park.

Paddling on Lake Coleridge

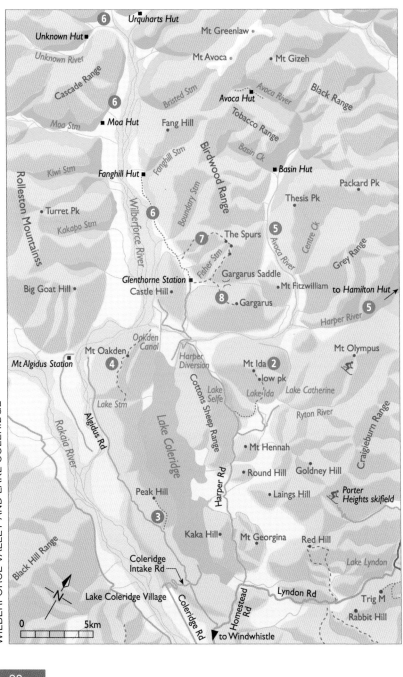

WILBERFORCE VALLEY AND LAKE COLERIDGE

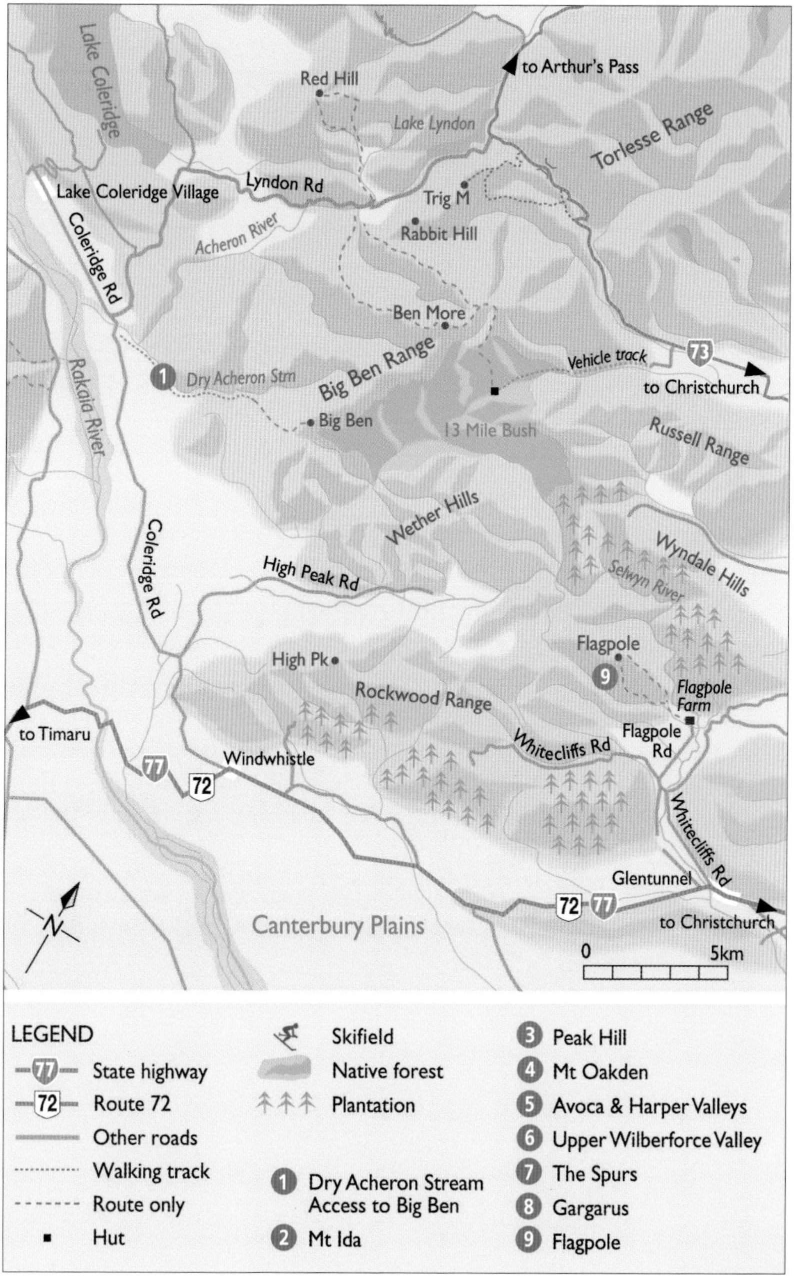

Lake Coleridge
Red Hill
to Arthur's Pass
Lake Lyndon
Torlesse Range
Lake Coleridge Village
Lyndon Rd
Trig M
Rabbit Hill
Acheron River
Coleridge Rd
Ben More
Big Ben Range
Vehicle track
73
to Christchurch
1
Dry Acheron Stm
Rakaia River
Big Ben
13 Mile Bush
Russell Range
Wether Hills
Wyndale Hills
Selwyn River
Coleridge Rd
High Peak Rd
Flagpole
High Pk
9
Flagpole Farm
Rockwood Range
to Timaru
Flagpole Rd
Whitecliffs Rd
77
72
Windwhistle
Whitecliffs Rd
Glentunnel
72
77
to Christchurch
Canterbury Plains
N
0
5km
LEGEND
77 State highway
72 Route 72
Other roads
Walking track
Route only
Hut
Skifield
Native forest
Plantation
1 Dry Acheron Stream Access to Big Ben
2 Mt Ida
3 Peak Hill
4 Mt Oakden
5 Avoca & Harper Valleys
6 Upper Wilberforce Valley
7 The Spurs
8 Gargarus
9 Flagpole

The route heads in off the road under a long row of pines, later dropping into the stream, which it then follows, twisting and turning, for some way to reach the meteorological station and base of Big Ben. On the way, two covenanted areas are passed; both are marked detours from the main route.

From the meteorological station the summit of Big Ben is readily accessed via a steep western spur, which climbs over Point 962m to a high shoulder and then onto the summit for outstanding views of the Coleridge Basin and Rakaia Valley.

2. Mt Ida
Lake Selfe to summit: 3–4 hours. **Hard**
Summit to Lake Catherine: 2 hours. **Moderate**
Summit to low peak: 1 hour. **Moderate**
Low peak to road: 2 hours. **Moderate**

This dramatic foothill stands directly behind Lake Selfe on the Harper Road and is characterised by high, bare, eroded faces, which usually carry heavy snow during the winter months. The mountain is isolated from its neighbours by the lakes and valleys that surround it, and it is this feature of its topography that make it eminently suitable as a day climb, because the view from any of its three summits is totally unobscured. While there are no tracks to the top, a good route is to follow the marked, poled track from the south end of Lake Selfe around to Lake Ida and from there to access the very steep southeast spur (more of a face until around 1200m) to gain the first summit at 1642m. Mt Ida lies about 1km away from here, at 1695m. The view is fantastic, and not only from the summit. Descend the same way or down the braid scree basin to Lake Catherine or, if you are keen, take the west ridge to the low peak (1570m).

Mt Ida and all the fishing access tracks here are on private land; please respect this.

NO IDLE MOMENTS ON MT IDA

There's a solid 900m slog awaiting those wishing to summit the isolated peak of Mt Ida in central Canterbury, just north of Lake Coleridge. It's untracked, unmarked and very steep, though there is no technical difficulty – just find a good line, hopefully clear of scrub, and head up. This is what Mike Latty and I did one autumn, when the idea of a walk in the hills on a sultry evening looked to be a good, albeit tough, option. Leaving our vehicle at Lake Selfe in mid-afternoon, we took the track around to Lake Ida and the base of the mount. I had deliberately chosen a late start so that we could cruise the shingle ridge crest between the peak's three summits in the early evening and perhaps catch the golden light of an autumn sunset from a lofty vantage. 'At least we'll get up here quickly', I remark to Mike as we labour over a rock outcrop to rest, turn from the slope and gape at the perspective we have gained of the basin and its numerous post-glacial mounds that sprout from the landscape like a series of massive beehives. It's a tawny, ragged and dusty topography in here, where rivers twist about the giant tors searching for an escape from the maze.

Traversing ridges of Mt Ida, Avoca Valley in background

The first summit is near, at 1642m, and 700m away, through a shallow saddle, is Mt Ida, just 53m higher. We reach it at 6pm, the light is lowering in the sky, the nor'west wind is but a faint memory, and we are positioned for a remarkable ramble in evening light along the 1.5km ridge crest to the low peak at 1570m. Our loosely formed plan has paid off handsomely. The ridge crest is spectacularly narrow, dropping rapidly from its two-boot-width 1000m northwest to the Harper River screes, and 1000m south to the Lake Selfe basin. 'Let's do it', I call to Mike, who is already heading away along the ridge, needing no encouragement. At the low peak a rocky corridor grants access to the summit, lit by the distant twinkle of the sun sinking below the alps. The route off requires some care – there are bluffs and steeper slopes ringing the south side where we plan to descend, so an assiduous line is chosen to skirt these obstacles and gain the great southwest scree face of Mt Ida. At 1400m we sidle out onto the face, perfectly located to take a direct line on the 700m descent – a scree run, and run it we do. Great leaping bounds in soft, finely grained scree take us from the sunlit heights onto the dark flanks of the lower mountain in barely 20 minutes.

It's getting late and the exhilaration of the descent is short-lived – a narrow band of tall matagouri bars our progress. Matagouri is a native shrub that grows to 2–3m and sports fearsomely long woody spines that tear and penetrate exposed flesh. I am wearing shorts, so by the time we are both spat out onto the easy tussock slope below the scrub band we are not a pretty sight.

'All in an evening's work', I comment to Mike as we limp away in the dark toward the car at the far end of the lake.

3. Peak Hill

Road to summit: 2–3 hours. **Moderate**

Peak Hill (1240m), centrally located on the southwestern shoreline of Lake Coleridge, grants an unsurpassed viewpoint of the Coleridge Basin, Southern Alps, Rakaia Valley and eastern foothills. Ratings of 'best' viewpoints are largely subjective and often heavily weighted with personal preferences, however Peak Hill is unequivocally outstanding. The summit view, with its clearly defined border between the broad, green-grey trench of the Rakaia watershed and the deep-blue bowl that holds Lake Coleridge, is both unexpected and visually stunning. Add to this feast a coating of snow punctuated by the yellow spray of alpine tussock and a deep corridor of mountains receding to the distant Main Divide and you may begin to realise the splendour of the scene. If, perchance, it all becomes a little too much, just choose one of the many small knolls overlooking the lake and pause for a moment, or even an afternoon, to absorb the immense grandeur of the scene revealed below.

Lake Coleridge and Peak Hill, left, from Mt Oakden

Wilberforce Valley from Mt Oakden

Peak Hill is one of those special places that is worth much more than just one chance visit. It is a place to which many will choose to return, especially at different seasons, to recapture the mood and the light.

It is accessed from Rakaia Gorge via Coleridge Road and then on to Algidus Road, or from Lake Coleridge village via Coleridge Intake Road and Algidus Road. Bypass the access to the intake itself and continue for approximately 5km until near the steep southern flanks of Peak Hill, where a small carpark and sign indicate the poled route through paddocks to the base of the mountain.

4. Mt Oakden

Lake Stream to summit: 4–5 hours. **Hard**

Standing at the northern end of Lake Coleridge, in the central Canterbury foothills, is the imposing summit of Mt Oakden (1633m). Actually, it's a

Climber on summit of Mt Oakden, Rakaia River beyond

twin-summited mountain, with a low peak, at 1590m, lying 800m east of the high peak across a great fault scarp that divides the summit plateau. The summit features are not the only attractions for climbing this modest outlier of the Main Divide, which is barely 30km away and dominated, at this locality, by the mighty swathe of the Rakaia and Wilberforce rivers. The Wilberforce laps the very foot of Mt Oakden, which acts as a barrier to the river's southeastward progress, sending it coursing off to the southwest before joining the Rakaia farther downstream. Thus, the scene is set for a visual feast of landscape features when climbing Mt Oakden, and more so from its summit ridge stretched out for a kilometre in a north–south direction above the valleys.

Plying the lower slopes of the mountain, however, is not easy. There are many approaches, with the least problematic being a direct line from the head of Lake Coleridge, where the Oakden Canal brings waters over from the Wilberforce to feed into the lake's hydro system. There are no tracks or signs here – it's the perennial solution of 'find a line and go'. However, the unmarked route via Lake Stream to the northern rib, marked by Point 1173, is the best option. This is reached by the Harper Road, past Lake Selfe, to the lakehead and Oakden Canal, where cars can be left.

Mt Oakden is not a serious climb, more of an enjoyable scramble, and there are numerous routes to the summit. However, if going in winter an ice axe and crampons will be necessary.

The peak can also be accessed from the south, via Algidus Road, to a high saddle at 100m and then by the southeast ridge over Points 1431m and 1460m to the summit. This is a longer and harder route.

Drive to the head of Lake Coleridge and Oakden Canal for access.

All routes are on private land; phone Mt Oakden Station (03 318 5809) for permission.

5. Avoca and Harper Valleys
Harper Diversion (head of Lake Coleridge) to Basin Hut, Avoca Valley: 5–6 hours. **Moderate**
Harper Diversion to Hamilton Hut (Harper Valley): 5–6 hours. **Moderate**

These two valleys, at the head of Lake Coleridge, grant access to the Craigieburn Range (Harper Valley) and Black Range and Arthur's Pass National Park (Avoca Valley). They are both large catchments and as such the rivers can prove impassable during and after heavy rain. 4WD trails run for much of the length of the lower valleys and can be either walked or biked, with the permission of the landowners (Upper Glenthorne Station, ph. 03 318 5801). Walking times to the valley mid-reaches are long, so these routes are not often favoured, with most accessing the upper valleys from either Arthur's Pass National Park or the Craigieburn Conservation Park. (See notes for 'Arthur's Pass National Park' and 'Craigieburn Conservation Park and Ranges' for relevant trips in the upper valleys.)

6. Upper Wilberforce Valley

Glenthorne shearers' quarters to Fanghill Hut: 2 hours. **Easy**
Moa Hut from Fanghill: 90 minutes. **Easy**
Unknown Hut or Urquharts Hut from Fanghill Hut: 4 hours. **Moderate**

Lying in a huge glacial trench almost 6km wide, the Wilberforce River Valley, immediately above Lake Coleridge, is a fascinating place to explore and experience the high-country grandeur and solitude. A visual treat of high-country beauty awaits those few explorers who venture this far. Beyond Glenthorne homestead an easy, graded vehicle track crosses the undulating tussock terraces before descending to the main river valley. Immense panoramas of valley flats, craggy peaks and distant glaciers fill the Wilberforce with an array of topography, colour and splendour.

Indeed, it is an awesome place, made all the more enjoyable by the ease of the walk into the first hut upvalley, Fanghill. This station hut rests on a grassy terrace set well back from the Wilberforce River and commands a dramatic spectacle of river, bush and mountain. A relic of mustering days, its corrugated walls and roof still provide welcome shelter from the elements, whilst inside a large open fireplace guarantees warmth on many a cold and frosty night.

If time permits it is possible to travel on upvalley to reach Moa Hut on the far bank. This entails crossing the main river, which should be treated with respect. The Wilberforce can carry a huge volume of water after rain or thaw and has claimed many lives; however, in average flow it should not present any problems for the experienced.

Trampers at Moa Hut

Unknown Hut (4 bunks) and Urquharts Hut (6 bunks) can be reached by following the river left, mostly on old 4WD trails, as far as Bristed Stream, where the river can be crossed, if low, to Logans Mistake and then to the Unknown/Wilberforce confluence, where a crossing is again made to reach either hut. Note that negotiating the upper valley requires sound river-crossing skills and judgement.

To access, drive to the head of Lake Coleridge on Harper Road, through Lake Coleridge Station, past Lake Ida turnoff. Drive over Harper River bridge, turn left and carry on for 4–5km up the hill to Glenthorne Station (phone 03 318 5801 for permission before arriving). Call at the house as a fee is charged for use of both Fanghill Hut and the access road beyond the house for vehicles.

Directly behind Glenthorne Station homestead stand two peaks, The Spurs and Gargarus. Both make excellent day trips, albeit rather strenuous ones.

7. The Spurs
To high peak via Point 1832m: 4–5 hours. **Hard**
Descent to farm via Spur 1902m: 3–4 hours. **Hard**

The Spurs is really a cluster of three summits, 1985m, 1964m and 1902m, standing above a series of deep, rugged gullies, the spurs of which provide good routes to or from the high basins and peaks.

The best and most ambitious option is to bag all the high peaks and their outliers in a complete traverse, beginning just to the west of the stream (unnamed) draining Spur 1964. Climb onto the ridge from here, through scattered scrub, passing over Points 1408m and 1587m before ascending the steepening ridge to Point 1832m.

This route, like all the other spurs, has panoramic views of the Wilberforce watershed, Boundary Stream and, as you approach the main range, stunning views into the Avoca catchment and Arthur's Pass region. With the hardest part of the climb now completed, a rewarding ridge trip ensues, heading due east over the two highest Spurs before turning south from the summit and descending to Spur 1902m. This Spur offers the most challenging part of the traverse, with some easy scrambling over and around rocky knobs. A very narrow section just before 1902m can be turned on the east through an easy basin and then to the peak via a steep shute. Take care when descending from the top down the ridge; it is very narrow here and loose.

Continue on down the ridge to Point 1706m, where the going is much easier, and drop down the steepening ridge on the river right of Gargarus Stream. A short, rough, bush section is required to cross Fisher Stream, and then back to the farm paddocks.

For those who do not wish to traverse the narrow ridge onto Spur 1902m, descend south into the basin beneath Spur 1985m and traverse south at about 1620m before climbing to the ridge again near Point 1706m. (In winter, beware of avalanche danger in this basin.)

8. Gargarus (1655m)

Glenthorne to summit: 3–4 hours. **Hard**

Descent from summit: 2–3 hours. **Moderate**

This lower summit is accessed over Fisher Stream and by ascending the open ridge toward the Spurs before crossing through bush at 940m to reach the open swampy clearing draining Gargarus Saddle. Cross Gargarus Stream near the bush edge and head directly up the steep southwestern face of Gargarus to the wide, rounded summit. Thre are wonderful views of the Harper, Avoca and Wilberforce rivers from here as well as Lake Coleridge.

Call Glenthorne Station (ph. 03 318 5801) for access.

INTO THE UNKNOWN

Unknown Hut is a special place, way up where the Wilberforce Valley is constricted between the flanks of the ranges and Canterbury's space is completely lost to view as the Unknown River curves in a wide arc beneath the Cascade Range. This is magnificent isolation, where the only track is the riverbed, and that at the whim of the river. So it is that three of us, Nick Ashley, Mike Latty and I, trek in one mid-winter's day, having taken to mountain bikes for the first section of the route. The road is frozen, fortunately, as without the freeze it would be a mud-slick, something we are to discover on the return leg. Mountain

Climbing to Moa Saddle from Unknown River

bikes are not normally a feature of tramps I do, but on this occasion we take them to speed our progress during the shorter winter days. They prove their worth, despite the packs we carry, and we reach Fanghill Stream in just over an hour, stash them and walk on. Farther up, Nick and I make a side trip to historic Urquharts Hut, a classic piece of high-country history dating to 1930, before heading into the Unknown and the objective for this trip, Unknown Hut.

Smoke curls from the chimney as we pull up off the last terrace, and there's a welcome 'Howdy boys' from Mike as we enter. 'Brew's on, so help yourself', he continues, as I familiarise myself with this rustic little refuge, legacy of the culler's era, dating to 1970. 'Hey, it's good to be back, Mike.' He was with me last time we passed this way, en route to Unknown Col and the Whitcombe, so our return is a shared memory of a good trip in the hills.

We schedule a pre-dawn start for our pass-day to Moa Stream and are greeted by darkness, light snowfall and cool winds as we make our way to the foot of Moa Saddle, where we locate a poled route winding up through the forest and bluffs. Mist drifts randomly about the tops, revealing snowy faces, or a window along the corridor of the Unknown. A kea calls, a breeze stirs the tussock, otherwise all is still. The pass summit is just 200m above the valley floor and we pause at the top in the stiff southerly flow pushing up from Moa Stream. South of the pass we enter the Moa Basins, a world of sub-alpine shrublands festooned with snow, where deep drifts make slow going, until we gain the bed of North Stream and are able to make better progress. Gold miners once fossicked here, over 100 years ago; they found scant pickings. We enter Moa Stream by mid-afternoon, Moa Hut is not far off, so we head over the river flats for a late lunch and some respite from the cold.

Dusk is stealing over the valley as we gain the Wilberforce and strike out across its bony wastes for Fanghill Stream. Though weary we're not beyond appreciating the marvellous space and beauty of the valley on a winter's evening, as intense sunlight falls on the shoulders of the peaks. At the bikes we mount up, 10 hours logged so far, and just 30 minutes of light left. Pedalling off into the dark, uphill on the mud-slick trail, where a crescent moon casts its faint light on our labours, Mike calls, 'Hey mate, this isn't just a good trip, it's a grand trip.'

9. Flagpole (896m)

Paddocks to summit: 3 hours round trip. **Moderate**

This attractive summit not only offers a superb and extensive view of the Canterbury Plains and mountains, but has an interesting round-trip route along the summit ridge.

Beginning from behind Flagpole Farm (see access notes), the unmarked route climbs from the back paddocks, 1km west of the homestead, onto a small saddle overlooking the Selwyn River Gorge. A 4WD track crosses the saddle to the river and another winds up the ridgeline to Flagpole. This is easy to follow and climbs steadily, passing through small saddles and tussock flats with the ever-expanding view of mountain and plain unfolding below. It seems that the view can hardly be bettered from the summit; a dramatic panorama is displayed of all the major foothill peaks, together with the Selwyn River catchment, Torlesse and Puketeraki Ranges, Mt Hutt and distant summits above the Rakaia River. Below the summit, to the east, lies a splendid view of farms and forests in the Whitecliffs/Coalgate area. Make sure you allow time to relax on the peak and enjoy this unparalleled spectacle. If you have timed your visit for sunrise, the additional dimension of brilliant early-morning light washing the hills and valleys is spell-binding and well worth the early start.

For the descent you can return via the ridgeline, the easiest option, or for the fit, a very steep descent begins right from the trig, to the south, dropping down a fenceline to the back paddocks of Flagpole Farm; a most enjoyable tramp.

Access is from Glentunnel on Route 72 to Whitecliffs and Flagpole Road and farm.

This route in on private land, phone Flagpole Farm (03 318 2352) for permission.

Tim Hayward fords Clyde River

Canterbury Plains and wind-scoured snow, Korowai/Torlesse Tussocklands Park

Waimakariri Plains Region

Korowai/Torlesse Tussocklands Park

This conservation area, covering 21,000 hectares on the Torlesse and Big Ben ranges, was New Zealand's first tussock grasslands conservation park and an exciting development in the protection and promotion of high-country areas.

It is located both to the north and south of SH73 as it climbs from the Canterbury Plains over Porters Pass en route to Arthur's Pass. As they near Porters Pass, travellers on this route will be familiar with the high, dry mountain ranges, their lower slopes carpeted with alpine tussock and scattered pockets of mountain beech, while the high ridges are devoid of vegetation and are often under heavy snow during the winter months.

It is a dramatic landscape and one of the most accessible mountain areas in New Zealand. As such it is popular with recreationalists year-round as they tramp, climb and ski-tour in the area.

The region also has a long association for Māori, who used its undulating basins and ridges for safe, seasonal access to their food-gathering areas. From this association has come the term 'Korowai', meaning cloak. Charles Torlesse, a surveyor, was led by local Māori to climb these mountains in 1849, where he viewed the alps, describing them as: 'the romantic and chaotic mass of mountains to the westward'. In 1858–59 a small band of government workers made the first rough road over Porters Pass using pick and shovel, and this original road, which was used by the Cobb & Co. coaches plying the route westwards, is still visible within the park near Porters Pass.

The park is especially important for the alpine plant associations found here, notably the unusual plants that have adapted to living on unstable screes, such as vegetable sheep, South Island edelweiss, and Haast's scree buttercup. There are also good numbers of native birds and insects to be found, especially kea, falcon, pipit and rifleman, along with wētā, lizards and grasshoppers.

The park has a few marked tracks and several access points off SH73, including Kowai River (private), Porters Pass, Lake Lyndon Road, Porter Heights skifield road (winter access only) and Craigieburn Road in the north.

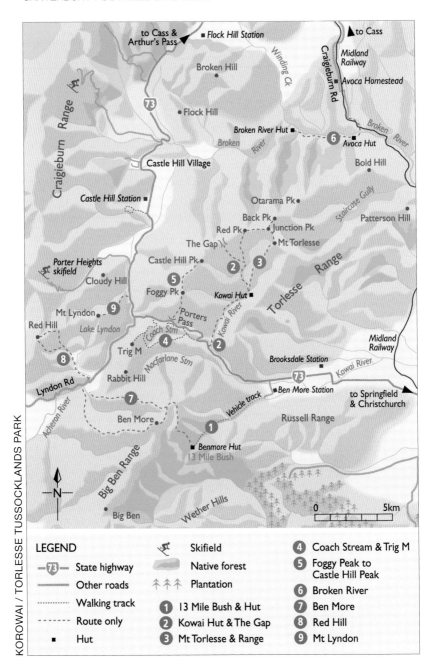

to Cass & Arthur's Pass
■ Flock Hill Station
▲ to Cass

Winding Ck

Craigieburn Rd
Midland Railway
■ Avoca Homestead

● Broken Hill

Craigieburn Range

73
● Flock Hill

Broken River Hut ■
6
■ Avoca Hut
Broken River

Broken River

● Bold Hill

Castle Hill Village

Castle Hill Station ■

● Otarama Pk
Back Pk ●
Staircase Gully
● Patterson Hill

Red Pk ● - - ● Junction Pk
The Gap ● Mt Torlesse

Porter Heights skifield
● Castle Hill Pk
2
3
Torlesse Range

● Cloudy Hill
5
● Foggy Pk
Kowai Hut ■

Mt Lyndon ● ●
9
Porters Pass
Kowai River

Red Hill ■
Lake Lyndon
Coach Stm
4
2

● Trig M
Macfarlane Stm
Midland Railway ■

8
● Rabbit Hill
Brooksdale Station ■
Kowai River

Lyndon Rd
7
Vehicle track
■ Ben More Station
73
to Springfield & Christchurch

● Ben More
1
Russell Range

Acheron River

■ Benmore Hut
13 Mile Bush

Big Ben Range

Wether Hills
0   5km

N
● Big Ben

LEGEND

🎿 Skifield

━73━ State highway

━━━ Other roads

Native forest

⋯⋯⋯ Walking track

🌲🌲🌲 Plantation

- - - Route only

■ Hut

❶ 13 Mile Bush & Hut

❷ Kowai Hut & The Gap

❸ Mt Torlesse & Range

❹ Coach Stream & Trig M

❺ Foggy Peak to Castle Hill Peak

❻ Broken River

❼ Ben More

❽ Red Hill

❾ Mt Lyndon

1. 13 Mile Bush and Hut

Carpark to hut: 2–3 hours. **Moderate**

Hut to Big Ben Range summit: 2–3 hours. **Moderate**

A large, densely forested catchment, 13 Mile Bush lies west of Springfield on SH73 and has an access easement through private land to reach the bush. It is a popular hunting area and has a small hut, Benmore Hut (4 bunks), owned by the New Zealand Deerstalkers' Association, located in a saddle at the head of 13 Mile Bush Stream. A marked track leads to the hut. From the hut various lightly marked trails head onto the Big Ben Range and into the Selwyn River catchment.

Access is off SH73 through Ben More Station to a carpark and signage. Permission is not required.

2. Kowai Hut and The Gap

SH73 to Kowai Hut: 2 hours. **Easy**

Kowai Hut to The Gap: 4–5 hours. **Hard**

Opposite a curve on busy SH73, at the foot of Porters Pass, beneath the spreading branches of a huge pine tree, a short gravel road, which passes over a minor ford, gives access to the Kowai River and the unique sub-alpine and alpine region of the Torlesse Range. The range itself is the last barrier to the westerly winds that sweep across the Southern Alps and, being detached from the alps, provides a unique and often sheltered environment.

After parking your car at the locked gate, an easy 4WD track can be followed on the river right. The track, though easy to follow, has some short, steep climbs from where you may look longingly to the flat riverbed mean-dering across the shingle below. On a fine, warm day the riverbed provides an interesting alternative, or could be added as a return route to your car, but it involves multiple river crossings and should not be attempted if the river is running high.

As the 4WD track winds toward the high peaks of the range, the valley begins to narrow and the terraces drop away to the riverbed, forcing the track out onto the bed itself. The route across the riverbed is indistinct, but of short duration, and at this stage of the walk the Kowai Hut (4 bunks) is plainly visible on the opposite bank, tucked against the hillside on a terrace a few metres above the river beneath the southern aspect of Mt Torlesse.

VEGETABLE SHEEP

On the slopes below the ridge-tops can be found one of the unusual attractions of this area: vegetable sheep. The name of this dense community of alpine cushion plants can be readily appreciated when they are seen at a distance: their pale green colour amid a sea of grey looks remarkably like a few scattered sheep.

On closer inspection you can but marvel at the closely interwoven, spongy surface of these hardy plants, which reach lengths of up to 1m. Their dense shape fends off grazing predators, forces out competitors and protects against winter blizzards. They are also drought resistant, as water in the ground beneath them cannot evaporate through the dense tangle of waterproof hairs on their leaves.

Vegetable sheep, Torlesse Range

The hut was originally built as quarters for research on the surrounding tussock and shingle slopes by the Tussock and Grasslands Division of the former DSIR. A great deal of work was carried out in this valley system to ascertain the rate of erosion to which these shattered greywacke mountains

Upper Kowai River, Porters Pass

are subjected. There are still a number of structures remaining in the area, immediately adjacent to the hut, which will capture your attention.

The view from the hut window on a fine, clear day is striking. At the head of the valley, which steepens rapidly once you leave the hut area, is the Torlesse Gap, a remarkable feature of the ranges that is visible from well out on the Canterbury Plains. It is this geographical landmark that attracts most visitors to the area: to reach 'The Gap'.

Be warned, though: once you leave the hut the terrain becomes considerably more difficult and continues so all the way to The Gap itself, which stands at approximately 1700m. In summer it is a tough scramble, with some route finding required in the bluffs at the valley head. Winter provides an altogether different challenge, with heavy snowfalls accumulating on this, the southern face, and ice sometimes freezing the streams. Yet to stand in the narrow defile that is The Gap is an amazing experience. Being approximately

30m across, with sheer rock walls either side and steep loose shingle slopes falling to north and south, the feeling of passing through a huge doorway is inescapable.

Beyond, to the north and west, loom the Southern Alps and Arthur's Pass National Park; to the south and east flows the Waimakariri River in a wide, graceful sweep to the sea, with Banks Peninsula floating like an island across the plains.

Rumour has it that a local daredevil flew a light aircraft through The Gap some years back. He would have needed a perfect day for such a stunt, as the updraughts can be fierce, as well as a very steady hand.

It is possible to reach Castle Hill Peak from The Gap via a short traverse to the southwest on the northern slopes of The Gap and then easily up to the ridgeline and over Point 1941m. This is a route for the experienced only. Options to continue farther afield are many, though most entail a fair degree of fitness and navigation in the open, untracked and very rugged upper valley.

3. Mt Torlesse and Range
Kowai Hut to Mt Torlesse: 3–4 hours. **Hard**
Mt Torlesse to Red Peak via Back Peak: 2–3 hours. **Hard**
Red Peak to hut: 2–3 hours. **Hard**

Northeast of Kowai Hut a steep scree ridge running to the left of the large basin draining the south face of Mt Torlesse (1961m) provides the most direct ascent route. From the hut the summit looks deceptively close; however, though not a technically difficult route and really just a steep scramble, it is an ascent of over 1160m.

In summer it is essential to carry water on these high, dry peaks, which shimmer under the intensity of the sun. In winter the ridges and basins are the focus for cross-country skiers. There are numerous variations on routes to the tops throughout the range, yet the steep, direct ridges are usually more favourable than the truncated streambeds and the small bluffs scattered throughout the watershed.

Summit views are of a nature not experienced on other higher peaks on the Divide to the north and west, the major difference being the immensity of space presented before you by the spectacle of the Canterbury Plains, which begin directly below the summit of Mt Torlesse. This sea of patterned

Pat Barrett on the summit of Castle Hill Peak

yellows, greens and blues arching away toward the distant ocean is breathtaking. Scything across the centre of the picture, the Waimakariri River boldly penetrates the plains in a grey sweep to the sea. North and west run the sister summits of Torlesse: Back Peak (1979m), Otarama Peak (1963m), Red Peak (1853m), Castle Hill Peak (1998m) and Foggy Peak (1741m) above Porters Pass. Beyond their weathered tops stand the Southern Alps, interspersed with the valleys and gorges of the Arthur's Pass and Wilberforce regions.

The ridge-top winds onward from Mt Torlesse and is readily followed to Back Peak or Otarama Peak, where good scrambling along the easy, narrow ridge crest provides an exhilarating traverse. Beyond Otarama Peak the ridgeline slowly descends over several kilometres to Bold Hill (1286m) and the Waimakariri River Gorge near Staircase Gully. This is a long route, with access out over Broken Hill River to Craigieburn Road.

Another option is to turn west at Point 1882m (Junction Peak) and follow the ridge over to Red Peak before exiting the tops down a steep southern spur into the upper Kowai River, passing over a remarkable area of deep red rock and scree from which the peak takes its name. The route beyond Red Peak is for more serious climbers and involves some rock scrambling as well as a descent and traverse, south of the ridge, to reach The Gap.

The upper region of the Kowai catchment contains all the attractions of a high-alpine cirque: waterfalls, tussock benches, bluffs and a degree of remoteness and beauty unexpected in a range so close to a major highway.

Once the streambed is reached, small pockets of mountain beech are negotiated until you reach the easier confines of the Kowai Gorge where it passes beneath grassy river terraces before re-joining the main river near Kowai Hut. Travel through this section is mostly on the river left.

The Kowai River is reached in 1 hour from Christchurch on SH73, the Arthur's Pass highway. Turn off under the big pine tree opposite the old

Lake Lyndon from Trig M, Porters Pass

roadman's hut below Porters Pass (eastern side). Cars must be left here. Contact Brookdale Station for permission (ph. 03 318 4748).

4. Coach Stream and Trig M

Trig M via Starvation Gully: 2 hours. **Moderate**

Trig M via Coach Stream: 2–3 hours. **Moderate**

Trig M to Rabbit Hill: 1–2 hours. **Moderate**

A series of hiking trails has been established off the Porters Pass highway, making possible some moderate walking routes on the low ranges above Lake Lyndon. With some basic tramping skills you can plan some excellent half- to full-day hikes here, using the road to return to your car.

Coach Stream is accessed at a small layby on a sharp corner on the eastern side of Porters Pass and has an easement through farmland to reach the conservation land near the head of the gully.

The track is gentle at first, then climbs steadily to Point 1079m and around the ridgeline and up again to the main ridge, where it intersects with the marked route coming over from Porters Pass through Starvation Gully. From here it is about another hour along the ridge to Trig M (1251m) and its grand views over the Lyndon Basin and Southern Alps. Either return the same way or, for the experienced, follow the ridge crest south to Rabbit Hill, and then descend steeply via a northerly spur to the Lyndon Road around the lake.

These trails are marked and signposted at access points either side of Porters Pass on SH73.

5. Foggy Peak to Castle Hill Peak

Porters Pass to Foggy Peak: 2–3 hours. **Hard**

Foggy Peak to Castle Hill Peak: 2–3 hours. **Hard**

Return via Foggy Peak: 3–4 hours. **Moderate**

One of the park's most popular tops routes is along the crest of the range from Porters Pass to the principal summit, Castle Hill Peak (1998m). For many, just to ascend the long, steep slopes of Foggy Peak (1741m) from the pass and savour the views from this lofty vantage is attraction enough to commit mind and body to this surprisingly strenuous ascent. If snow lies on the route, and your party is experienced at winter travel on the open tops,

Climbing to Foggy Peak

this ridge traverse is one of the best and most exhilarating ascents to be found anywhere in the Canterbury foothills.

From Porters Pass, the route up and over Foggy Peak is a steady and steepening haul, with a false summit providing some frustration for those who are anxious to reach the top. The ridge is straightforward but can be very icy under winter conditions.

Past Foggy Peak, the main range is followed, descending at first to a broad saddle and then climbing more gently over an undulating ridgetop. In summer this is easy travel, but under snow it can be either exceptionally fast, or a frustratingly slow plod in soft snow where skis would be a major advantage.

It is approximately 3km along the ridge to Castle Hill Peak, the final section of the climb being up a steep, narrow ridge with drop-offs either side. It can be icy and care is needed. It is not difficult, but can be a little intimidating in winter conditions.

Lake Lyndon and the Southern Alps from Foggy Peak

The summit view is stunning. The ridge falls away rapidly to the north and west, conveying the impression of being on the prow of a great ship forging through the mottled and lake-speckled landscape below. The whole Torlesse Range is visible from here, as well as Christchurch, the plains and the full stretch of the alps; a magnificent sight.

Pause a while and relish in the challenge obtained and the reward. However, if the wind is up, this is no place to linger and it will be wise to retrace your steps along the ridge and over Foggy Peak to the road.

For most parties, this is a long day trip. If you are inexperienced, it should not be attempted under adverse conditions, and not at all in winter, when ice axe and crampons are essential.

CASTLE HILL PEAK CLASSIC

The Foggy Peak to Castle Hill Peak route is, I believe, a classic Canterbury foothills traverse, and a perennial favourite among the local fraternity of recreationalists, be they trampers, skiers or climbers, at every season and in almost any weather. Personally, I have completed the traverse, or variants of it, in high summer, dead of winter, at night, under a full moon, camping out, in fog, gales, and in sublime quiet. It's just that sort of trip, challenging enough, especially under snow, to make any trip here worth the effort, but not so difficult as to make it only possible under ideal conditions. Its accessibility is another factor in adding to its popularity as, unless you want a serious vertical challenge, Porters Pass provides the logical jump-off point for the summit, with its bonus altitude of 942m.

On this attempt I've come in the pre-dawn hours of early winter to begin my fight to the summit through deep powder snow and to concentrate on the emerging dawn colours beginning to soak from the sky onto the snowy landscape to my south and west. Christchurch is a dazzling web of light away to the east, backed by the great black shadow of Banks Peninsula, while below my feet I can hear a B-train hauling its load up the incline of Porters Pass, headlights probing the dark slope.

Alone on the mountain, I set up tripod and camera and await the waxing light over the Big Ben Range, out to Mt Hutt, and on into the headwaters of the Rakaia watershed, where the great wedges of Whitcombe and Evans dominate. It's a fantastic scene and despite the cold and wooden legs, eminently worth capturing. For all that, I am still pleased when I can holster my camera and head up-slope to Foggy Peak, the effort rapidly warming my limbs. I tell myself that once I reach Foggy, I'll flag the traverse, as the snow is like porridge and saps both my energy and my resolve. Foggy, as I well know, has at least two false summits, but this matters little when you just want to be there and another crest hoves into view. Topping out is a bit of an anti-climax when you are feeling a bit wrecked from the effort and just want to sit down, which I do.

Big Ben Range from Foggy Peak at dawn

I coax myself to roll off some more film of the familiar yet transfixing scene around me and then relax for a cuppa and an early lunch. It's just 9am.

Sustenance and the splendid surroundings rekindle my interest in the traverse, that and a little talisman of promise that I spy out along the ridge-crest traverse – black rock protruding through the snow. This gives substance to the hope of improving conditions and I set off, slowly at first, wading off the far side of Foggy, quickly progressing to easier travel until my boots are skimming the snow, leaving behind a neat 20mm-deep imprint, and my first sense of delight all day. This ridge is magnificent. Poised between plain and mountain it ascends in a slow curve to the base of Castle Hill Peak, which juts from the crest, a beautiful 200m pyramid of snow and ice with a fine approach up its south ridge.

The approach is steep, much steeper than Foggy Peak, and can be intimidating under winter conditions, often requiring step-kicking or even crampons, but it's not dangerous and the snow grants me

Sub-alpine plants

a rapid, if tiring, ascent. The angle eases as I reach the summit step and then walk out onto the broad, gently sloping peak.

It's exhilarating to be back, and some years since my last climb of this mountain. Furthermore the day has improved, with no sign of the nor'wester predicted to rise by early afternoon. A rest is both desired and deserved, so I shed my pack onto the snow, pull out the remaining lunch and thermos, and sit back to enjoy the high location and beauty of a winter's day.

Descent is marked by more careful foot placement than the ascent, and that wind has finally arrived, stripping snow from the ridge in growing plumes, some of which I have to pass through. They inject fingers of chill, laden with snow particles, into my parka hood, pressing me onward to escape the attack. I pause on the final slope to the main ridge back to Foggy to batten down the hatches for the more open traverse ahead. I needn't have worried though as I manage to pass on along the ridge in the lee of the wind and escape its growing strength until I reach Foggy.

Its broad, soft slopes are fully exposed to the nor'wester, which is gusting in powerful bursts over the summit cone, lifting ever-increasing amounts of snow skyward and creating a ground blizzard that obscures my boots in a white blur, making it easy to stumble as I can't always see the terrain I am about to walk on. It's a taxing ascent back onto Foggy Peak, and tough work on the long drop to Porters Pass, where shifting wind gusts, dense snow plumes and tired limbs keep me on my mettle.

Though many times ascended, the mountain is having the final say.

6. Broken River

Railway line to Avoca Homestead: 1 hour. **Easy**

Broken River Hut from homestead: 2–3 hours. **Moderate**

Running along the northern boundary of the Torlesse Park, Broken River provides a remote experience for tramping parties. It is accessed via the Craigieburn Road near Cass, driving down alongside the Midland Railway line (through many gates!) to the railway viaduct over Slovens Stream. The homestead is an ideal destination for families with young children, provided care is taken with the river crossing near the hut.

Access is along a 4WD trail, under the viaduct, to a ford of Broken River (often very swift) to the old homestead on the south bank. This building (built in 1909) was once part of Flock Hill Station, one of the most isolated farms in the region. Now managed by DOC, it is an historic building and open for use. Broken River Hut lies 2–3 hours walk upstream on a southerly terrace at the junction with Winding Creek, this unmarked route can only be used in low river flows.

Dominique Barrett arriving at Avoca Homestead

7. Ben More

Lake Lyndon Road to Ben More: 3–4 hours. **Moderate**
Big Ben from Ben More: 2 hours. **Moderate**
Return to Lake Lyndon Road from Big Ben via Point 1660m and ridge over Point 1327m: 2–3 hours. **Moderate**

In the southern section of the park, the Big Ben Range separates Lake Lyndon from the Canterbury Plains. This long, flat-topped range has two principal summits: Ben More (1655m) and Big Ben (1416m). The undulating ridge has several points of access from the Lake Lyndon Road and from the upper Macfarlane Stream near the Porters Pass Road. This makes possible long traverses of the summit area, which extends for over 6km to Big Ben in the extreme south.

The tops provide very pleasant travel, though it is a fair upward haul to reach them, with over 800m of ascent. They have grand panoramas of the Korowai/Torlesse Tussocklands Park, the Canterbury Plains, Lake Coleridge basin and Rakaia River, and are a popular destination for committed ski tourers during winter.

For Ben More the best route lies approximately 2km south of Lake Lyndon, where the road takes a sharp turn to the right (north) into the upper Acheron River. A vehicle track in the bottom of the gully will take you, on foot, over the Acheron and a small stream draining Ben More. Once on the large terrace above the stream junction, proceed south to the toe of the long ridge that runs east over Points 1465m, 1555m, 1510m and 1624m to the summit. This is a long but not too strenuous route, granting wonderful views as you ascend. From Ben More you can continue southwest to Big Ben or northeast to Point 1660m and return to the road via the ridge north of, and opposite, the one you ascended.

It is also possible to reach Benmore Hut by continuing north from Point 1660m and then swinging south around the ridge-top and descending scree, tussock and bush to the hut. This route is not marked. The hut is a small A-frame structure, which stands on a bush saddle between the upper Selwyn River and 13 Mile Bush Stream. There is a marked track back out to the road from here down 13 Mile Bush Stream. This area of predominantly beech forest is one of the largest forested areas of the park.

Ben More is reached by the Lake Lyndon Road, over Porters Pass.

8. Red Hill

Acheron River to summit: 2–3 hours. **Moderate**
Return via ridge over Points 1488m and 1494m: 2–3 hours. **Moderate**

Red Hill (1641m) is a modest peak southeast of Lake Lyndon in the Korowai/Torlesse Tussocklands Park. It has an easy approach via the Acheron River, which is largely sheltered from the nor'wester, making it a good choice in very windy conditions. The upper valley is bush fringed and leads out, eventually, to open ridges adjoining the upper mountain and Red Hill.

At the top you can rest and enjoy the view out over the incredibly varied topography of the Ryton Basin, where unusual, cone-shaped peaks dot the landscape beside the great blue canal of Lake Coleridge, backed by the ragged, cloud-topped Southern Alps and faraway valleys of the Wilberforce and Rakaia. You could make a round trip from the summit, north via several sub-summits to the Acheron River, or go all the way out to Mt Lyndon and descend to the lake.

From the sharp bend in the Lyndon Road at the Acheron River, park your car and ascend the riverbed into the upper valley.

Access is also possible from Porter Heights skifield road to the upper Porter River. Walk to Coleridge Pass and south to the summit (winter access only).

9. Mt Lyndon

Lake to summit: 2.5 hours. **Moderate**

For a spectacular view from a relatively easily reached foothill, Mt Lyndon (1489m) offers an excellent day excursion to gain its wide, shingly summit and grand views of the Lake Coleridge basin.

Access is from the northwestern end of Lake Lyndon, just off SH73, and onto a small spur, which has a rough trail on its lower section, running up onto the eastern face of the mountain. The ridge-top can be followed southwest to Red Hill.

TRAVERSE TROUBLES – MT LYNDON

Gale-force winds rip over the high ground on Mt Lyndon, near Porters Pass, as a nor'west front gains force in the Southern Alps, west of the Korowai/Torlesse Tussocklands Park, through which I am attempting a late evening tramp. It's one of those last-minute things, to get in during daylight saving hours, and to savour the beauty of the high country under evening light. The route up is direct, straight up a likely looking spur from the northern end of Lake Lyndon. A couple of campervan owners cast a sceptical gaze in my direction as I head skywards on this sultry evening. They are enjoying dinner at lakeside; no hard-out effort for them tonight.

The vans rapidly shrink to less that match-box size, while the lake spreads out below and the plains lift into view over the summit of Porters Pass. It's a tad over 500m height gain from lake to summit, a distance that can be comfortably covered in around 60 minutes, depending on how you feel and what you have on your back. This is a lightweight mission, save for the camera gear, and I seem to be going well.

At the ridge crest the nor'west finds me and delivers a couple of blows to my stability and progress. I hove to for a rest, fuel-up, and pull on a parka to ward off the chill. It's only here that I begin to notice the rapid accumulation of wave-form clouds soaring into the stratosphere. These giant stacks of lenticular, or hogsback, clouds as they are commonly known, reach exceptional heights and magnificent proportions, appearing like gigantic castles in the air. Mountains of cloud, flat-topped and razor-tipped, merging on the edge of the jet-stream, fearsomely handsome, they are portents of an approaching storm. I head on, cloud-cliffs towering at my back, and skirt the low knobs on the ridge-top, intent on travelling as far as time and light will allow before exiting to the lake below.

Unexpectedly, I'm bombed. Six kea come curving at me on the gale, shrieking and flashing their vermilion underwings at me. They mean business; this is no curiosity call, as they level out at head height for a strike. I fling my arms up, shout into the gale, and run, hard left,

Nor'west wave cloud over Porters Pass

not easy in these conditions. The kea follow, chasing me for a few hundred metres along the crest, swooping at me as they drive me away from their nest site. Escape is relief; I scan for the mini-F16s and breathe easy when they fail to appear. More ridge looms ahead, now in the lee I make better progress and climb out onto another knob, where the wind returns and I consider my descent.

Turning northeastwards along a sub-ridge I am treated to a fantastic spectacle. The wave-form clouds have grown and now radiate the setting sun, appearing like enormous aerial explosions arrayed in light. Luminous and otherworldly, they reflect pale yellows through deepest ruby tones, and as the light wanes they fade out into bruised towers of vapour. At a half-run I scamper down easy scree into a shallow valley, cut through a bush remnant, and climb to a low saddle leading to Lake Lyndon.

A final hour takes me back, around the shore in the dark, headlamp wavering, as a thousand spiders' eyes gleam at me from their lairs under the lakeside rocks.

Pat Barrett on Mt Oxford at dawn

North Canterbury Foothills and Lees Valley

Curving in an arc around the northwestern edge of the Canterbury Plains is a series of foothill forests, all of which lie either north or east of the Waimakariri River, and by virtue of their proximity to Christchurch are well known and frequented by trampers and picnickers.

Oxford Forest (11,350 hectares), in the southwestern corner of the region, is perhaps the most popular as it includes Mt Oxford (1364m), a well-tracked foothill summit, and the popular Wharfedale and Ryde Falls tracks.

Mt Thomas Forest (10,800 hectares) has two attractive picnic areas and several short loop tracks around its principal summits, Mt Richardson (1047m) and Mt Thomas (1023m).

Ashley Forest (15,487 hectares) encompasses both a commercial forestry block owned and managed by Carter Holt Harvey and a DOC estate covering approximately 1700 hectares. As such, it contains large areas of exotic forests as well as some scenic native forests and tussock tops on Mt Grey (934m) and Mt Karetu (972m).

Puketeraki Forest (6750 hectares) lies on the flanks of the Puketeraki Range in Lees Valley and contains tramping tracks and huts. There is also scope for extended tramping traverses of the Puketeraki Range, including the highest summit, Chest Peak (1936m).

Oxford Forest

Once described as 'The most magnificent stand of virgin bush in Canterbury' by early visitors, Oxford Forest has lost none of its charm and still contains the most extensive area of lowland forest, as well as the largest track and hut network, of all the northern forests. There are, however, no designated picnic areas.

A large timber mill worked the Coopers Creek area until 1912. Now walkers are greeted by a pervading silence, save for the wind in the trees, as they draw up at Coopers Creek or View Hill carparks, the two southern entrances to the forest. Lees Valley provides the northern entrance.

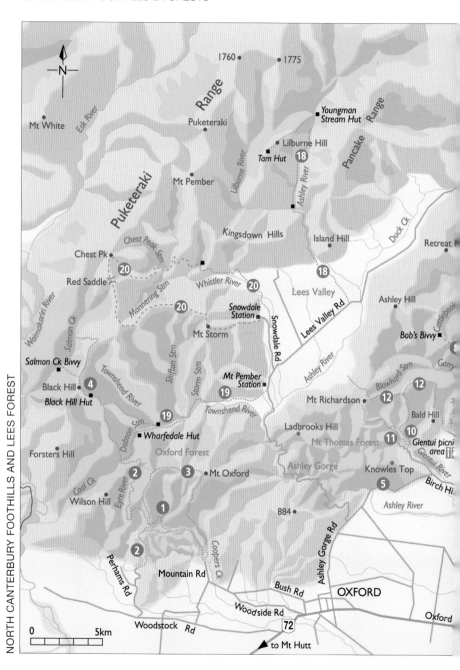

LEGEND

72 —	Route 72	
	Other roads	
....	Walking track	
- - - -	Route only	
▪	Hut	
🚻	Public toilet	
🏕	Picnic area	
🏕	Camping area	
	Native forest	
🌲🌲	Plantation	

1 Ryde Falls
2 Wharfedale Track
3 Mt Oxford
4 Black Hill Hut & Salmon Creek
5 Ashley Gorge Waterfall Track
6 Wooded Gully Track & Mt Thomas
7 Mt Thomas Loop Tracks
8 Bob's Bivvy
9 Pinchgut Hut
10 Glentui Loop Track

11 Glentui Waterfall Track
12 Richardson & Blowhard Tracks
13 Lake Janet Picnic Area & Track
14a Mt Grey Track
14b Red Beech Track
15 Grey River Nature Trail
16 Scout Road Track
17 Mt Karetu
18 Upper Ashley River
19 Townshend River
20 Whistler River & Chest Peak

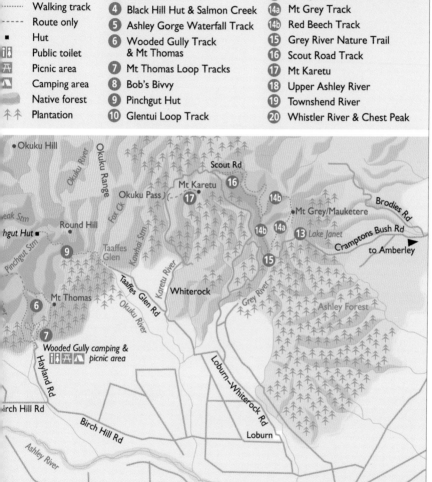

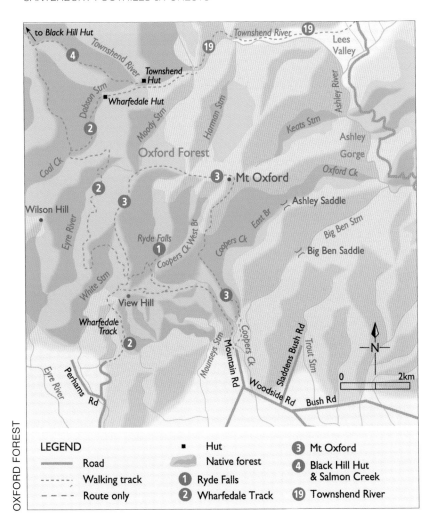

LEGEND

- Road
- Walking track
- Route only
- ■ Hut
- Native forest
- 1 Ryde Falls
- 2 Wharfedale Track
- 3 Mt Oxford
- 4 Black Hill Hut & Salmon Creek
- 19 Townshend River

1. Ryde Falls

Ryde Falls from View Hill: 2 hours. **Easy**
Ryde Falls from Coopers Creek: 2.5 hours. **Easy**
View Hill to Ryde Falls back to View Hill (loop walk): 4 hours. **Moderate**

These small, attractive waterfalls are accessed through either View Hill or Coopers Creek. Both routes begin on farmland and later enter the mixed beech/podocarp forests that are a feature of Mt Oxford.

The View Hill entrance follows the first part of the Wharfedale Track, passing the link track to Coopers Creek, and later descending into the upper West Branch where the falls are located. This is a pleasant track, particularly on a hot day, when the cool, shady forest, large trees and banks of forest ferns are a delight to walk through.

From the falls you can return via the same route or, for a round trip, take the track that travels down the West Branch and later zigzags up onto the link track between Coopers Creek and View Hill. This track follows a low bush ridge between the two carparks and so allows for a satisfying loop walk from either end, both of which take in the falls.

2. Wharfedale Track

View Hill to Wharfedale Hut (10 bunks): 4–5 hours. **Moderate**
Wharfedale Hut to Lees Valley: 2.5 hours. **Easy**

Originally developed as a proposed road link between the plains and Lees Valley (this idea was abandoned in 1886 after a huge sum had been spent) and later used as a stock route, the well-graded Wharfedale Track begins at View Hill, contours along the hillside above the Eyre River, crosses a bush saddle and descends to Dobson Stream and Townshend River in Lees Valley.

It is a long, easy bush walk with a shelter (containing sleeping bench and stove) 30 minutes from the Townshend River junction. From here the route follows open country and a 4WD track to the Lees Valley Road, crossing Shifton Stream on a footbridge.

Note: A flood route exists, on the river left, from Shifton Stream swing-bridge to Storm Stream, across the hillside above Townshend River. The route out from Wharfedale Hut to Lees Valley crosses private land and permission is required (phone 03 312 4351).

3. Mt Oxford

Coopers Creek to Mt Oxford: 3–4 hours. **Moderate**
Mt Oxford to Wharfedale Track: 2–3 hours. **Moderate**
Link track to Coopers Creek (not via Ryde Falls): 1–2 hours. **Easy**

This is the best sub-alpine walk in the region and encompasses the greatest diversity of terrain and vegetation to be found and, accordingly, some of the most expansive views. It can be walked via Coopers Creek or View Hill carparks, with the latter offering a slightly shorter ascent time. However, because of the increased travel time to View Hill, Coopers Creek is the preferred route and the trip is described from here.

From the carpark, cross the creek on the wooden bridge and follow the road to the scout camp. A marked track descends into the East Branch of Coopers Creek, crosses a footbridge and ascends a long spur through pockets

Mt Oxford summit trig

ACCESS FOR THE MT OXFORD AREA

View Hill: via Oxford township and west on Route 72 for about 3km and right onto Woodstock Road for 10km. Turn right up Perhams Road, where a road sign indicates the Wharfedale Track. Perhams Road crosses farmland, through two fords (impassable after heavy rain) and through several farm gates (leave as found), before reaching the carpark on the ridge.

Coopers Creek: via Oxford township. On the west side of Oxford, Woodside Road branches northwest (right) for 7km to Mountain Road. Turn right here and travel up through farmland to the carpark.

Ashley Gorge Waterfall is signposted 1km east of the Ashley Gorge Bridge.

Black Hill Hut and **Salmon Creek** are accessed via Lees Valley Road (see notes for 'Puketeraki Forest and Range').

of scrub and bush until continuous forest cover is reached on the upper mountain. This gives way to sub-alpine tussock grasslands, which lead over small rocky outcrops to the summit plateau. A grand spectacle of the Canterbury Plains and alps awaits you, and it is a fitting place for lunch. Note that there is no water at the summit.

Continuing west, the poled route traverses open tussock tops with more vistas of the plains and climbs over Point 1300m, before dropping into the bush and down to the track junction with the Lees Valley end of the Wharfedale Track (1–2 hours to Wharfedale Hut via an overgrown route). Carry on past the junction and down through open beech forest, where old man's beard moss will be found festooned on the tree trunks. This ridgeline remains almost level for 1–2km until it begins to drop steeply down the ridge to reach the View Hill end of the Wharfedale Track. Follow this out to View Hill or return to Coopers Creek via the link track.

Note: Under severe nor'west conditions the upper parts of Mt Oxford are exposed to gale-force winds and sometimes heavy rain. This may not be apparent at Coopers Creek, which is on the lee side of the mountain.

4. Black Hill Hut and Salmon Creek

Wharfedale Hut to Black Hill Hut: 3 hours. **Moderate**

Wharfedale Track (in upper Dobson Stream) to Black Hill Hut: 3 hours. **Moderate**

Wharfedale Track to Wharfedale Hut: 1–2 hours. **Easy**

Loop from Black Hill Hut to Salmon Creek Bivvy and out via the upper poled route to the ridgeline and back to Black Hill Hut: 5–6 hours. **Moderate/Hard**

This is an interesting tramping route for more active parties, which climbs to the open tussock tops above the Townshend River via steep bush spurs off the Wharfedale Track. These allow for a return loop back to the river, taking in the hut and a side trip to the top of Black Hill (1335m).

The mountain beech forest encountered here, as on Mt Oxford, has an eerie feel to it, especially if the wind is up, sighing through the stunted trees and waving the long green wisps of old man's beard moss like fingers on the breeze.

Black Hill Hut, a traditional trampers' hut, sleeps six and is a cosy shelter nestled on the bush edge, with expansive views out over Mt Oxford and Lees Valley. Beyond the hut a poled route continues on to Black Hill and along the easy open ridge-top above Salmon Creek. There are wonderful views from here into the hidden reaches of the Waimakariri River Gorge and across to the Torlesse and Craigieburn ranges.

About 1km north of Black Hill a poled and marked route descends to Salmon Creek and the lower Salmon Creek Bivvy (sleeps 2) just downstream, on the river left, where the route meets the river.

Salmon Creek can be followed upstream for approximately 2km to where a second marked route ascends back to the ridgeline and along to Black Hill. The upper Salmon Creek Bivvy has been removed.

5. Ashley Gorge Waterfall Track

30–40 minutes one way. **Moderate**

This short, steep, forest track climbs from the main road (signposted) into a narrow ravine, dominated by mountain beech with some podocarp species present, where a 12m waterfall cascades into a clearing of fuchsias.

Mt Thomas Forest

Like Ashley Forest, Mt Thomas Forest contains large areas of exotic plantations, which in the case of Mt Thomas extend right to the summit. There are three access points: Wooded Gully camping and picnic area, Glentui picnic area and Taaffes Glen Road. The two picnic areas are popular destinations in their own right for visitors as they have tables, toilets and well set-out grass areas. Wooded Gully also has a small attractive stream that is popular with children.

Mt Thomas Forest is reached either through Rangiora/Loburn or Oxford/Ashley Gorge, where the two major access points are signposted off the Oxford to Loburn road. Wooded Gully is accessed via Hayland Road and Glentui is accessed via Glentui Bush Road. Pinchgut Hut is accessed from the Taaffes Glen Road (off the Loburn to Whiterock Road).

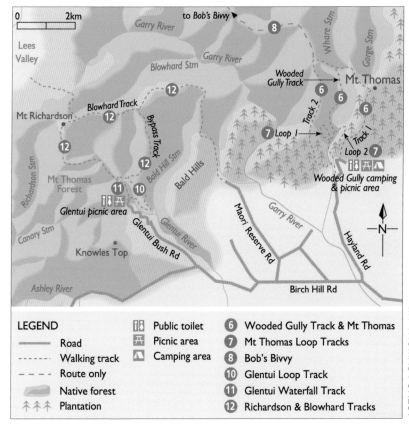

LEGEND

———— Road
- - - - - - Walking track
– – – – Route only
Native forest
🌲🌲🌲 Plantation

🚻 Public toilet
⛱ Picnic area
⛺ Camping area

6 Wooded Gully Track & Mt Thomas
7 Mt Thomas Loop Tracks
8 Bob's Bivvy
10 Glentui Loop Track
11 Glentui Waterfall Track
12 Richardson & Blowhard Tracks

MT THOMAS FOREST

6. Wooded Gully Track and Mt Thomas

Wooded Gully to Mt Thomas: 2–3 hours. **Moderate**

Track 1 to Mt Thomas: 2.5 hours. **Moderate**

Track 1 to picnic area from junction with Wooded Gully Track: 2.5 hours. **Moderate**

This forest and riverside walk climbs up though the gully, which steepens near the top, to reach the ridge-top west of Mt Thomas, in mountain beech forest. From here you can turn right (east) and follow Track 1 up, out of the forest, onto the tussock-covered shoulder of Mt Thomas and then to the summit (1023m). Alternatively, you can turn left (west) and climb onto an unnamed tussock top (1043m), and descend Track 2 along the ridge crest, and down to the forestry road, which is followed out to the Wooded Gully picnic area.

From Mt Thomas summit, which commands views over the Canterbury Plains to the sea, into Lees Valley and the upper Okuku River, you can also descend directly back to Wooded Gully picnic area by going down the forestry road that runs south from the summit (signposted) toward the plains for 300–400m, to where a track marker indicates right, down a steep, rocky road, which later becomes a track through the pine plantation. This also makes a much faster ascent route for Mt Thomas.

7. Mt Thomas Loop Tracks

Loop 1: 1 hour. **Easy**

Loop 2: 2 hours. **Easy**

From the Wooded Gully picnic area there are two short walks up the sides of the gully, linking with the Wooded Gully Track.

Loop 1 begins a little way up the west side of the main track and is suitable for less-fit walkers. Loop 2 begins farther up the main track and makes its way across to Track 1, which descends from Mt Thomas.

8. Bob's Bivvy

3–4 hours via Track 2. **Moderate**

From Point 1043m, west of Mt Thomas, on Track 1, a marked route exists to the west, out over Points 953m and 1046m to Bob's Bivvy (2 bunks) hunting hut. This track follows the ridgeline all the way to the hut, finally dropping into a bush saddle at the head of the Garry River, where the bivvy is sited. It makes an interesting return day trip or an overnight tramp to a seldom-visited part of the forest.

9. Pinchgut Hut
Taaffes Glen Road road-end to hut: 3.5 hours. **Moderate**
Hut to Point 953m: 2–3 hours. **Moderate**

One of the few huts in the northern foothills, Pinchgut Hut (10 bunks) is reached by a moderately easy, marked track along the banks of the Okuku River, from where it climbs steeply over a high ridgeline and then sidles down into Pinchgut Stream and the hut. This is a very scenic trail, passing through mature kānuka forest and later mixed beech forest. The hut is set in a small grassy clearing on the banks of Pinchgut Stream. The Okuku River is a moderately sized, attractive river draining much of the Mt Thomas Forest, and may become impassable after heavy rain.

A high route exists from Pinchgut Hut to Wooded Gully. This begins at a junction about 100m back along the main Okuku River Track behind the hut and climbs up onto the ridge-top on the river right of Pinchgut Stream. Follow this southwestwards over Points 552m, 793m and 953m to where it links with the Bob's Bivvy Track. Head southeast over Point 1043m to Track 2.

Another marked track climbs onto the ridgeline between Cattlepeak and Pinchgut streams, opposite the hut, and heads southwest to Point 1081m.

To access this area, take Taaffes Glen Road, from near Whiterock, north of Lowburn, to Fox Creek (two fords are necessary). It is possible to drive farther, to a small clearing beside the road at a sign saying, 'Light No Fires'. Leave cars here and follow the vehicle track on, past beehives, and down to a small creek entering the Okuku River. Walk out onto the riverbank and look for marker posts (steel standards with yellow pipe on top) on the far bank (river right). Cross here and pick up the track, which climbs onto a terrace above the river. A track sign on the riverbank indicates it is 4–6 hours to Pinchgut Hut, but this is incorrect.

A BIT OF A PINCH

It's a stiflingly hot day, one of the few I can remember this past summer, and though a welcome reprieve from the often cool weeks we have been having it makes for trying tramping conditions as Bernadette, my eight-year-old daughter, and I make our way along the Okuku Valley Track. Pinchgut Hut is our destination, a nice little lockwood-style structure that resides in Pinchgut Stream, a feeder in the mid-reaches of the Okuku.

The Okuku is a surprise, as it channels down through a deep gorge in the Mt Thomas Forest Conservation Area after draining the northern end of Lees Valley. Consequently it is a moderately large river and would be fearsome to enter after heavy rain. For the most part the trail is well defined, but it presents a solid tramping experience as it climbs above various sections of the gorge on steep, rough trails, fording several side creeks and eventually sidling out high above the river to reach the hut.

Bernadette is feeling the pinch, and so am I. The heat is taking its toll on our energy so we stop at riverside and splash some water over our faces, wet our hats, and fill up our bottles. The river here is constricted between high, bush-covered faces and there is only one way out, a steep climb over loose scree to access the high sidle. The sidle proves easygoing, but as we round a corner on the narrow track we are confronted with a large and active wasp nest in a dead tree beside the track. I shepherd Bernadette as we hurry past, keeping well over, and scamper off down to the track to get as much distance between us and the wasps as possible.

Not long after this we reach the hut, set in a grassy glade beside its namesake stream, and at 2 hours 40 minutes we are well under the 5 hours the signpost advises at the road-end. There are a couple of hunters at home and once we introduce ourselves and set up our sleeping bags and food we have a free afternoon ahead of us. This is just as well as the heat is intense now, making the hut interior like a sauna, so we escape to the riverbank and paddle our feet in an attempt to cool down. Reading and relaxing fill in the latter part of the

Bernadette Barrett at Pinchgut Hut

day until it's time for dinner and a good night's sleep. Just on dusk, a family of four arrives; they are spent and pleased to see the hut.

The heat remains well into the night, making for a restless sleep, until the cool of night finally settles into the valley. A fine day dawns, and as we have only to return down the track, Bernadette and I take our time over breakfast, reading, and watching the busy exit of the other groups until we are by ourselves once more. We have a special plan this day though; a cooling swim in the deep green pools near the road, followed by lunch at a café in Rangiora. What could be better! There's just that wasp nest to pass.

Mt Richardson and Glentui Picnic Area

The Glentui picnic area is another sheltered, picturesque location for family picnics, or just to enjoy a little peace and quiet as you commence or complete walks in the area. There are tables and toilets here. Two short walks are possible from the carpark: Glentui Loop Track and Glentui Waterfall Track.

10. Glentui Loop Track

90 minutes return. **Easy**

This is a pleasant forest and fern walk, which descends from the carpark into the Glentui River Gorge, crosses the river on a bridge, and climbs up and around the eastern side of the gorge before linking with, first, the Bypass Track, then the Richardson Track, before returning to the carpark/picnic area.

11. Glentui Waterfall Track

20 minutes return. **Easy**

This is a very easy stroll from the carpark, upstream above the river, through beech forest to a steep-walled, mossy gorge and cascade.

12. The Richardson and Blowhard Tracks

Glentui carpark to Mt Richardson: 2–3 hours. **Moderate**
Mt Richardson to Lees Valley: 2 hours. **Moderate**
Mt Richardson to Bypass Track/Glentui: 2 hours. **Moderate**
Blowhard Track to Boys Brigade Camp from Bypass Track junction: 2–3 hours. **Moderate**

This is one of the most popular tracks in the Glentui watershed, leading onto one of the most accessible foothill summits. The track forms an interesting loop trip via the ridge-top and provides a very satisfying short tramp. It starts from the carpark and follows the Waterfall Track before climbing steadily up the ridgeline above the river, where there are some moderately steep sections. The forest here is predominantly mountain beech, giving way to dracophyllum scrub and tussock grasslands near the summit of Mt Richardson (1047m). This modest hill provides sweeping views of the Puketeraki Range and Lees Valley. From the summit, active walkers can continue east, along the ridgeline, on the Blowhard Track. There are three options here:

Mt Richardson

(i) Approximately 500m east of the summit a marked track descends to Lees Valley through bush and later farmland. This is a seldom-used route, requiring a long drive in/out of Lees Valley, crossing the Ashley River, and permission from the farmer (Mt Pember Station, Lees Valley, phone 03 312 4351).

(ii) The Bypass Track is the best option. Continue on along the scenic ridge-top through forest and open grassland, where a large fire once destroyed the bush cover, for 2km past the Lees Valley junction, to where a marked track descends back to the Glentui picnic area.

(iii) Follow the Blowhard Track through thick ridge-top forest, later dropping down a ridge to the Boys Brigade Camp at the end of Maori Reserve Road. This will necessitate a car shuttle or walk between the camp and Glentui River.

Ashley Forest

Ashley Forest lies at the northeastern extremity of this guide. It contains several walking tracks and two sheltered picnic areas, as well as the best view, I believe, of any of the northern foothill summits. The forest is mostly exotic pines, but a small section of native bush has been preserved on the western flanks of Mt Grey and the tracks are located here. Māori named the mountain 'Mauketere', floating mountain, as they believed the spirits of their dead left the summit for the long journey to Cape Reinga.

Access to Mt Grey is via Amberley. Turn left (west) in the centre of the village, past the domain onto Douglas Road and through Broomfield onto Cramptons Bush Road at the Brodies Road intersection. Follow this up through plantation forest to Lake Janet at the top of the hill.

Note: Ashley Forest is often closed to all public access during high fire risk periods. Contact Rayonier NZ Ltd (phone 03 310 7612) during office hours for the latest update.

13. Lake Janet Picnic Area and Track

Lake Janet Track: 10 minutes. **Easy**

An idyllic picnic area, secluded and picturesque, Lake Janet has picnic tables, toilets and a short 'round the lake' track. In late autumn and winter, however, the lake area receives little sun and can be very cold. It is sited at the top of Cramptons Bush Road on the south side of Mt Grey.

14. Mt Grey Summit and Tracks

Mt Grey from Grey River picnic area: 2–3 hours. **Moderate**
Red Beech Track to Mt Grey: 3–4 hours. **Moderate**

Interestingly, Mt Grey (934m), the lowest northern foothill, has the best view and one of the easiest summit tracks. It is located well to the northeast of the other foothills, the most distant from the alps and correspondingly the closest to the coast and the view of plains, mountains and sea is outstanding, stretching from the Kaikoura mountains to Lake Ellesmere, as well as the foothills south to Mt Hutt. Keen photographers could try camping on the summit, but beware of the wind. Nor'west sunrises are dramatic! Also, there is no water available here.

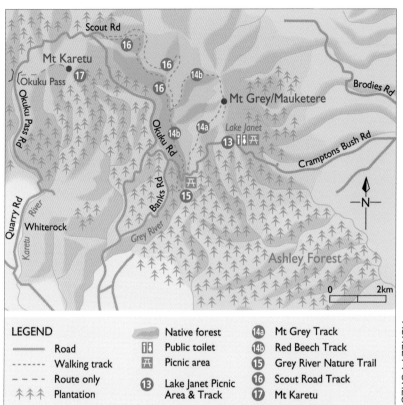

Relaxing in a field of gently waving tussock at the summit, while enjoying lunch and the 360-degree panorama on a flawless summer's day, is an experience to be relished – and repeated.

There are two marked tracks to the summit, both leaving from the Grey River picnic area – the Red Beech Track and Mt Grey Track.

The Red Beech Track heads into the upper Grey River catchment and passes through beautiful forest, which includes red beech, Hall's tōtara, matai, rimu and some kahikatea. The Grey River is especially attractive, and a small hut, constructed out of petrol cans by scout groups in the mid-1920s, will be encountered not far above the picnic area. Beyond here the track sidles upvalley above the gorge, crosses the river at the intersection with the Scout Track, and climbs steadily to the high, open ridge north of Mt Grey.

Mt Grey summit in winter

The Mt Grey Track also climbs through forest from the picnic area, but is much more direct and heads up onto the south side of the mountain and then via the ridge to the summit, passing the TV translator en route.

15. Grey River Nature Trail
1 hour. **Easy**

A short walk beginning and ending in the Grey River picnic area, this trail grants visitors a brief introduction to the diversity of forest types found on Mt Grey and throughout Canterbury. Of special interest are the shell banks embedded in the soil at 700m above sea level, and a small cave created by water erosion.

16. Scout Road Track
6–8 hours. **Moderate/Hard**

Located in the upper Grey River catchment, this track is mostly only of interest to hunters. It links the lower section of the Red Beech Track with a forestry road (Scout Road) on the north side of Mt Karetu, in Ashley Forest plantation. It forms a continuous loop, traversing both banks of the river and climbing into some tributary catchments. There are some good stands of red beech through here.

17. Mt Karetu
Okuku Pass to summit: 1.5–2 hours. **Moderate**
Return via road: 90 minutes

West of Mt Grey stands Mt Karetu (972m), a tussock-covered foothill with good views of the plains, Okuku headwaters and north Canterbury. It is a short, easy tramp over open tops from Okuku Pass. A round trip can be completed by descending to the forestry roads north of the peak via any convenient spur and following these, west, back to Okuku Pass. Scout Road and track are also a short distance northeast from the summit.

Puketeraki Forest and Range
In remote Lees Valley stands the Puketeraki Range, a barrier of high ridge-tops and rounded summits reaching 1600–1900m and running northeastwards all the way to the Hurunui River. The range acts as a bulwark against the prevailing northwesterly winds sweeping down from Arthur's Pass and so the valley floors are often sheltered from the rain, but not always the wind. There are two tracked catchments here: Townshend River and upper Ashley River.

Access is via Oxford onto Ashley Gorge Road, left onto Lees Valley Road, and through the gorge to Lees Valley. (Take special care as this is a narrow, winding road and slips are common.)

Note: Much of Lees Valley has recently been sold to foreign interests and access for recreation is currently being re-negotiated. Contact New Zealand Walking Access Commission (www.walkingaccess.govt.nz) for further updates and call Mt Pember Station for access 03 312 4351.

18. Upper Ashley River and Puketeraki Forest

Farmland gate to Youngman Stream Hut: 4–5 hours. **Moderate**
Youngman Stream Hut to Tarn Hut via Lilburne Hill: 2–3 hours. **Moderate**

This area provides a good opportunity for a moderately hard tramp in pretty country with good tracks and huts.

An interesting marked tramping track begins on the river right at the top of the farmland flats at the base of the hills, where the Ashley River issues from an open gorge. The track keeps to the river right all the way to Youngman Stream Hut (6 bunks), fording the Lilburne River past the first gorge. The Lilburne River is swift and a better ford exists approximately 1km upstream. Past the ford a poled route continues along the flats and riverbank, where several short, sharp climbs avoid small gorges and bluffs. A final climb, before the hut, sidles high to avoid more extensive bluffs, and descends to the hut standing in peaceful surroundings on a grassy flat across the river.

From the hut a marked and poled route can be followed, across the river, climbing up onto Lilburne Hill (1405m) and down to a small tarn at 1280m and Tarn Hut. There are also good campsites here and some wonderful views of the main range, especially if there is snow about. This is a lovely place to stay, in good weather, and experience an easy tops camp. Return must be via the same route.

To access the upper Ashley River, continue past Snowdale Road over Whistler River on Lees Valley Road to 1km before the Ashley River bridge (the second one), where poles mark the public access vehicle track, on the left, over farm flats to a locked gate. Permission is not required for this route.

Note: Access out via the farm track, south of the tarn, to the Lilburne River ford is not permitted by Kingsdown Station. Tarn Hut may be re-sited in the near future.

19. Townshend River

This grants access to the northern end of the Wharfedale Track, Townshend Hut and Black Hill Hut. See track notes for walks under 'Oxford Forest'.

Access to Townshend River is 1km north of the concrete bridge over the Ashley River, at the beginning of the flats in Lees Valley, where a locked gate will be seen on the left (west). Permission from Mt Pember Station (phone 03 312 4351) and a key for the gate are required if using 4WD.

20. Whistler River and Chest Peak

Chest Peak from farm flats: 5–6 hours. **Hard**

Return via same route: 4–5 hours, or via Red Saddle and Mt Storm: 6–7 hours. **Hard**

Chest Peak (1936m) is the principal summit on the Puketeraki Range and is a common goal for fit, active trampers. The route is unmarked, steep in places, and during winter can carry moderate to heavy snow. Under summer conditions it is not hard, just a steady uphill push.

From the Snowdale Station flats walk up the Whistler River over farm tracks on terraces on the river left. These later climb over a series of small hillocks above the river on the north bank and descend to the Whistler River/Chest Peak Stream junction. A track continues up Chest Peak Stream and then climbs through bush, up onto the spur dividing Chest Peak and Mannering Streams. From Point 1225m on this ridge a steep spur is climbed directly to the summit shoulder, traversing the edge of a large basin on the south face of Chest Peak. This basin and spur are clearly visible to the northwest from suburban Christchurch, especially in winter. There is one small bluff on the spur here, which is easily negotiated, and then a final steep pinch leads to the summit plateau.

Magnificent views await you here: the Canterbury Plains, Waimakariri Basin, Arthur's Pass National Park and Craigieburn Range. Chest Peak is a strategic mountain, granting amazing views out over the interface of plains, foothills and alps, and is certainly worth the energy expended to reach the summit.

Descend via the same route or, for those experienced in ridge travel, a long, relatively easy route is possible, under good conditions, south to Red Saddle (1544m), then to Point 1668m, and then east to Mt Storm (1254m), descending back to Snowdale Station.

To access Whistler River and Chest Peak, 1km past Mt Pember Station turn left up Snowdale Road to Whistler River. This route crosses private land and permission is required (phone 03 312 4351).

Twin Fall Stream, Hawdon Valley

Waimakariri Basin and Arthur's Pass National Park

Craigieburn Conservation Park and Ranges

Known as Canterbury's hidden wonderland, Craigieburn Conservation Park offers trampers, skiers and walkers wide-ranging opportunities to explore and enjoy the outdoors through the park's varied landscapes. It lies 110km northwest of Christchurch and 42km south of Arthur's Pass, occupying 44,000 hectares of high country between the Waimakariri and Wilberforce rivers, east of the Southern Alps. Peaks range from 1700m to 2294m at Mt Greenlaw, in the extreme northwest of the region.

The park was formally gazetted in 1967, with additional areas being added in 1979 and 1984 (Bealey and Wilberforce). Prior to this it was pastoral lease, which was the predominant factor influencing the present-day landscape, particularly the forest cover. The introduction of red deer and possums in the early 20th century continued the modification of the vegetative cover, with the present-day forest confined to the mid and upper reaches of the Harper/Avoca catchment and eastern Craigieburn Range.

For most visitors the Craigieburn Range and skifields are the primary focus. Running parallel to SH73, this high, eroded range, with Mt Enys (2195m) its highest summit (which, incidentally, is not in the park), offers everything from easy day walks to challenging winter and summer tramps on the exposed ridge-tops, as well as a variety of skiing terrain. Three club skifields are located on the eastern flanks of the range, Cheeseman, Broken River and Craigieburn, and one commercial field, Porter Heights, is at the southern end. It is a magnet for avid skiers during the winter months, with generally good snow conditions from July to early September, and a sheltered aspect from the northwest gales.

However, the park offers much more for those who want to explore the Harper and Avoca forests, which lie beyond the Craigieburn Range. Here the real character of the park is revealed, with wide, braided, U-shaped valleys, typical of past glaciation, extending well back into the sub-ranges, where

LEGEND

1. Craigieburn Valley Walking Track
2. Lyndon Saddle to Helicopter Hill
3. Jacks Pass to Dracophyllum Flat
4. Hut Creek Track
5. Lyndon Saddle– Camp Saddle
6. Cass to Lagoon Saddle Circuit
7. Mt Bruce
8. Avoca River
9. Half Moon Saddle
10. Mt Enys, Craigieburn Range
11. Castle Hill Nature & Scenic Reserve
12. Cave Stream Scenic Reserve
13. Purple Hill & Lake Pearson

State highway — 73 —
Other roads
Walking track
Route only
Hut ∎
Skifield
  Broken River   BR
  Cheeseman   CH
  Craigieburn   CR
  Porter Heights PH
Native forest
Plantation

0   5km

Barker Hut · Anti-Crow Hut · Mt Murchison · White Col · Greenlaw Ck · Avoca Col · Anti-Crow River · Mt Greenlaw · Gizeh Col · Jordan Stream · Bea Spur · Mt Gizeh · Sphinx Saddle · Mt Avoca · Easy Stream · Jordan Saddle · Power · Burnett Stm · Avoca River · Avoca Hut · Tobacco Range · Long · Bristed Stm · Half Moon Saddle · Hanging Valley Ck · Basin Ck · Packa · Basin Hut · Thesis Pk · Fanghill Stm · Birdwood Range · Grey · Fanghill Hut (Private) · The Spurs · Avoca River · Wilberforce River · Gargarus Saddle · Hor · Gargarus · Mt Ida · Cottons Sheep Range · Mt Oakden · Rytor · N · Lake Coleridge · Rakaia River · to Christchurch

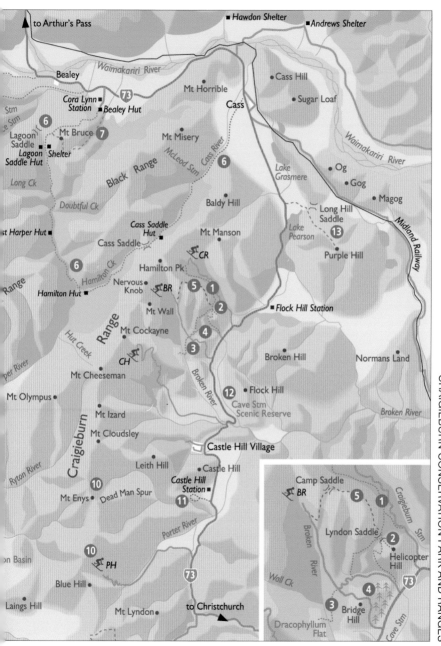

Fr Antoine Thomas on Craigieburn Range at dusk

the highest peaks stand, some with small summit glaciers. Dense forests of mountain and silver beech fill the upper Harper and Avoca valleys, which in their lower reaches are dominated by open, grassy floors and magnificent vistas of the high peaks and passes.

Craigieburn is, above all, a park of manageable proportions, without many of the obstacles that could intimidate would-be explorers. The rivers do not carry large volumes of water, except in flood, and therefore are an easy gateway to the valley heads. There are few real gorges, with none to be found in the major catchments, and the majority of high passes and peaks are accessible for most averagely experienced parties. Long ridge traverses are possible, especially in the eastern and southern sections. Distances are not great, with most trips across the ranges possible in the space of a weekend.

Craigieburn contains a remarkable cross-section of landforms, with space, tranquillity and seclusion to be found for those seeking the wilderness but perhaps not desiring an overly challenging experience. It is a park for all seasons and for all people.

Short Walks and Tramps

Short walks on formed tracks are confined to the eastern flanks of the Craigieburn Range, where a series of inter-linking trails run between the Broken River and Craigieburn Stream watersheds. These short walks, up to 2 hours, meander through the beech forests beside picturesque streams, with occasional views of peaks on the range. They are sheltered from the wind and are ideal family excursions.

1. Craigieburn Valley Walking Track
70 minutes. **Easy**

Originally cut to allow walking access to the skifield, the signposted track climbs upvalley from below Lyndon Saddle, with which it has a branch track, through mountain beech to the alpine tussock zone and skifield buildings. This track also links with Camp Saddle.

2. Lyndon Saddle to Helicopter Hill
15 minutes. **Easy**

This is a short, steep track ascending through mountain beech to the open tussock top of Helicopter Hill (1262m). There are good views from here over the Broken River Basin and Torlesse Range.

3. Jacks Pass to Dracophyllum Flat
45 minutes. **Easy**

Accessed off the Broken River skifield road, this pleasant forest walk passes through attractive mountain beech forest on a gentle downhill gradient to Broken River Stream. Ford the stream and climb onto the terrace opposite, where a large scrubby flat is covered with scattered pockets of dracophyllum shrubs. When snow is on the peaks, this is a most agreeable setting for a leisurely lunch on a fine day.

4. Hut Creek Track
25 minutes. **Easy**

A short loop track from the carpark located off the Broken River skifield road about 2km from SH73. This walk passes through an area of forest used for trial plantings to establish the suitability of exotic species for placement above the bushline. Fortunately, little of this was ever carried out in the Craigieburn Park.

Longer Walks and Tramps

5. Lyndon Saddle–Camp Saddle Traverse
3–4 hours round trip. **Moderate**
Bush track between Lyndon and Camp saddles: 70 minutes

I am always surprised to discover additional opportunities for interesting trips in a familiar tramping area that I presumed I knew well, especially when I have visited the region on many occasions. So, when looking for a short trip on the tops in winter for a snatched break during mid-week, I was pleased to discover the popular Lyndon Saddle to Camp Saddle traverse along an outlying ridge of the main Craigieburn Range. With access to both saddles facilitated by excellent bush tracks, and easy, open beech forest above these, joining the tussock and scree, the round trip provides a satisfying short walk.

Although the undulating ridge-top is only just above 1500m altitude, its proximity to the 1800–1900m main range and peaks infuses a sense of expectation at the spectacle of craggy summits and sweeping snow faces (during winter), seemingly a hand's breadth away.

Three small peaks on the 2km ridgeline provide additional viewpoints, especially to the south and east over the dense forests of the Craigieburn Park

Mountain daisies,
Craigieburn Range

and on to the open tussock landscapes of the Waimakariri Basin and distant Torlesse and Puketeraki ranges.

Sandwiched between this panorama and the Craigieburn peaks there is much of visual interest as you wend your way along the mixed scree and hard snow of the ridge crest, pausing regularly to admire the view and the associations of tussocks and alpine herbs scattered in pockets on the tops. As the walk is short, there is time to enjoy the view, the sun, and the peace.

Alpine vegetation, Craigieburn Conservation Park

This is one of its major advantages; there is no particular rush to go anywhere.

The descent from Camp Saddle, above which vegetable sheep and other alpine plant species are plentiful, follows a good track through an attractive tussock basin and into the forest once more, before finally reaching the Broken River skifield road.

Access for this walk, and the other short walks in this section, is from SH73, turning off at Cave Stream Shelter, just before the Craigieburn cutting, and driving slowly up the road looking out for the signposted track on the right to Lyndon Saddle. This can also be accessed off the Broken River skifield road and signposted track to Camp Saddle.

Note: The ridge between the saddles may be difficult to follow in misty conditions; an alternative bush track also links the saddles, to the north, on the Craigieburn Valley face.

6. Cass to Lagoon Saddle Circuit

Cass to Cass Saddle: 3–4 hours. **Moderate**
Cass Saddle to Hamilton Hut: 3 hours. **Moderate**
Hamilton Hut to West Harper Hut: 2 hours. **Easy**
West Harper Hut to Lagoon Saddle Shelter: 3–4 hours. **Moderate**
Shelter to Cora Lynn Station: 2–3 hours. **Moderate**

By far the most popular overnight tramp, this moderate 2–3-day trip is facilitated by well-spaced, comfortable huts, and traverses two saddles and three river valleys in the east of the park. It is an ideal tramp in its own right, and is especially attractive if nor'west weather precludes a trip farther to the west. The final section of the track, above Lagoon Saddle, has a grand view over Arthur's Pass National Park.

The track is usually walked from Cass to Cora Lynn Station in the west; road transport will be required between the tracks. A marked route exists on the river right of Cass River beside pines and later onto the open, bouldery

Mike Latty at Lagoon Saddle

riverbed, which is followed for some distance (about 4km), crossing as necessary, until the marked track is picked up on the left (river right) near the junction with McLeod Stream. This track climbs and sidles above a small gorge and crosses the river twice on bridges before reaching the secluded Cass Saddle Hut (3 bunks). Above here open tussock travel (poled) in beautiful surroundings leads to Cass Saddle (1326m), which the track crosses and then descends sharply into the Hamilton Creek bush and picturesque tussock flats.

Hamilton Hut (20 bunks), a large, well-constructed hut on a terrace on the south bank of the creek, commands a good view of the Black and Grey ranges.

Above the hut the well-marked track crosses both Hamilton Creek and then Harper River (footbridge). Harper River lies in a narrow defile beneath the spurs of the Black Range, and the track follows its sinuous length all the way to its source at Lagoon Saddle. En route it passes historic West Harper Hut (5 bunks), set in a small clearing, and Lagoon Saddle Shelter (A-frame, no bunks). Lagoon Saddle Hut (3 bunks) is located just across the stream, opposite the shelter. It is rather run down.

Beyond the shelter the track sidles to the bush edge above Lagoon Saddle and it is here that the best views on the walk are obtained, especially if the weather is fine and clear to the west. A dramatic spectacle of Arthur's Pass is gained from here, and farther on, as the track sidles along the open hillside below Mt Bruce. It is a refreshing contrast to the shady, narrow confines of the upper Harper River. A poled route continues around the hillside, before dropping down an easy bush spur, where there are some pines, and exiting past the Bealey Hut (6 bunks), 300m from the road-end at Cora Lynn Station.

Access for each end of this track is either from Cass or Cora Lynn, both of which are on SH73. From Cass the track starts at a small carpark 400m south of the Cass River road bridge on SH73. From Cora Lynn the track starts on Cora Lynn Road 1km east of Bruce Stream Bridge through marked access on the station. (Also see 'Wilberforce Valley and Lake Coleridge' for notes on alternative access.)

Waimakariri headwaters and the Southern Alps from Mt Bruce

7. Mt Bruce

Mt Bruce from Lagoon Saddle: 1–2 hours. **Moderate**

Summit to saddle south of peak and out via Bruce Stream: 2–3 hours. **Moderate**

Mt Bruce (1630m) rises sharply in a broad face above the poled route from Lagoon Saddle Shelter to the bush spur descending to Cora Lynn Station. It makes a worthwhile side-trip for those walking the track, or a day trip from the highway, offering superb panoramas of Arthur's Pass and Craigieburn parks from its rounded summit. Although of modest altitude, it stands well back from the main ranges and has one of the best views possible of the eastern regions of the parks.

The route ascends the broad spur/face above Lagoon Saddle and steepens over mixed scree and tussock to the summit. A round trip/descent route is possible to the low saddle on the Black Range, south of the summit at 1360m, via steep scree/snow, and then into Broad Stream, where a marked route exists from the bush edge. Walk down the bush spur and streambed to a major fork, and then to the highway.

SUMMIT SURPRISE – MT BRUCE

Dense mist swirls about us as we exit my ute at the foot of Mt Bruce in Arthur's Pass National Park. It's still fully dark, frigid, and no time to be waiting about, as the three of us, Nick and Zac Ashley and I, tighten pack straps, pull on gloves and adjust our headlamps, before stepping out into the mist. The climb begins immediately, but fortunately is moderated by the gradient of the Lagoon Saddle Track, which ascends the hillside above the flats of Cora Lynn Station before traversing west across the face of Mt Bruce, our objective for sunrise. The track spurs our progress heavenwards and in under an hour we clamber out of the bush, and the mist, and can begin to enjoy this night-time perspective of the Waimakariri Valley. The valley floor is filled with the dense bank of mist that had so chilled us on arrival at Cora Lynn, but the peaks are clear and even now, still an hour off sunrise, there is a steady lightening of the eastern horizon. No time to linger, should we hope to crest the top before sun-up.

At this point, around halfway along the traverse towards Lagoon Saddle, we leave the easy line of the track to strike out directly for the east shoulder of Mt Bruce. It's not an easy approach, not due to

Sunrise over Waimakariri Valley from Mt Bruce

Lagoon Saddle Shelter

any technical difficulty, but in the dark, holes, clumps of tussock, and half-frozen scree make for a frustrating passage upwards.

Dawn is coming as we reach the shoulder and make a final burst for the peak, where a snowy, corniced ridge suggests caution.

At just a smidgen over 1600m we gain the broad summit, not overly high for peaks in the Arthur's Pass region, but amply elevated and sufficiently distant from the Divide to allow for unobstructed views along the corridor of the Waimak' Valley – and we are in time for dawn. It creeps in over the Poulter Valley peaks to the east, sending shafts of light onto the Divide and scattered patterns over the misty valley. I find there is nothing quite like being on a summit at dawn, especially if it has been hard-won due to timing and unexpected delays en route as ours has been this day. The cold, fatigue and general discomfort evaporate with the promise of rubescent light sweeping in and transforming the scene before you. Places both familiar and unfamiliar gain a spectacular dimension at this time and plant seeds of endeavour for additional forays.

As the dawn light ebbs, to be replaced by brighter tones, we edge down from the summit, westwards again, to pick up the track and explore the frozen tarns of Lagoon Saddle, lunch in the freezer-like interior of Lagoon Saddle Shelter, and strike 'gold' again, photographically speaking, with the frozen waterfalls of the upper Harper Valley.

It's been a varied day, undoubtedly capped by the dawn, but full of surprises in a wintry landscape.

8. Avoca River

2–3 days to access the river head and return. **Moderate/Hard**

This large western catchment contains the park's most remote tramps. It is a very scenic region and worthy of a visit on this basis alone. There are few huts, but idyllic forest camps are numerous, as are the possibilities for pass-hopping trips into Arthur's Pass National Park or the upper Wilberforce Valley.

The Sphinx Saddle–Jordan Saddle route (see notes for 'Bealey Hut and Spur') is well used by tramping parties and makes a visit into the upper Avoca possible, over 2 days, from the Arthur's Pass highway, without involving an extended valley walk.

Sphinx Saddle (1539m) is accessed from Easy Stream to Anti-Crow River, a tributary of the Waimakariri.

Further north, harder possibilities exist for a similar circuit over Gizeh and Avoca cols, but these are steep, difficult routes requiring care and good navigation. The head of the Avoca River is a dramatic place, with sheer rock walls standing as mighty bastions beneath high glaciers and rugged summits.

(See notes for 'Wilberforce Valley and Lake Coleridge' for alternative access.)

9. Half Moon Saddle

3–4 days to cross the pass. **Hard**

A challenging transalpine route leads from a headwater creek of the Avoca River, Hanging Valley Creek, over Half Moon Saddle (1851m) to Bristed Stream and the Wilberforce River. Avoca Hut (6 bunks), in the upper Avoca River, provides good shelter for tramping parties.

This trip passes through an isolated region of the park, where rock summits and rugged gorges predominate. It will take 3–4 days to complete, returning via the lower Wilberforce Valley or back to Arthur's Pass National Park via Burnett Stream and White Col.

This is suitable for experienced parties only. White Col is an alpine route.

(See notes for Fanghill Hut in 'Upper Wilberforce Valley' for access.)

EVENING RANGE-ROVERS

There's a plan afoot – sunset on the crest of the Craigieburn Range, via the Mt Cheeseman access road, with a late start thrown in, timed nicely for that golden glow of the evening as the sunlight melts into the horizon. A last-minute addition to this formula is Fr Antoine Thomas – a companion with whom to share the moment at the ridge-top. A warm afternoon greets us as we wend our way along the access road, through the beech forest and clearings, until we reach the first locked gate. It's much lower than expected and adds a sudden cloud of doubt as to the viability of our excursion (it's already 6pm) to reach the summit before dark. Still, neither of us is easily deterred, so we don our boots and packs, camera and food, and soldier on, the short hop to the top having now turned into a 5km walk, climbing 900m.

It's easy though and we cut out some of the zigzags by taking a direct line up the tussock slopes to reach the snowline and base buildings of the skifield. From here it's less than 1km and 300m to the ridge-top. There's not a soul to be seen and the warmth of the evening makes for delightful walking conditions. The only problem is the soft snow pack that fills the upper basin.

With a little assiduous route selection we scamper up almost to the ridge-top by following thawed-out sections of the basin where rock and tussock are exposed. The last steep pinch is tough going, but we swap the lead to keep up the pace and arrive at the final slope to the crest. At this point the sun's action and wind deposition have created a crusty layer that eases our progress towards the ridge and we ratchet up the pace to arrive slightly out of breath at the top.

The sun's still up but sinking fast, creating some wonderful lighting effects over the alps and Harper River catchment directly below us, and best of all it's still warm. In fact, a magnificent evening is seeping into the ranges, a somnolent breeze is wafting out of the Harper, and we are good to go for a wander along the crest where more views await. This snowy landscape is a far cry from the busy streets of Riccarton in Christchurch, which we left just 4 hours earlier, and a

Moonrise over Puketeraki Range

welcome reminder of what can be achieved in an afternoon from the city centre if you set your mind to it. Fr Antoine agrees and heads off at a steady clip along the top to a nearby peak, where we catch another glimpse into Arthur's Pass National Park and the great lumpy canvas of the Waimakariri Basin. Moonrise sets the scene – its great baleful eye rising in the east and we snap a few shots, down some orange juice, and share a sandwich as the day retreats.

The time is closing on 9pm and we are vaguely aware, in all the excitement of having claimed our prize, that we have yet to descend to the vehicle, drive home and have dinner somewhere. That last marker is a forlorn hope, however, and we suffice with snack bars and a half-cold cuppa at the car, but that registers no complaint from us after our range-roving at dusk.

Summit Walks

Throughout the area, easily reached peaks up to 2000m can be gained by fit parties in a day or a weekend. The skifield access roads grant excellent access (in summer, Porter Heights and Cheeseman skifields roads are locked and access may not be granted), from a high level, to the open tops, and as such provide exciting ridge-top traverses both in summer and winter. Numerous summits can be bagged in a day, in good conditions, from the skifields, with a complete traverse of the range possible in 2–3 days. The views from the ridge crests are one of the most remarkable experiences of a visit to this part of the park, and encompass the Canterbury Plains, the Pacific Ocean and the Southern Alps.

Leading ridges provide direct access to the summits, with some easy scrambling necessary to gain the top. The Craigieburn and Black ranges are the best options and can be traversed to provide satisfying ridge trips.

Some of the best climbs are Mt Enys from Porter Heights, Mt Cheeseman from Cheeseman skifield, Hamilton Peak traverse to Nervous Knob to Mt Wall from Broken River skifield, Hamilton Peak and Mt Manson from Craigieburn Valley skifield, Black Range from Lagoon Saddle, either southwest to Bruce Saddle or south and east from Mt Bruce, and Mt Olympus from Mt Cheeseman skifield or from Mt Olympus skifield/Ryton Basin, although both these routes will require permission for access during summer.

In winter all routes attain a moderate degree of difficulty, and a sound knowledge of basic alpine skills, involving ice axe and crampons, together with avalanche awareness and good conditions, are essential for all parties venturing onto the tops.

Access to peaks on the southern end of the range, Cheeseman, Cloudesley, Enys etc., is via Castle Hill Station and permission will be required to access them (ph. 03 318 8466).

10. Mt Enys, Craigieburn Range

Porter Heights skifield carpark to summit: 4–5 hours. **Hard**
Return: 2–3 hours

Standing near the southern end of the Craigieburn Range above SH73 (Arthur's Pass highway), Mt Enys (2194m) is the highest foothill summit directly accessible from a major highway and skifield. However, its

Climbing onto Craigieburn Range, with Torlesse Range beyond

accessibility is belied by its height, heavy winter snowfalls and, most significantly, its exposure to gale- or storm-force westerly winds. These factors make this relatively easy summit worthy of respect and have seen this writer retreat from several attempts to gain the summit, especially during winter.

The curving sweep of the Craigieburn Range, gained in the south from Porter Heights skifield, provides an exciting high traverse to the summit, passing over several lower 1900–2000m peaks en route. The range crest is broad, with some narrow rocky outcrops, and in good conditions provides fast access to the square-shaped summit, where a final steep 200m ascent leads to Mt Enys.

Views from the peak cover a huge tract of the South Island, stretching along the Divide from Mts Cook and Tasman (which are prominent on a fine, clear day), over the Rakaia peaks to Mt Rolleston, and beyond to the peaks at the head of Lake Sumner.

At your feet lies the complex mountain, lake and river landscape of the Harper, Avoca and Wilberforce valleys and Lake Coleridge, while eastward the horizon stretches all the way to Christchurch and the Pacific Ocean, including the Torlesse Range and Canterbury foothills.

As other more westerly summits are more challenging than Mt Enys, and therefore deemed better objectives, Mt Enys is often left to be climbed on those marginal days when the weather precludes attempts on higher and harder summits. Therefore, it is often climbed in less than ideal conditions, which does not do justice to this spectacular viewpoint.

Best access is during winter, via SH73 to Porters Pass and the Porter Heights skifield road carpark and up through the field to the range crest. If you arrive an hour before the tows start you will have the field to yourself. Follow the ridge north over several intermediate summits to the top.

Other routes are via Mt Cloudesley (2107m) to the north on the range. Another easier spur exists, south of Dead Man Spur, and is approached from the skifield road and Porter River. This road is closed in summer. Other routes are possible from the west.

As a winter climb, ice axe and crampons should be carried and consideration given to avalanche conditions, which can be extreme in some seasons.

Access for Mt Enys is through Castle Hill Station; phone 03 318 8466 for permission.

Castle Hill Reserve

Reserves and Lakes

11. Castle Hill Nature and Scenic Reserve
1 hour to all day. **Easy**

Two adjacent recreational areas immediately bordering the park are worthy of mention: Castle Hill Nature and Scenic Reserve, and Cave Stream, both on SH73. Castle Hill Nature and Scenic Reserve contains spectacular limestone tors and is popular with rock climbers and botanists. It is signposted on SH73 and has a large carpark and interpretation panels.

12. Cave Stream Scenic Reserve
1 hour to traverse cave. **Moderate.**
Good agility needed.

Described as one of the most exciting natural features in Canterbury, Cave Stream flows underground for 362m and exits through an imposing tunnel, where it joins Broken Hill Stream. The reserve is also of scientific importance as the limestone formations both above and below ground are classic karst topography.

Although the cave is the focal point of the reserve, spectacular limestone outcrops, canyons and cliffs above ground form a veritable maze of passages and open boulder fields over which a day or more can be spent exploring or climbing.

The cave is accessed via a short track from the carpark on SH73 to the downstream end. Here a shallow stream issues from the mouth of the cave. Inside the cave soon narrows and begins a series of tortuous bends, while climbing steadily to the upper end. The force of water can sometimes be difficult to negotiate, so if you have any doubts, do not enter. It can be difficult and dangerous to turn and come back with the water behind you. In normal flow, however, the cave is an exciting place to visit and the short, sharp climb up a steel ladder at the upstream end, and emergence back into the sunlight, brings a great sense of achievement for those who complete the underground passage.

Access is off SH73, 500m east of the access road to Mt Cheeseman skifield.

Take a good torch (and backup), warm clothes and a change of clothes. It can be very cold in the underground stream, sometimes up to your thighs.

13. Purple Hill and Lake Pearson

Lake Pearson to summit: 3–4 hours, descent: 2 hours. **Hard**
Via scree and lake-shore: 3–4 hours. **Moderate**

In the centre of the Waimakariri Basin, Purple Hill (1680m) ramps up above the shores of Lake Pearson, a wildlife reserve and popular camping and fishing destination for Cantabrians. This high, bare mountain is isolated from all surrounding ranges by the streams that flow beneath its steep spurs and ridges. It is a demanding climb to reach the long summit ridge, and in summer provides an unrelenting 1000m ascent from the lake-shore. As you climb the broad north ridge, first on tussock and later on scree and rock, the varied topography of the landscape below becomes ever more apparent. The cones of Sugar Loaf, Og, Gog and Magog recede below and merge with the great sweep of the Waimakariri River as it surges past the flanks of Mt Binser.

Lake Pearson's hourglass shape flashes invitingly from the tawny meadows, as does the long lazy form of Lake Grasmere, a little farther to the north. Although hardly a climber's mountain, Purple Hill grants a stunning spectacle over this landscape, dissected by the twin ribbons of SH73 and the TranzAlpine Railway. Even up here the unmistakable sound of the locomotives plying the track waft past; they seem rather apt as you puff and pant upwards to the summit, which recedes against the banner of sky.

There is no water on this climb, so make sure you are well provisioned for lunch and a well-earned rest at the top.

An option for descent, other than returning via the north ridge and face, is to drop down the steep scree face west of the summit, through scrub, to the shore of Lake Pearson. This can then be followed north, with some shallow wading or scrub bashing required (depending on the lake level), to the vehicle tracks where you began at the lakehead.

Access is off SH73 at the northern end of the lake and follow vehicle tracks to the lake-shore. Ascend from near Long Hill Saddle, south, to the summit. Although Purple Hill is on private land, permission is not required. Please respect this and do not disturb stock.

SHADES OF PURPLE – PURPLE HILL

A steepening snow-covered ridgeline rises from the broad shoulder I am traversing at 1400m on the nor'west slopes of Purple Hill in the Waimakariri Basin. Though just over 1600m, Purple Hill guards the eastern shoreline of Lake Pearson, which any traveller to Arthur's Pass will be familiar with, and is one of those 'island summits' unconnected to any main ranges and therefore offering a unique spectacle of the landscape in this quadrant of the high country.

I started from the lake-shore on a fine winter's morning, its perfect picture-card setting framed by ridges decked with snow, courtesy of a huge dump that has plastered the surrounding ranges but surprisingly left out Purple Hill. However, the rain associated with the snow at lower altitudes has produced a firm crust on the snow, and this requires care and an ice axe and crampons to safely negotiate. It's been a tough pull up the trackless hillside to gain the high shoulder and I'm thankful there hasn't been thick snow cover on the slopes to slow my passage further.

Lake Pearson from Purple Hill

A light southerly brushes the ridge crest as I creep ever higher, the basin and lake arrayed about the spurs of Purple Hill in a collage of colours and textures, drawing my eyes away to the Southern Alps, now revealing their winter splendour from behind the clouds. It's enough to push me on, picking past rocky sections, over small snowy bluffs, sidling past larger ones, until I arrive at the summit ridge, where a short traverse on easy-angled slopes brings me to the top. A fine view awaits – Lake Pearson's hourglass shape curves through the plains below, alongside which SH73 traces its route out toward the clustered snowy ridges of Arthur's Pass. East and south lie sub-ranges loaded with snow and topped by cloud banks still being pushed by the dying southerly. It's a familiar yet lonely landscape, cold and uninviting, wintry and inhospitable.

Lunch is my call, that and a photo shoot from the top, where the cloud and changing light produce some dramatic effects. It's too cold to stay long, sitting on spare clothing in the snow, so I down a quick hot drink, stuff a few snack bars in the pockets of my parka and head off. The top section requires even more care on the descent, but I make it readily enough and rest again lower down to remove some clothing in the warming temperatures.

Lake Pearson still looks inviting below, but a winter wade is not on my wish-list today. Wading the lake-shore is an option for returning from the summit and will grant a round trip by descending to the south and then west from the top to access the large basin on Purple Hill's west face. Not far off the high shoulder I traverse into a shallow gully and head directly down. In doing so I pick up the 'escalator' – a recent rainwater gut that has eroded the face and left deep, soft, muddy soil in its bed, which is ideal for an easy and fast descent.

The lake-shore comes up rapidly and in moments I'm heading across the flats – homeward bound.

Arthur's Pass National Park

Next morning we went up the stream as far as it was possible … cutting our way with billhooks. It was hard work, and though we had light swags, it took the greater part of the day to get out of the bush into the scrub, where we found we had arrived at a swampy valley about a mile in length which evidently had once been the bed of a glacier.

… The barometer registered about 3000ft above sea level. This was evidently an available saddle with very little difficulties on the east side, the heavy work would be on the west side, where there was a precipitous descent into a long narrow gorge, the head of the Otira River.

From *Memoirs*, Arthur Dudley Dobson, 12 March 1864

The highway aside, very little has changed since Arthur Dudley Dobson and friends crested the Main Divide at what has become known as Arthur's Pass. His comments on the breathtaking view down the ragged gulch of the Otira Gorge are as apt today as in 1864. Perhaps the rata is not quite as profuse, perhaps the glaciers are smaller, but the sigh of the wind through the crags, the call of the kea above and the roar of the river below are as real and as uplifting for the soul.

Arthur's Pass National Park was officially created in 1929 and today remains the most easily accessible of all New Zealand National Parks to a major population base. The pass itself is still an important transalpine road crossing.

The park covers an area of approximately 95,000 hectares of extremely rugged terrain between the headwaters of the Waimakariri and Taramakau rivers. The peaks of the park are between 1600m and 2400m elevation, with the highest, Mt Murchison (2408m), standing at the head of the White River, a feeder of the Waimakariri.

These factors account for a major part of the popularity of the region, especially amongst West Coasters and Cantabrians. The park cannot boast of a singular scenic monument or feature; it does not have a Mt Cook or a Milford Sound. Yet it possesses a timeless quality, underpinned by a diverse landscape and climate, which embraces both the eastern and western aspects of the alps. Huge braided riverbeds, rock gorges, peaks, passes and glaciers (the most northern to be found in the South Island), waterfalls, tarns, secluded river flats, alpine lakes and gentle, flower-filled meadows have all helped create a special affection in the hearts of those who visit or venture into the park.

The Waimakariri and Poulter are the major rivers dissecting the park in the east, whilst the Otira and Taramakau rivers cut through the ranges to the west. Between these major catchments lie a host of smaller rivers and streams draining rugged mountain ranges that are characterised by steep forested flanks rising to tussock basins, scree faces and ridges and, near the Divide, snowfields and glaciers. It is a region that offers endless variety for those who aspire to explore the hinterland beyond the highway that bisects the park.

Early History

The Main Divide of the South Island formed a formidable deterrent to any interaction between eastern and western Māori tribes until the 18th century, when Ngāi Tahu from the east had forged several routes through the mountain chain granting them access to the prized greenstone lands of the Ngāi Wairangi tribe in the west.

Māori favoured the more northern and easier Hurunui–Taramakau crossing of the Divide rather than the steep, rugged Arthur's Pass route, largely because it provided better access to food sources en route and a gentler gradient to climb on the return trip when heavily laden with greenstone. Arthur's Pass, it seems, was used infrequently as a speedier route to the west. But soon all was to change.

Arthur Dobson, while on a survey through the Taramakau Valley with his Māori guide, Tarapuhi, son of Tuhuru, was shown the pass at the head of the Otira River. However, this was prior to the discovery of gold on the West Coast so there seemed little incentive to develop further access, especially when the Hurunui crossing via Harper Pass provided a comparatively much easier route. Gold was discovered in Westland in 1864 and immediately there was much interest in developing direct access to the goldfields. After a 3-week examination of all the passes out of the Waimakariri, Poutler, Minga and Hawdon valleys, George Dobson (Arthur's brother), when reporting to his father, said, 'Arthur's Pass is the best route'. So the pass was named and the rush was on.

A workforce of over 1000 men was soon spread along the 160km route from Porters Pass in western Canterbury to Hokitika. They toiled through a severe winter with pick and shovel, scant shelter and inadequate food to complete the road, in less than a year, on 20 March 1866 – a remarkable achievement!

The Coaching Era

Miners, sheep, cattle and later horse-drawn coaches were soon plying the newly opened route. These coaches were operated by Cobb & Co. and ran an unbroken service from 1866 to 1923. The journey of 270km took 3 days, unless delayed by flood, storm or snow, which was not uncommon. All who travelled were fearful of the most dramatic part of the trip: the Otira Gorge. The gorge held those who travelled it in awe and dread of its terrific precipices and hairpin corners, so acute that 'the leading horses disappeared from sight', and by the adze-carved 'track' that sufficed for a road; it was so narrow that scant inches separated distressed passengers, bucking coach and 'the shortest way to the bottom'. It was a journey of pioneering tradition.

For all its terrifying reputation, there was never a life lost in the gorge and only one fatality recorded on the road over Arthur's Pass, when a child was hurled from an overturning coach at Warden's Creek.

The Otira Gorge Viaduct is but the latest development in the history of the highway and was completed in 1999. It bypasses the infamous zigzag section, which had been under threat of collapse. It is 35m high and 440m long.

Railway and Tunnel

The possibility of a railway link between Canterbury and Westland was considered as early as 1865, and although it was begun in 1886 it was not until 1900 that much progress was made on the easier approaches across the valley flats in the Taramakau and Waimakariri. Work began on the construction of the Otira Tunnel in 1908 but fell so far behind that the original contractors were relieved of the job and the government was forced to complete the task itself. It proved a difficult and time-consuming task. Above ground the political and economic situation between the counties was a continual source of disagreement, while in the tunnel itself fractured rock, seeping water and heavy timbering of the walls and roof, to prevent collapse, added to the hardships endured. The onset of war in Europe added labour shortages, so it was not until 1923, 37 years after commencement of work, that the tunnel and railway link were finally opened. The tunnel is 8.5km long and has a gradient of 1 in 33.

TranzAlpine Express

Today a modern, comfortable tourist train, the TranzAlpine Express, plys the rail link between Christchurch and Greymouth. The return trip can be made in a day, however to fully appreciate this unique rail journey it is best to spend a night in Greymouth or Arthur's Pass and have the time, especially at Arthur's Pass, to explore the mountain environment. Contact KiwiRail for details.

Arthur's Pass and Village

Arthur's Pass is a wonderful alpine village set amidst the rugged grandeur of the Southern Alps, in the heart of Arthur's Pass National Park, where man's footprint on the land is seemingly insignificant against the vastness of the South Island's hinterland.

The roading contractor, J. Smith, set up a camp at Camping Flat, the site of the present village, to enable his men to complete the project. It was this and the subsequent Midland Rail route and Otira Tunnel contract that set the foundations for the small hamlet that has survived into the 21st century.

Arthur's Pass has lost none of its simple alpine charm throughout the intervening years, and with the present national focus on promoting tourism, it is refreshing to discover that this small hamlet, of approximately 50 permanent inhabitants, remains as an unsophisticated mountain retreat, where those who enjoy some of life's simpler pleasures – such as walking and botanising – can wander without the disruption and glitter of tourist amenities. The small coffee houses cum restaurants, situated on the main highway, are greatly outnumbered by the various basic cottages owned by the locals and transient visitors from both east and west coasts, and all are lorded over by the great dark forests and sheer-sided peaks of the pass.

It seems that everything here is vertical. There are few real tourist walks available, the most notable being to the Devil's Punchbowl and Bridal Veil falls, and into the fearsomely named Bealey Chasm. These short, well-maintained tracks can be completed in the course of a morning or afternoon's stroll, and many of those who visit on the daily TranzAlpine rail trip do just this.

View into Arthur's Pass National Park up the Waimakariri River

Bernadette Barrett in Hawdon Valley

For the more adventurous visitor there is excitement and endeavour waiting at the road's edge. Numerous alpine tracks scale the valley walls, at an unrelenting gradient, direct to the alpine grasslands and snowy summits unseen above the village. Tracks with names like Avalanche Peak, Con's Track, Mt Aicken and Rome Ridge will spirit the energetic into bright alpine gardens, waterfalls and snowfields, where the view and challenge are limited only by the weather, conditions and your ability. There are return trips, round trips and ridge trips, where the tramper can really test his or her mettle on rickety crests far above the defile of the valley, where kea call from distant crags and the mountain winds sigh over the landscape. Beware, though: there is real and present danger here, from the wind and cloud. Nor'west gales pummel these tops with a frequency and ferocity unsuspected by the casual visitor and they often arrive with little advance warning, trapping the unwary in a scorching gale and swathing the peaks in a sea of cloud.

Arthur's Pass has a place in the heart of many trampers and walkers; simple, yet secure in its setting beneath the peaks.

Mt Alexander

Taramakau River

Taramakau River

73

Taipo River

to Greymouth

37

Seven Mile Ck

35

Lake Ck

35

Lake Kaurapataka

Otira River

Pfeifer Stm

Rocky Ck Hut

Dillons Hut

Taipo Hut

Carroll Hut

Kelly Saddle

34

Pfeifer Bivvy

36

Mt Pfeifer

Griffin Ck Hut

Scottys Bivvy

Kelly Range

Kellys Ck

33

Goat Ck

Tara Tama

Hunt Saddle

34

30

Mt Barron

Goat Hill

Otira

31

Dunns Ck Hut

Dunns Ck

37

Taipo River

Deception River

Otehake Hut

Otehake River

Hura Ck

Mid Taipo Hut

Hunt Ridge

Hunts Creek Hut

Hunts Ck

Rolleston River

Mt Franklin

33

Julia Hut

32

Mt Armstrong

Waimakariri Col

Arthur's Pass

Temple Basin

Upper Deception Hut

Falling Mtn

Tarn Col

Taruahuna Pass

Julia Creek

Carrington Pk

Mt Rolleston

GPH

Goat Pass

15

Lake Mavis

Crow Glacier

Rome Ridge

Mt Cassidy

MB

Mt Oates

Mt Scott

Mt Wilson

24

Sudden Valley

Waimakariri Falls Hut

Mt Aicken

Mingha River

Sudden Valley Stm

Harman Pass

Avalanche Pk

Crow Hut

Arthur's Pass

EH

Polar

White River

Mt Guinevere

Crow River

14

Williams Saddle

Mt Williams

Mt Davie

Carrington Hut

18

Mt Bealey

Bealey River

Edwards River

16

17

Dome Pk

Barker Hut

Greyneys Shelter

Mt Harper

White Col

Greenlaw Ck

Anti-Crow Hut

Waimakariri River

Klondyke Corner

Klondyke Shelter

Mt Murchison

Anti-Crow River

18

Bealey

Mt Horrible

Jordan Stm

Bealey Spur

19

Cora Lynn Station

Bealey Hut

Mt Misery

Jordan Saddle

Power Stm

Bealey Spur Hut

Mt Bruce

Avoca River

Bruce Stm

Lagoon Saddle

Avoca Hut

Lagoon Saddle Hut

Lagoon Saddle Shelter

—N—

0

ARTHUR'S PASS NATIONAL PARK

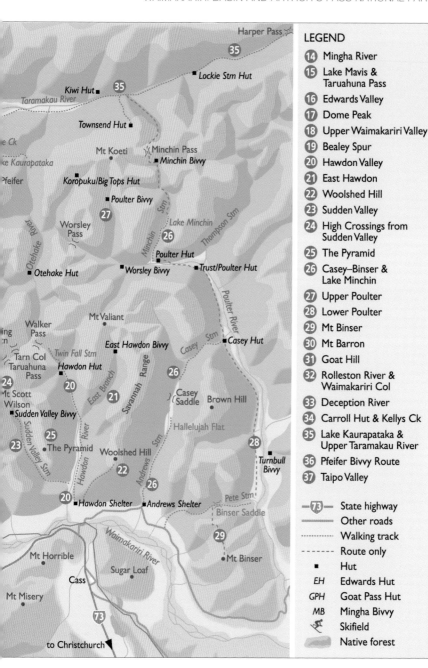

LEGEND

14 Mingha River

15 Lake Mavis & Taruahuna Pass

16 Edwards Valley

17 Dome Peak

18 Upper Waimakariri Valley

19 Bealey Spur

20 Hawdon Valley

21 East Hawdon

22 Woolshed Hill

23 Sudden Valley

24 High Crossings from Sudden Valley

25 The Pyramid

26 Casey–Binser & Lake Minchin

27 Upper Poulter

28 Lower Poulter

29 Mt Binser

30 Mt Barron

31 Goat Hill

32 Rolleston River & Waimakariri Col

33 Deception River

34 Carroll Hut & Kellys Ck

35 Lake Kaurapataka & Upper Taramakau River

36 Pfeifer Bivvy Route

37 Taipo Valley

—73— State highway

Other roads

.... Walking track

------- Route only

■ Hut

EH Edwards Hut

GPH Goat Pass Hut

MB Mingha Bivvy

Skifield

Native forest

ARTHUR'S PASS NATIONAL PARK

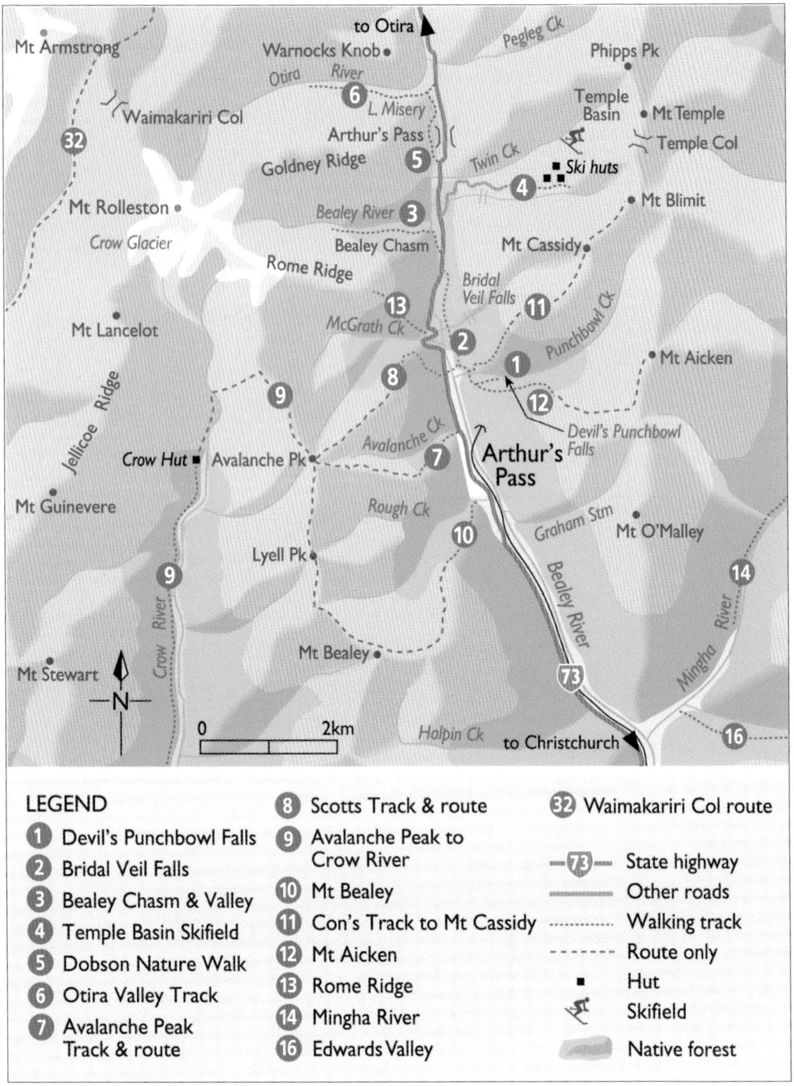

to Otira

Mt Armstrong
Warnocks Knob •
Pegleg Ck
Phipps Pk

Otira River
6
L. Misery
Temple Basin
• Mt Temple

Waimakariri Col
Arthur's Pass
Twin Ck
Temple Col

32
Goldney Ridge
5
▪▪ Ski huts
4

Mt Rolleston •
Bealey River **3**
• Mt Blimit

Crow Glacier
Bealey Chasm
Mt Cassidy •

Rome Ridge
Bridal Veil Falls
11
Punchbowl Ck

Mt Lancelot •
McGrath Ck
13
2

Jellicoe Ridge
9
8
1
• Mt Aicken

12
Devil's Punchbowl Falls

Crow Hut ▪ Avalanche Pk •
Avalanche Ck
7
Arthur's Pass

Mt Guinevere •
Rough Ck
Graham Stm
Mt O'Malley •

Lyell Pk •
10

Crow River
9
14

Mt Stewart •
—N—
Bealey River

Mt Bealey •
73

0   2km
Halpin Ck
to Christchurch

Mingha River
16

LEGEND

1 Devil's Punchbowl Falls
2 Bridal Veil Falls
3 Bealey Chasm & Valley
4 Temple Basin Skifield
5 Dobson Nature Walk
6 Otira Valley Track
7 Avalanche Peak Track & route

8 Scotts Track & route
9 Avalanche Peak to Crow River
10 Mt Bealey
11 Con's Track to Mt Cassidy
12 Mt Aicken
13 Rome Ridge
14 Mingha River
16 Edwards Valley

32 Waimakariri Col route

—**73**— State highway
——— Other roads
·········· Walking track
------ Route only
▪ Hut
🎿 Skifield
Native forest

Eastern Arthur's Pass National Park

Short Walks and Day Tramps from Arthur's Pass Village

Branching off SH73, as it passes through Arthur's Pass village and the sub-alpine zone, are many short walks and day tramps, all of which are well signposted and marked along their routes. This section highlights these tracks and some alternative routes on the tops. For most people the Arthur's Pass National Park Visitor Centre and museum are of special interest on a visit to the park, with track, weather and route information available.

1 & 2. Devil's Punchbowl Falls and Bridal Veil Falls
Both walks take approximately 1 hour each. **Easy**

Both of these spectacular cascades are set among beech forest and rocky bluffs, where well-formed tracks are, as in the case of the Devil's Punchbowl Falls, ascended right up to the plummeting curtain of water.

Access bridge to the Devil's Punchbowl Falls

Devil's Punchbowl Falls

These tracks are accessed at the northern end of the village, over a gravel road onto the Bealey riverbed. A footbridge gives access to the west bank, where track signs indicate the various trails.

The Devil's Punchbowl Falls (112m) are the premier attraction for all visitors to the village. The walk is short and sharp, and has recently been upgraded by constructing a wide staircase over the course of the old rocky trail to access the base of the falls. Steep flights of stairs, bridges, boardwalks, and a final viewing platform make the trek in as much an adventure as the final destination, with airy views of the Bealey Valley through the canopy. At the end of the walk a large platform perched on the edge of Devil's Punchbowl Creek grants a mesmerising vista of the mighty drop of the falls. A powerful jet of water spills from the lip of the creek, pulsing out between solid rock walls crowned with forest and smeared with ferns and mosses. As water cascades down the face, rivulets fan out to broaden the cascade from a single jet into a river surging into the pool at the base of the cliff. Gusts of wind carry spray far down the valley and up into the trees lining the ridge above. From this point you can stand and gaze directly up into the great ribbon of white water pouring from the rent in the face high above. Take care here, though, as rockfalls are not uncommon.

The Bridal Veil Falls Track offers an interesting walk through sub-alpine forest, with a short, rocky scramble up the stream to view the falls. All the stream crossings are bridged. This delightful track can then be followed up toward the pass, exiting farther up onto the highway.

3. Bealey Chasm and Valley
15 minutes to Chasm. **Easy/Moderate**
1–2 hours to upper valley.

The Chasm, a small, rocky gorge in the Bealey River, is reached after only a few minutes' walk through attractive beech forest. One track cuts through the forest to a small clearing above the gorge and bridge, while the other crosses the footbridge and ascends easily through bush and sub-alpine vegetation zones. Later it moves out onto the riverbed and ends beneath the sheer Bealey Face of Mt Rolleston. Care must be used here during winter and spring due to avalanche danger. Good views are obtained from the upper valley of the Arthur's Pass mountains.

Bealey Chasm in flood

This walk is accessed a few hundred metres up the highway from the northern entrance to the Bridal Veil Track, on the opposite side of the road.

4. Temple Basin Skifield

Carpark to skifield lodges: 1–2 hours. **Moderate/Hard**
Lodges to Col: 1–2 hours.

Near the summit of Arthur's Pass, a carpark, right on the bush edge, marks the beginning of the Temple Basin Track. This gives access to the skifield, which has a walk-in option only. A goods lift is available during winter for ski equipment. Skiing first came to Arthur's Pass in 1927, when Guy Butler, who owned the hostel, bought eight pairs of Norwegian hickory skis. Later Oscar Coberger arrived from Mt Cook and set up a ski and mountaineering depot in the village. He was an amazing individual who completed a grand traverse of Mt Cook when in his 70s. The first ski hut was opened at Temple Basin in 1933 and there have been many additions to the complex since then, with two lodges now available.

The walk is spectacular as you climb high above the valley and into the alpine meadows below the skifield buildings. Numerous waterfalls leap from the rock faces above, and extensive panoramas of the Arthur's Pass mountains are revealed. This includes one of the best viewpoints of Mt Rolleston, directly across the valley. Temple Basin is a highlight of a visit to the pass and is one of the easiest and safest places to reach the tops. A day shelter is available just below the skifield buildings, from where a further hour's walk will take you to the upper ski basin below Mt Temple. Here the Page Shelter is sited. It is open to the public and is reputed to be haunted.

For keen trampers Temple Col (1774m) is now within reach at the top of the tow-line, making for a rewarding, if strenuous, climb to the crest of the Main Divide and a lofty viewpoint of peaks, passes and valleys. (This route can be linked to Goat Pass, see notes for 'Mingha River and Hut'.)

Twin Stream and Mt Rolleston, Temple Basin

The basins of the skifield are a special place to observe alpine plants and perhaps kea.

5. Dobson Nature Walk and Lake Misery Track
Nature walk: 30 minutes. **Easy**
Lake Misery Track extension: 30 minutes. **Easy**

A few hundred metres north of the skifield carpark stands the summit of Arthur's Pass and the monument to Arthur Dudley Dobson. Across the road the Dobson Nature Walk begins, an easy trail through alpine plants, tussock and boglands on the pass summit. Beyond the pass to the west, mountains and valleys beckon, towering above the alpine grasslands that the road traverses. This walk links with the Otira Valley Track via the Lake Misery Track and also back down the western side of the highway to Temple Basin carpark and Arthur's Pass Village.

The extension track to Lake Misery is well worth the extra time spent exploring these beautiful alpine bog lands and tarns.

6. Otira Valley Track and Mt Rolleston
Road to footbridge: 1 hour. **Moderate**
Bridge to upper valley: 1 hour.
Road to Low Peak Mt Rolleston: 4–6 hours. **Hard+**

Just before the road dips in a steep gradient to Pegleg Flat, a small layby on the left (west) provides parking and access to the Otira Valley. This, I believe, is the premier short walk in the park, especially in late spring and early summer when Mt Cook lilies flower in profusion along the track. It will take up to 2 hours to reach the valley head, where the forbidding Otira Face of Mt Rolleston towers above. This is also the most frequented access route to climb the mountain, via the Otira Slide – a relatively straightforward route in good snow and weather conditions. However, this is an alpine ascent, requiring experience, fitness, alpine equipment (including a rope), and favourable weather.

The lower valley presents an array of colour and pattern as you wander among small cascades and rolling tussock knolls beneath ice-smoothed rock faces. A whole day can be spent absorbing the beauty and tranquillity of this special alpine garden. Warnocks Knob (1167m) can be ascended, to the north via steep scree, about an hour up the track to gain a view of the Otira Gorge and highway.

7 & 8. Avalanche Peak Tracks
Avalanche Peak Track to summit: 3–4 hours. **Moderate/Hard**
Descent via Scotts Track: 2–3 hours.

Avalanche Peak is the best-known and most frequented of the major day trips in Arthur's Pass National Park. Being sited in the very centre of the village on SH73, it lends itself to day-tripping.

There are two tracks on the peak; both grant good access through the bush to the tussock, from where poled routes lead onto the rocky summit at 1833m.

Mt Rolleston from Avalanche Peak

The steep and direct Avalanche Peak Track begins between the chapel and the visitor centre and ascends a rocky track beside Avalanche Creek, where there are several spectacular waterfalls in a deep gut to the north of the track. However, be careful approaching these ravines for a closer view, as there have been fatalities here.

Higher up, the track sidles out onto a narrow spur and climbs above Rough Creek, which is visible beyond large bluffs in the valley below. If there is snow on this spur an ice axe should be used. The spur levels off after about 300m, giving access to the top basin just beneath the summit. The route climbs the steep snow grass and rock face above, joining with Scotts Track. This track, which begins just north of Wardens Creek on SH73, opposite the Devil's Punchbowl Falls, climbs a more gentle ridge track. The two tracks can be linked for a satisfying round trip.

The final ridge to the summit of the mountain is loose and quite narrow in places and care is needed. The summit itself is broad and allows room to sit and study the wonderful sweep of mountain country it commands. Mt Rolleston and the Crow Glacier dominate the scene, while farther west the rock and snow summits of the upper Waimakariri River crowd the horizon. Below in the deep trench of the Bealey River sits Arthur's Pass village and the pass itself, the highway cutting through forest and tussock to disappear north into the Otira Valley. Southeastwards the gentler, drier Craigieburn Range blocks out the valley.

The descent down Scotts Track is relatively easy, considering the steepness of the ascent route, and allows time to wander and enjoy the mountain spectacle from the broad, easy-angled ridge-top. This eventually drops via a series of short zigzags and easy spurs into the bush, where a long sidle across the hillside and down to Wardens Creek saves energy, and your knees.

Once back at the road, the village centre is less than a kilometre away, south, down the highway.

9. Avalanche Peak to Crow River

Avalanche Peak to Crow Hut: 2–3 hours. **Hard**
Crow Hut to Waimakariri River: 3 hours. **Moderate**
Waimakariri to Klondyke Corner: 2 hours. **Easy**

This moderately difficult route is suitable for fit trampers with some experience of open, untracked tops. It continues west and then north of Avalanche Peak for approximately 1.5 km along the ridge-top to just north of Point 1658m, where a scree slope, which broadens toward the bottom, is descended directly to the upper Crow River. This scree slope, one of several along the ridge, is recognisable as the correct route as it is the only one that can be viewed clearly as a safe route all the way to the Crow River. The others have bluffs on them and are dangerous.

A cairn marks the top of the route. The trek to this point on the ridge has outstanding views of Mt Rolleston and the large Crow Glacier perched above immense bluffs on the southern aspect. There are also grand views of Arthur's Pass highway and attendant summits, as well as west into the hinterland of the park.

The scree slope has some large, rough boulders to scramble over at the bottom, but once the river is reached, easier going will be found down to Crow Hut (10 bunks) on a grassy terrace above the river. Good views are obtained of Mt Rolleston from the hut, but much of the glacier has receded from sight, onto the shelf beneath the peak.

Downstream a marked track holds to the river right bank for some distance, crossing to the left (east) as the valley broadens. Alternating flats and bush sections are encountered as you draw near to the Waimakariri River, and these continue for some kilometres along the north bank of the river. Eventually, the steepening riverbank forces you out into the main river, where meandering channels are crossed to link with the flats once more. In average flow, these channels present little difficulty.

Finally, the river moves away to the south and a bouldery riverbed is crossed to the access road at Klondyke Corner. Transport will need to be arranged to return to Arthur's Pass village.

Other Day Tramps from Arthur's Pass Village

There are several other full-day walks leading from the village to the high tops.

10. Mt Bealey (1836m)
Road to summit: 3–4 hours. **Hard**
Summit to Avalanche Peak: 2–3 hours. **Hard**
Low peak of Bealey to Rough Creek and road: 2–3 hours. **Moderate**

On the south side of Rough Creek, at the end of the road past the houses, a steep, rocky track heads up a spur through forest to the open tops. The ridgeline is then followed south and west over Point 1760m (low peak) to the summit. This ridge provides easy rock scrambling with magnificent views of the pass and alps.

It is possible to continue around the ridge, sidling past rocky outcrops as necessary, over Point 1778m, Lyell Peak, and onto Avalanche Peak, thereby completing a rewarding tops route with superb views into the Crow and Waimakariri rivers.

Alternatively, a direct descent can be made from the low peak of Mt Bealey down steep scree into Rough Creek, which is then followed back to the road.

11. Con's Track to Mt Cassidy (1850m)
Bealey River to Mt Cassidy: 3–4 hours. **Hard**
Mt Cassidy to Mt Blimit to Temple Basin skifield: 2–3 hours. **Hard**

At the beginning of the track to Devil's Punchbowl Falls, a sign indicates Cons Track to Mt Cassidy. This track climbs directly up the spur above Punchbowl Creek and once at the bush edge traverses north over open rocky terrain past a trig point, from where direct access leads up onto the main ridge and back to Mt Cassidy. This part of the route is quite demanding and steep. In snow or ice, an ice axe and crampons will be essential. The peak lies well back along the ridge and grants an interesting perspective of the upper part of Punchbowl Creek. It is possible to continue on along the ridge and scramble up Mt Blimit (1920m) and then descend north, through easy tarn basins and gullies, to Temple Basin skifield. This is a spectacular traverse.

Climbing up to Mt Blimit

12. Mt Aicken (1858m)

Bealey River to Mt Aicken: 3–4 hours. **Hard**

At the highest point of the Devil's Punchbowl Falls Track, where it descends and sidles into the canyon, a track junction indicates a climb to Mt Aicken. This ascends steadily through bush and sub-alpine vegetation, over small rocky knolls to the open tussock, and later rock, of the ridge-top. This is readily followed northeast around the ridge crest and over Points 1844m and 1863m to the true summit, which is a short rocky scramble 500m east of the main ridge. This overlooks the Mingha Valley. There are grand views of Mt Rolleston from the ridge.

13. Rome Ridge

Road to flat-topped ridge: 2–3 hours. **Hard**

The Coral Track, which begins north of McGrath Creek on an uphill section of SH73, is an exceptionally steep climbers' track, in some places resembling a ladder through the forest, to access Rome Ridge and Mt Rolleston. Both of these objectives are relatively serious undertakings and most trampers on this track would be well advised to return via the same route. The track is easy enough to follow, and once above the bushline a steep, stepped spur climbs to the table-topped ridgeline, where spectacular close-up views of Mt Rolleston are obtained. Above here the ridge narrows and rises sharply as it climbs toward the peak.

Only competent climbing parties should continue above the 1500m contour.

HIGH AND MIGHTY – MT CASSIDY

Dense cloud fills the Bealey Valley in Arthur's Pass National Park, reducing visibility to some 200m or less, as we climb through the sub-alpine forest of Cons Track below the summit of Mt Cassidy. Fr Kevin Mears is my companion on this outing. We last did a climb of Mt Rolleston when he was in his late 60s; now, at 75, I am amazed at his strength and vitality, he may be slower than I am, but is no less determined to reach the summit, 1100m above and over 2km away along the broken ridge crest.

View of Arthur's Pass village under mist, from Mt Cassidy

We exit the bush as the cloud begins to dissipate and the opposite valley walls materialise into the welcome and familiar cones of Mt Rolleston and Avalanche Peak. Just a whisper of wind here, enough to stir the murk and reveal the view, dramatic as it is, with the highway snaking through the forest below, and the near-vertical slopes of Cassidy granting an aerial perspective and a reminder to take care as we traverse out to the north, searching for the rocky gut that accesses the ridge crest. Broken talus slopes rear heavenward as we ascend, slowly picking our way through the terrain until the angle eases and we haul out onto the large plateau above the gullies.

Roaming onward, we clamber over rocky tors with high and mighty views into the head of Devil's Punchbowl Creek and into distant Westland. The summit is near now, barely 100m of ascent to the cairned peak, where we can gaze into Paddy's Basin and just beyond to the far side of Temple Basin, wherein the skifield lies.

Spying a direct descent into the lower skifield basin, we scoot on down over rock and easy scree, tussock and stream, to gain the first footbridge over Twin Creek, and beyond the wide skifield access trail. Save for a short descent of the highway to the village, we're homeward bound.

Other Tramps Near Arthur's Pass

14. Mingha River and Hut

Road to Mingha Bivvy: 3 hours. **Moderate**
Bivvy to Goat Pass Hut: 1–2 hours. **Moderate**

This valley is the route of the Coast to Coast mountain run held in February each year. A consequence of this is the media attention it receives, and due to this it is perhaps viewed by some trampers as of less interest than other valleys. Yet the upper section is very rugged and a beautiful location in which to wander and savour the dramatic scenery of the alps.

The first section of the route lies in the riverbed for nearly 3km above its junction with the Edwards, after which a marked track begins on the river right, at the top of a small terrace just past where a major side-stream enters the valley from the northwest. The track then climbs and sidles upvalley, to avoid a gorge, passes over the stunted vegetation on Dudley Knob, and gradually descends to the upper valley flats where Mingha Bivvy (2 bunks) is located on a grassy terrace. This is a pleasant place for lunch or even an overnight stay if you don't mind its rustic nature. Blue duck, New Zealand's native torrent duck, are regularly seen in the river near here.

Above the bivvy the track follows the riverbed for 1km, with numerous easy fords necessary until a small gorge is encountered as the valley begins to swing left (west). A marked and poled track, and later boardwalk, climbs out of the river (river left) and sidles around onto Goat Pass (1070m). If the day is fine, this section of the track is the highlight of the trip. Goat Pass, which

MINGHA AND EDWARDS VALLEYS

These two large catchments issue from the mountains just east of Arthur's Pass and are readily accessible from SH73, where open river-bed travel leads to the junction of the two rivers, 1km northeast of the road. Both rivers are key entry points for several extended tramping trips in the park, to the west and east.

Entry to the valleys entails crossing the Bealey River just above its junction with the Mingha. This is normally an easy ford, but the river rises very rapidly after heavy rain.

Goat Pass Hut

was surveyed by the Dobson brothers (Arthur Dobson gave his name to Arthur's Pass) as a possible route for a dray track to the west, lies on the crest of the Main Divide beneath the towering precipices of Mts Oates, Temple, and Franklin to the west.

The pass is vegetated with luxuriant alpine tussock, Spaniard grass, and in summer, alpine daisies, buttercups and the delicate Mt Cook lily. It is a stunningly beautiful location on a clear day in any season. Goat Pass Hut (20 bunks) is sited in the sub-alpine scrub just north of the pass, as the boardwalk begins to descend to the Deception River.

Routes out from here include:

(i) Deception River to the west and SH73 north of Otira
Goat Pass Hut to SH73 via Deception River: 6–8 hours. **Moderate/Hard**

A rugged, mostly untracked valley with rough going and some swift fords to negotiate.

Lake Mavis, Mingha Valley

(ii) **Temple Col (1774m)**
Goat Pass to Temple Col: 5–6 hours. **Hard+**

A high, moderately difficult, unmarked alpine crossing, to the west, into Temple Basin skifield summit. Experienced parties only.

15. Lake Mavis and Taruahuna Pass
Goat Pass to Lake Mavis: 1–2 hours. **Moderate**
Lake Mavis to Taruahuna Pass: 3–4 hours. **Hard**

Many of the visitors who trek through Goat Pass take a side-trip up to beautiful and spectacularly set Lake Mavis, just 500m above the hut. The route, though steep at the bottom where it climbs through sub-alpine vegetation, soon eases back as it ascends the broad, easy ridge crest to the lake basin. It is possible to camp here, but be careful with toilet waste and food scraps; such a beautiful location needs to be preserved.

From the lake there are two possible routes out:

(i) Williams Saddle
Lake Mavis to Williams Saddle: 3–4 hours; saddle to Edwards Hut: 1 hour.
Hard+

(ii) A tops route from Lake Mavis (1600m)
5–6 hours. **Hard**

Head south through basins on the southwest side of Mt Oates to the ridgeline near Point 1869m. From here descend the broadening ridge to Williams Saddle (1327m), and drop down through scrub to Edwards Hut. This is a long, difficult route, over untracked tops, with some rock scrambling required. Good fitness and navigational skills are needed. Ice axe and crampons are required in winter.

Lake Mavis to Taruahuna Pass is another high route, climbing above the lake along the Main Divide to 1850m, north of Point 1978m, and then descending through a high basin to a small lake (snow covered in winter and spring) and following a feeder stream down towards Taruahuna Pass. Note that this route is bluffed lower down and requires a high sidle at 1500m out to the north (look for cairns here) and a descent through a line of bluffs back to the slopes above the pass. Though not a difficult route, it could be hard to find in poor weather.

16. Edwards Valley
Bealey River to Edwards River East Branch: 2 hours. **Moderate**
East Branch to Edwards Hut: 2–3 hours. **Moderate**
Hut to Taruahuna Pass: 2 hours. **Moderate**

This companion valley of the Mingha has a similar route, beginning at the forks with the latter, and traversing through easy bush (river left) above a small gorge to a stony flat, which is followed for 2km until its junction with the Edwards River East Branch. Here a steep track climbs the spur between the streams (just upstream of the forks in the East Branch), high above the main valley so as to avoid a spectacular gorge and waterfalls, some of which can be glimpsed from the sidle track as it contours over the mountainside, still in bush, to reach the upper lip of the valley.

Wire rope aids have been placed on this track to assist with some of the steeper sections. The track emerges from the beech forest into an attractive park-like upper valley, where wide tussock flats and terraces stretch away to the northeast and distant Taruahuna Pass (1252m).

Edwards Hut (14 bunks) stands just ahead, on a flat beside the sparkling Edwards River, which meanders through waving tussocks and, in summer, a profusion of alpine flowers. It is a captivating setting and well worth a stopover for a night or two, so as to explore the upper valley.

Taruahuna Pass, at the valley head, is an incredible spectacle, and for those with the time, highly recommended. The easy route traverses a well-trodden path through the tussock valley head below the massive bluff faces of Mt Oates (2041m) for 5–6km, ascending gradually to the pass. Taruahuna Pass is a staggering legacy of the forces of nature unleashed in the 1929 Arthur's Pass earthquake, which sent a torrent of rock debris (estimated at 60 million cubic metres) from the northwest face of Falling Mountain (1901m), coursing down onto the pass and over 3km into the Otehake Valley. The force virtually 'split' the mountain in two and the resultant devastation is astonishing.

Alternative routes out from Edwards Hut include:

(i) Taruahuna Pass to Tarn Col to Walker Pass to Hawdon Hut

Taruahuna Pass to Tarn Col: 1 hour. **Hard**

Tarn Col to Walker Pass: 3 hours. **Hard**

Walker Pass to Hawdon Hut: 2–3 hours. **Moderate**

From the pass a moderately challenging route continues east, climbing steeply onto Tarn Col (1368m), opposite Taruahuna Pass, and descending through tussock and streambed to the Otehake River East Branch. Turn south here and climb up from the river (river right) over the low, scrub-covered Walker Pass (1095m) on a sparsely marked trail to the pass summit and attractive tarns. Descend through scrub and streambed to the lip of the gorge overlooking Hawdon Valley. Follow a track, marked and poled, up onto the shoulder (river left) of Twin Stream, which drains the pass, to the Hawdon Valley and hut.

(ii) **Williams Saddle to Mingha River**
Edwards Hut to Williams Pass: 1–2 hours. **Hard**
Williams Pass to Mingha River: 2 hours.

This untracked route begins across the Edwards River, south of Edwards Hut, and climbs a steep streambed and scrubby gully draining the low pass. Tarns here make this an attractive setting, with good views over the Mingha River.

It is necessary to travel south, along the bush edge, for 1km towards Mt Williams before descending the bush face to the Mingha. This avoids bluffs in the bush below the pass.

17. Dome Peak
Railway bridge to bushline: 2–3 hours; bushline to summit: 2–3 hours. **Hard**
Summit to Edwards East Branch forks: 2–3 hours. **Hard**

Dome Peak (1938m) is a prominent mountain, visible across the Waimaka-riri River from SH73 near Mt White bridge as you approach the national park from the south. It shadows the route of the highway all the way to the Waimakariri River bridge, to the north, as a mighty rampart of bush faces, hanging valleys and steep screes and rock buttresses. In winter it is an impos-ing spectacle.

A relatively easy, unmarked route begins from the Bealey River railway bridge, ascending the long west ridge to the summit. This is accessed south of the bridge, up beside a small bluff and into the beech forest, which covers the flanks of the ridge. It is generally easy going as it leads to the bush edge, although some small areas of windthrow and regrowth will need to be skirted to find open bush travel.

Above the bush edge, sweeping panoramas of the park and environs are gained, and these increase in magnitude and splendour as you ascend the undulating ridge eastwards over Points 1484m, 1759m and 1920m.

Easy scree slopes lie to the north of the ridge, contrasted against plum-meting bluffs and gullies on the southern aspects. The ridge is delightfully easy and leads directly to the summit, where Dome Peak's significance as a landmark, around which the southern catchments of the park revolve, is immediately apparent. Waimakariri, Mingha, Edwards, Bealey, Hawdon and Sudden valleys curl around various aspects of Dome Peak, and numerous routes and passes can be identified. It is a marvellous viewpoint.

Descent is possible north of the peak, first scrambling from the summit down onto the ridgeline, heading northeast, and then dropping from here down scree and tussock to the Edwards River East Branch. Some careful route-finding will locate good access off the upper bluffy faces of the many scree gullies, through bush, to the valley floor. Follow this out to the Edwards junction. (See notes for 'Edwards Valley' for the route out.)

18. Upper Waimakariri Valley and Huts

Highway bridge to Anti-Crow Hut: 2–3 hours. **Moderate**
Anti-Crow Hut to Carrington Hut: 2–3 hours. **Moderate**

The Waimakariri River is the major watershed in Arthur's Pass National Park, and tramping into the mountain vastness that surrounds it provides a rewarding and spectacular introduction to the Southern Alps. There are two reasonably accessible huts on the valley floor, Anti-Crow and Carrington, and two others, Barker and Waimakariri Falls, located high in the valley

Waimakariri Valley from Klondyke Corner

headwaters. These latter two huts are only accessible for experienced parties over challenging routes in the upper valley.

Anti-Crow Hut (6 bunks) has good, year-round access along the south bank of the river, beginning at a hidden picnic area on the south side of the highway bridge over the Waimakariri River. Here a well-marked track climbs and sidles above the riverbed, west, along the hillside, where expansive views of the river are gained.

This track drops onto grassy flats where delightfully easy travel leads on toward the mountains. A stony ford of Jordan Stream interrupts this meander, however it resumes on the far bank and continues, descending gradually, toward the bush edge ahead. Once this is reached, a rough, steep track climbs over a low shoulder and descends to the hut.

A better option, if the rivers are low, is to continue on along the base of the small hill, over the open riverbed, fording streams as necessary, until the hut is sighted, on the left in the bush. There are excellent views up the Crow River opposite, to Mt Rolleston and the Crow Glacier.

Beyond the hut the track cuts through a section of forest to the Anti-Crow River. This river is usually relatively easy to cross if low (although it is often swift), however if it is high it can be dangerous and several lives have been lost here through misjudging the force of the water.

Once you are over, a low spur is crossed to the main Waimakariri River. Continuing on to Carrington Hut from here is not a route for the inexperienced. In autumn and winter the river will often be very low and present a straightforward route to the hut, with at least two crossings of the main stream necessary. This will vary from season to season. A rough, overgrown flood track does still exist on the river right bank around to Greenlaw Creek (Greenlaw Hut no longer exists) and beyond. This can be used if the river is high, but it is very slow going in places.

The best route is up the riverbed, but be warned: the Waimakariri can be dangerous and only experienced trampers should continue.

Carrington Hut (36 bunks) is located in scattered bush at the junction of the White and Waimakariri rivers, and commands a stunning view of the sheer southern face and bluffs of Carrington Peak in the upper valley. It has a wonderful setting and is a fine place to spend a day or so, relaxing or exploring.

Partially marked routes continue to the bushline of the upper valleys to

Waimakariri Falls Hut and Waimakariri Col, Barker Hut and White Col, and Taipoiti River and Harman Pass. These are all difficult transalpine crossings for experienced parties only.

Access is from SH73 at the Waimakariri River highway bridge, south side, to the carpark and track. Access is also via Klondyke Corner access road on the north side. This is a much shorter route but entails crossing the main river to the south bank.

AS THE CROW FLIES

Crow River enters the Waimakariri River just five bouldery kilometres from the Klondyke Corner road-end in Arthur's Pass National Park. It then heads due north for a further 7km to drain the ragged buttresses of Mt Rolleston and the Crow Glacier, one of the park's largest and most striking ice flows, resting on the southern flanks of Mt Rolleston and imbuing the upper valley with a special beauty. It is a place of typical mountain vastness, yet made accessible by a rough track to a comfortable new hut. Crow Hut, a 2002 replacement for an earlier structure that had resided here since 1958, is nestled into the bush edge at 1020m, on a small tussock-strewn clearing beneath the bluffs of Mt Guinevere. It is a magnificent setting. The first hut was built by the New Zealand Alpine Club and this latest version is the first hut to be built in the park for 30 years.

Many parties visit as part of the Avalanche Peak traverse from Arthur's Pass village, and many more as competitors in the annual mountain run over the same route, but for me it was purely to visit old haunts and check-out the 'new' hut as a day trip. Low river levels allowed me to pursue a ruler-straight dash over the interminable rock flats of the riverbed from Klondyke. Having spent many days tramping with a heavy pack on Canterbury's finest alluvial fans, I was determined not to let this particular sortie wear me down. So I set the watch, the pace, and the route, and went for it. The river was a cruise to cross, but oh so cold! However, a few metres up the far bank and the numbing sensation was soon gone. Onwards – southwest cloud filling the sky and gales raking the summits. The wind was forecast to reach 120kph, but there was barely a breeze here in the valley and I hoped to reach the hut at least before the wind was up. Crow River soon appeared and the grassy flats at the rivermouth were welcome. Then another five 'k' to the hut, and with the sun out. The Crow was named by an early pass explorer, probably J. Browning, in reference to the South Island kōkako or 'native crow', long-since died out here and now thought to be extinct.

It's an easy valley to walk, as long as you don't mind a few cold fords, rough riverbed and a lumpy track, but believe me, compared to some valley routes in the mountains this one is 'easy'. So again the pace was on for the hut-check. It is a delight to travel light and fast through the hills, observing the passage of the landscape while you reel in the goal. It wasn't long in arriving.

Crow Hut is trim and spartan, clean and very welcoming in the high valley. A couple of overnighters were just leaving as I arrived so I had it all to myself, not an uncommon occurrence here. Snow lay about the hut, following the recent spell of unseasonal weather, an additional touch of interest to the scene. It is necessary to go just beyond the hut to view the Crow Glacier and face of Mt Rolleston, and here the presence of the wind could no longer be ignored. It was scouring the summits, lifting fresh snow from the glacier high into the air, but aside from the odd gust through the valley the gale was maintaining altitude so I would avoid another pasting. I took

Crow Hut, Crow Valley

lunch in the sun on the hut step and then packed for the drift back down the track to the Waimak', taking it a little easier now I had the measure of the distance.

At the confluence with the Waimakariri I spied another old mate, Anti-Crow Hut, two 'k' away on the far bank. I'd heard it had been spruced up so I decided to pop over for another hut-check – as the crow flies.

19. Bealey Spur and Hut

Bealey settlement to hut: 1.5–2 hours; viewpoint at 900m: 1 hour. **Moderate**

Climbing up through the deep, shadowed forest along the flanks of Bealey Spur in the southeastern corner of Arthur's Pass National Park is an easy track that accesses the high, open tussock fields of the upper spur. It is a popular

Waimakariri River headwaters from Bealey Spur

Bealey Spur Hut

walk for day visitors, with the added attraction of a bush-edge musterers' hut and grand panoramas of the park. For a family walk in the mountains, it is outstanding.

The track begins at the upper limit of the Bealey settlement and enters the cool forest immediately off the road. It is a steepish and, in places, rough trail, leading in through the delightful beech forest, which is remarkable for the good numbers of forest birds to be seen and heard among the trees. The track continues though the forest, undulating along the ridge-top, with intermittent windows out on the Waimakariri River, to the right, and Bruce Stream and gorge on the left.

The bush cover is interrupted at several points along the ridge by extensive open tussock areas, and these are one of the highlights of the walk, for here magnificent panoramas stretch away to the alps and river valleys.

At around 900m the ridge narrows and bends slightly to the south, before continuing on westwards toward the Bealey Spur Hut. Here, by virtue of the unobstructed foreground, is the best viewpoint on the entire ridgeline.

Bealey Spur Hut stands on the edge of a clearing in mountain beech forest and is a rewarding destination for day-trippers, or as an overnight tramp. There are extensive views of the Arthur's Pass region from the open ridgeline above the hut.

Access is off SH73, up a narrow, steep road on the western side of the Bruce Stream highway bridge, approximately 13km south of Arthur's Pass township.

There are two options for continuing up along the untracked ridge above the hut:

(i) Hut Spur to Jordan Saddle and Stream
2 days. **Moderate/Hard**

This is a 2-day tramp involving a traverse of the ridge to Point 1875m and descent to Jordan Saddle (1469m), and then down into Jordan Stream, which is followed out to the Waimakariri River flats and back to the highway. This route requires good tramping and navigational skills, on open tops, as well as clear weather to find your way along the ridge. Jordan Stream provides good untracked travel, with multiple river crossings, and some limited camping about halfway down to the Waimakariri River.

(ii) From Point 1875m, above Jordan Saddle
Bealey Spur Hut to Point 1907m: 3–4 hours. **Hard+**
Point 1907m to Bruce and Power streams forks: 3–4 hours.
Forks to highway: 1–2 hours.

Competent parties in fine weather can continue on around the ridge, to the south, scrambling over Point 1907m (which has unequalled views of the upper Avoca catchment and peaks) and descending Blind Spur over Points 1750m and 1737m to the bushline. Keep to the ridge-top in the forest, which is quite open, dropping down to the forks of Power Stream and Bruce Stream. A slip on the end of this spur can be bypassed in the bush on the south side (right side going down) and into Bruce Stream, which is followed through the gorge to the highway bridge.

20. Hawdon Valley

Hawdon Shelter (carpark) to Hawdon Hut: 2–3 hours. **Easy**
Hawdon Hut to Walker Pass: 2–3 hours. **Moderate**

There is no doubt that often the most easily accessible huts and valleys are overlooked by those seeking wilderness and solitude, yet they too can offer both an introduction to the great outdoors for familes and younger trampers as well as opportunities to access more remote and difficult routes. The new Hawdon Hut (20 bunks) in Arthur's Pass National Park provides such an experience, and this valley is, arguably, the most scenic in the eastern part of the park.

An easy route wanders the flats into the valley head, at first passing through scattered matagouri and boulders, after a ford of the river, which can be difficult after heavy rain. There are many delightful forest glades farther upvalley, where filtered sunlight probes the understorey littered with leaves and sometimes snow in winter. Later the valley narrows and becomes cluttered with boulder-strewn terraces. Nearing the hut the valley opens out once more as the route crosses Discovery Stream (which accesses high unmarked

Pat and Bernadette Barrett at Hawdon Hut

routes onto the Polar Range, see notes for 'Sudden Valley') and then heads onto a bush terrace containing the large, well-appointed hut. The hut has a grand setting, looking directly into the Upper Hawdon and onto Trudge Col, a high and difficult route to Poulter Valley.

There is much to occupy your time here, especially if you have an extra day. An excursion onto the Main Divide via Walker Pass is an excellent way to experience the sub-alpine zone and spectacular scenery. This route is tracked and poled from the hut, and heads up onto the high shoulder of Twin Fall Stream catchment and then back to the pass and its beautiful summit tarns at 1095m.

It is possible to link Hawdon Valley with Taruahuna Pass (see notes for 'Edwards Valley').

21. East Hawdon
2–3 hours from junction with Hawdon. **Moderate**

An untracked, though easy, route exists into the East Hawdon to the small bivvy (2 bunks) at the valley head.

East Hawdon Bivvy

The valley is attractive and its head is easily reached, allowing for access to Mt Valiant and other peaks on the Savannah Range.

This valley is one of the last refuges for orange-fronted parakeet (kākāriki) and DOC is engaged in intensive predator trapping and monitoring of these birds throughout the catchment.

22. Woolshed Hill

Shelter to Woolshed Hill: 2–3 hours. **Moderate**

A modest summit accessed from the Hawdon Shelter carpark, Woolshed Hill (1429m) has a marked track through the beech forest on its southern flanks to bush-edge clearings and a flat tussock top, providing good views over the Waimakariri/Hawdon confluence and into the upper reaches of Sudden Valley. It is possible to traverse the ridge beyond Woolshed Hill, the Savannah Range, into the upper reaches of East Hawdon Stream. This is a long route requiring some rock scrambling to avoid rocky knobs on the ridge, and good navigational skills to reach the upper valley.

23. Sudden Valley

Hawdon Shelter to Sudden Valley Bivvy: 3–4 hours. **Moderate**
Bivvy to valley head: 1 hour; valley head to ridge crest: 1–2 hours. **Hard**
Ridge-top to Point 1844m: 1–2 hours; Point 1844m to Hawdon Hut: 2–3 hours. **Hard+**
With snow on the tops, an ice axe, crampons and alpine experience will be required for safe passage.

The hanging valley of Sudden Valley, a remnant of glacial times, lies in the southeastern corner of Arthur's Pass National Park. It is a valley of large proportions, which is surprising considering the modest stream that drains to the Hawdon River across the stony flats at the mouth of the valley. Yet beyond the barrier gorge, in the lower reaches of the catchment, lies a large and spectacular alpine valley head.

The tramp begins with a brief section of forest that gives way to an open, bouldery riverbed and a rough bulldozer track that leads toward the Hawdon River, which must be forded to gain the left bank (river right). Approximately 1km upstream from the shelter, Sudden Valley emerges to the west beneath steep bushclad hillsides and can be entered immediately to gain easy access upriver, over terraces and boulder banks. After 2km and approximately 30 minutes' travel, the valley is closed off by towering bluffs. Here the first of many short sections of track begin, again on the left (river right), taking you up and through the spectacular gorge, which can be glimpsed through the trees as the river pulses down among huge boulders.

It is a tiring route, which winds in and around the gorge, and care must be taken on the numerous stream crossings. You will be surprised how the nature of the easy stream you crossed on the flats has changed into a boisterous, swift mountain torrent. This, in fact, is one of the dangers of a visit to this hidden valley; you could easily become trapped by bad weather, as it takes only a little rain in the valley head for the Sudden Valley gorge to become impassable. Therefore, plan your visit accordingly.

After 2 hours from the road shelter, 'Devil's Chute' is reached. The way ahead in the stream is closed off by Barrier Falls, however the chute provides a route to the valley head. This begins on the right (river left) and can be easily missed, though there is a track marker and cairn. From here scramble up a steep, slippery gut to reach the track, which sidles out high above the gorge to again reach open streambed and pleasant beech forest, which will lead you to the first flats of upper Sudden Valley.

The view ahead is dramatic and unexpected after emerging from the damp confines of the gorge. An open, park-like valley stretches ahead, drenched in sunlight, with large stands of beech forest clothing the steep hillsides, small tussock flats dotting the riverbank, and on one of these resides Sudden Valley Bivvy, a small 2-person bivvy.

If you have time there is much to recommend travelling farther into the valley head, which can be reached in another hour where it steepens into bluffs and scree slopes. Here the massive block mountains of Scott (2009m) and Wilson (2035m) dominate, together with numerous lower summits, rock faces, gullies and ridges.

If your visit is in early summer, much of the upper valley will still be under snow, with avalanche chutes descending onto the valley floor. It is a breathtaking alpine scene, heightened by the alpine flowers, which include Mt Cook lily, that adorn the river terraces.

Returning via the same track is considerably easier and quicker than the inward journey.

VALLEY SURPRISE – SUDDEN VALLEY BIV

Deep in the hills of Arthur's Pass National Park is a secluded post-glacial valley, Sudden Valley. A hanging valley, so named because it 'hangs' at a higher elevation above the course of its lower reaches and that of the Hawdon River into which it flows.

The valley head is beautiful and its relative isolation lends it a special character not found in many of the more-open neighbouring watersheds. It also boasts a rough sort of a route and a new 2-bunk bivvy near the bush edge. Winter is not the best time to visit the valley, as snow often lies thickly throughout this catchment, including the valley floor, as it sees little sun, and the full beauty of the area is hidden beneath a white carpet. Undeterred and with time to spend on a day outing, I ventured into the mouth of the valley, planning to visit the new bivvy and familiarise myself again with the upper valley. I struck snow almost immediately, boot-deep on the flats, but, thankfully, almost non-existent along the forest track that climbs the valley sides and fords the cold flow of the river at various junctures en route to the falls.

Sudden Valley Biv

Once in the gorge, the light is reduced, the sound of water is amplified, and the sky becomes a narrow slot above. Half-way through, 'The Chute' enters the canyon, a steep, stony gully that grants access to the waterfall bypass track 150m above the gorge to the northeast. This route is the key to the upper valley, and once above the gorge the trail becomes steadily easier.

The bivvy lies 2.5km upvalley from here and it is cold. Snow lies deep around the small hut and I take lunch quickly, shivering inside on one of the benches. Outside the sun is trying to make an appearance, weakly penetrating the high overcast with faint shadows on the forest floor. I've done my dash for the day, there's little to linger for here, but the walk and new discoveries have been energising enough for a quick romp home.

24. High Crossings from Sudden Valley
Allow a full day. **Hard**

A high alpine crossing can be made from the head of the valley via steep scree and rock to the Edwards River and track, to the west, via a high col at 1840m just northeast of Mt Scott, and a direct descent to a feeder creek of the Edwards draining Amber Col.

Alternatively, for those with good navigational skills on the open tops, a route to the north and east can be tackled that leads along the Polar Range to the head of Discovery Stream, which drains to the Hawdon River upstream of Hawdon Hut. This route begins with a long, wrenching ascent of the steep, loose scree immediately north of Mt Scott. The ridge-top is gained at 1800m and then followed over Points 1876m and 1937m in a northeasterly direction to the southern head of Discovery Stream. Care must be used here to find a safe route off the ridge; this exists just southwest of Point 1844m, where rock and scree lead to easier slopes, which are descended to the valley floor. At the bush edge, a 30m waterfall is bypassed on the river right, after which delightful stream travel leads to open going and the Hawdon River below the hut. (See notes for 'Hawdon Valley' for the route out from here.)

This route was completed on a long autumn day trip, though it could be made easier by a high camp en route. However you choose to visit Sudden Valley, it is an isolated and enchanting region of the national park.

25. The Pyramid

The Pyramid from Hawdon Shelter: 2–3.5 hours. **Hard**
Descent via chute: 1.5–2 hours.

Standing above the confluence of the Hawdon and Sudden Valley rivers, the Pyramid (1608m) is immediately identifiable, when approaching the park from the south, by its angular-shaped ridges falling from a small, open top in steep, bush-covered spurs.

The southeast spur begins from the flats slightly north and west of the river confluence and climbs in virtually one long, steep ascent to the bush edge. Here the angle eases for a short distance before climbing even more directly around a small bluff and onto the summit ridge, where an easy scramble leads northwest to the main summit.

The Pyramid, despite its modest height, commands an unobstructed view of the Waimakariri basin and attendant peaks, as well as of the Hawdon and Sudden Valley watersheds and a spectacular 'aerial' view of the Hawdon and Waimakariri river flats.

The Pyramid route is gained at the very foot of the southeast ridge in the mouth of Sudden Valley Stream. This is then followed, via an old, rough

Hawdon Valley and Main Divide

track, to the bush edge and summit ridge. The descent is via the same route or via the steep, narrow scree shute, which drops into the stream draining the south face of the low peak. This scree is very obvious from the Hawdon Valley. A small waterfall part way down is easily negotiated.

For access to the Hawdon Valley tracks, turn off SH73 at the Mt White Bridge junction (signposted) and descend to the bridge. Turn left 500m east of Mt White Bridge and follow the access road, north, over flats to Hawdon Shelter and carpark.

Follow the bush track, north, along the river terrace to the open river and ford it well upstream of the wire fence. Care is needed here. The river right gives the best travel on terraces for most of the way. The track is not always well defined, however the riverbed provides easy access. The valley is prone to flooding during and after nor'west conditions and some parties have become stranded at the hut during these times. It's accessibility belies the fact that this is an isolated mountain region and appropriate care should be taken.

26. Casey–Binser and Lake Minchin

Andrews Shelter to Casey Saddle: 3–4 hours; saddle to Casey Hut: 2–3 hours. **Moderate**

Casey Hut to Lake Minchin: 2–3 hours one way. **Easy**

Casey Hut to Pete Stream: 3–4 hours; Pete Stream to Binser Saddle: 1–2 hours
Saddle to road: 1–2 hours. **Moderate**

A popular and easy tramp in the eastern section of the park, the Casey–Binser Track provides a good round trip over two moderate passes without the need to cross any major rivers. As such it is a viable option when high river levels or strong nor'west conditions preclude trips into the valley headwaters, which require fording of the main rivers.

Beginning at Andrews Shelter on the Mt White Road, the well-marked track climbs, at an easy gradient, through the bush above Andrews Stream and along a terrace until Hallelujah Flat is reached. This is an attractive area of spacious tussock flats, backed by the Savannah Range peaks. Continuing on, the track passes over Casey Saddle (777m), an almost imperceptible climb, and descends much more steeply down Casey Stream to the Casey Hut (16 bunks), set on a large grassy flat well back from the river. Here the wide sweep of the Poulter Valley dominates the view to the north and east, where high bare tops extend far back toward distant craggy summits near the Main Divide.

This is a lovely, peaceful location for the night and if you have time, and the Poulter River is not high, a day trip upriver to beautiful, secluded Lake Minchin and its nearby hut is an excellent side-trip.

The route crosses Casey Stream opposite the hut and follows markers through bush to the valley flats, where an indistinct vehicle track leads through easy terrain to Trust/Poulter Hut (6 bunks) set on the bush fringe. From the hut continue to the wide sweeping bend in the Poulter River where an unmarked route crosses the stony bed to the north bank (easily accomplished except in high flow) and the new Poulter Hut (10 bunks) set on the bush fringe and with grand views of the upper valley. Minchin Stream enters the Poulter Valley just upstream of the hut, but the track to the lake heads into the bush just near the hut.

Once on the well-marked track, tramp up through a beautiful stand of beech forest, on a very easy gradient, until the lake is reached over a low mound in the bush. Lake Minchin's setting is dramatic: bush fringed with steep, craggy mountains rearing above the lake-shore, where waterfalls descend gullies on the faces. An open valley-head directs Minchin Stream into the north side of the lake, and this can be reached by following the track along the eastern shoreline.

There is no hut at the lake but reasonable campsites can be found along the north shore and farther up Minchin Stream. This is a wild, remote location and worth spending time to savour and explore. Beyond the lakehead a track and route continue to Minchin Pass and the Taramakau River (experienced parties only).

27. Upper Poulter and Poulter Bivvy
Poulter Hut to Worsley Bivvy: 40 minutes. **Easy**
Worsley Bivvy to Poulter Bivvy: 1–2 hours. **Moderate**
Poulter Bivvy to Townsend Hut: 4–5 hours. **Hard**

The extreme head of the Poulter is also worth visiting, passing two small huts en route – Worsley Bivvy (4 bunks), about 40 minutes upvalley from Minchin Hut, and Poulter Bivvy (2 bunks), a further 1–2 hours on above the bush edge in the upper valley. The head of the Poulter forms a narrow canyon and is dramatic country, however to reach both huts, and especially

Poulter Bivvy, requires fording the river several times, with some quite tight sections below Worsley Pass (this pass has a difficult and untracked route to the Otehake), which would be impassable in high flows. This is worth remembering if you plan to stay at the upper bivvy in threatening weather.

From Poulter Bivvy a high, steep route leads out of the valley head, over a col just west of Mt Koeti, to alpine basins above the Taramakau River, from where an easy descent, in fine weather, can be made to Townsend Hut.

28. Lower Poulter
7 hours. **Moderate**

Downstream from Casey Hut, old farm tracks are followed alongside the Poulter River, heading south. These head up away from the river through a bush corridor to a large bush tarn. Beyond this the farm tracks continue beside the river on grassy flats to Mt Brown Creek, the site of the old Minchin Homestead, which was abandoned in 1870.

At Pete Stream, 5–6km below Mt Brown Creek, poles on the terrace on the river right of the stream indicate the start of the track up and over Binser Saddle (1085m).

This climbs for 600m to the bushy saddle, where a small clearing just west of the saddle grants limited views of the surrounding mountains. The track then descends steeply to Lower Farm Creek and Mt White Road, from where you can walk back to your car at Andrews Shelter.

See notes for 'Hawdon Valley' for access.

29. Mt Binser
Binser Saddle from road: 1 hour. **Hard**
Saddle to Mt Binser via ridgeline: 3–4 hours.
Descent via southwest spur: 3 hours.
This peak receives large amounts of winter snow, and travel times to and along the ridge will vary considerably. In summer conditions it should not present a problem in fine weather.

Bold ridges fall sheer to the open plains and twisted fingers of the Waimaka-riri riverbed, flashing silver in the mid-morning sunlight as the river surges eastwards. Beyond the flats, steep mountain flanks rise in ranks either side of the valley, drawing your gaze beyond the yellow and grey of the floodplain to the high peaks closing off the valley head in the west and north. Here the glaciated summits of Mts Harper (2222m), Davie (2280m), Murchison (2400m) and Franklin (2145m) preside in silent splendour above the snow-filled valleys. The scene is magnificent and one of the most all-encompassing in Arthur's Pass National Park, viewed from the easily accessed summits of Mt Binser (1860m), on the southern border of the park.

The peak has three summits, ranging from 1753m to 1860m and connected by an undulating 2km ridge that runs above the confluence of the Waimakariri and Poulter rivers. Under its winter mantle the spectacle is enhanced by an alpine dimension that exaggerates the steepness of the mountains flanks, with smooth faces of wind-packed snow, a corniced ridge crest, and a striking contrast between valley floor and the peak. The overall sense imparted to those who venture here is one of immense space and depth, viewing the landscape under your gaze as you traverse the ridgeline.

The route begins over the moderately steep, marked track to Binser Saddle (1100m), from the Mt White Road, beside the Waimakariri River. From the saddle the route (unmarked) strikes out through bush and onto the open northern flanks of the mountain. Steep snow/scree slopes, depending on season, lead directly up to the ridge and the low summit. A deep saddle must be negotiated between the low and middle peaks (1831m), with a final short climb to Mt Binser.

There are various options for the return, aside from retracing your upward route, with the best being a direct, though very steep, descent to the southwest, from the principal summit, to the Mt White Road. This is then followed back to your car.

Mt Binser and the saddle track are accessed across the Mt White Bridge, off SH73, a few kilometres north of Cass. The Mt White Road is followed to Andrews Shelter, and it is approximately 3km further to the track (signposted), which begins at the bush edge up a vehicle track (north side of road).

Note

Various extended tramps are possible in Arthur's Pass National Park east of the Poulter River through the Thompson, East Poulter (via McArthur Gorge) and Cox rivers and Bull Creek. Some small huts/bivvies are available. Generally, the valleys provide excellent travel.

Western Arthur's Pass National Park

This section of the national park lies north of the pass and centres around SH73, from where several marked tracks climb through very steep forest and tussock to reach the open tops. There are also some lightly tracked routes up the major valleys of the Rolleston River, Kellys Creek, Deception River, Taramakau and Taipo rivers. These last two valleys are outside of the park boundary but offer popular tramping routes and so are included here for completeness. In general, tracks and routes here are much harder than those found on the eastern side of the pass, the rainfall is much higher and the rivers are swifter.

TRACKS TO THE TOPS AND WALKS IN THE OTIRA VALLEY OFF SH73

The Otira Valley is the primary access point for routes and tracks in the western portion of the park. Mostly these are characterised by marked tracks, which ascend very steep faces and spurs from the highway to the bushline. Above this point unmarked routes can be followed to the peaks. Experience, good fitness and judgement, and basic alpine skills are prerequisites for attempting these summits. There are also several tramping routes in the valleys off the Otira River.

30. Mt Barron (1730m)

Highway to the summit: 6 hours. **Hard+**
Descent: 4–5 hours.

This is a challenging climb up a steep, lightly marked and sometimes over-grown track to the ridge-top and large basin south of the peak. This is a difficult route in winter, with heavy snowfalls making the going slow and avalanche prone. Although not far in distance, being only 3km from the road, the long ascent (1300m) and rugged nature of the route make this trip suitable for fit, experienced parties only.

The route to the peak is not obvious from the bush edge and further climbing is required to reach the 1500m contour, from where a long, curving spur heads into the south face of the peak and a large basin. This high basin grants access to the summit ridge via an exposed rock scramble from the west.

To reach Goat Creek descend from the ridge crest, west of the summit, into a large basin above Kellys Creek, and then across the ridgeline into the head of Goat Creek. Sidle northeast on easy terraces, above bluffs, for about 1km to reach the bush edge and steep spur on the river left of Goat Creek running down into the lower creek.

Good visibility is required to find this route.

The track is signposted on SH73, south of Otira, a few hundred metres north of the railway underpass. It is also accessible from the water supply intake on Goat Creek, 1km south of Otira.

31. Goat Hill (1656m)

Highway to summit: 4–5 hours. **Hard**
Descent: 3 hours.

Goat Hill offers a straightforward route to a high foothill and magnificent views over the upper Otira and Deception valleys and Mt Rolleston.

A well-marked track climbs through bush to sub-alpine scrub and open tussock, from where an unmarked route climbs steadily northwards, through large basins and past several tarns, to reach the summit ridge. The final section of the ridge, running east to the summit, is a rock scramble, which, if you choose, can be bypassed by descending into the scree basins north of the peak and climbing back up steep scree to reach the summit. Mt Alexander dominates the northern horizon and offers a challenge to those who wish to climb harder mountains.

Access is off SH73 at the Otira highway bridge, 2km south of Otira township. A hidden layby can be found on the eastern side of the road, where cars can be left. Walk through the gateway, beside the road, and head into the shingle gully of Barrack Creek. Head upstream for approximately 300m to where a large orange triangle, on the northern bank, indicates the start of the track to the bush edge.

MT BARRON, LORDING IT OVER OTIRA, WESTLAND

Steep, relentless climbs are an intrinsic part of many trips to the hills, and when the hills in question happen to be in Westland you can virtually guarantee that any pursuit of the vertical will be a solid physical challenge. Mt Barron (1730m), which looms directly above Otira village on the western side of the highway, is one such peak and can be observed, in fine conditions, from Arthur's Pass highway as you descend towards the viaduct. Sprawling ridgelines, high basins and dramatically steep shoulders falling to the valley mark this mountain out.

Setting off with two companions, Fr Antoine Thomas and Tony Jenkinson, in late summer I was keen to revisit this summit, having not been near it for many years, following one success and a series of attempts during winter when deep soft snow had turned me back on several occasions. This time the mountain is bereft of such hazards and the weather clement enough to give us a good opportunity to

Pat Barrett on the summit of Mt Barron

attain the summit. There's just that steep grind to contend with – over 800m just to reach the first basins. It surely makes good keen men of us – up through forest and sub-alpine vegetation to gain the final shattered ridge on the lip of the basin, where there is a soaring view of Arthur's Pass highway and the Otira Valley cutting down beneath our feet.

Care is required near the top as the rock is poorly bonded and ragged, and stony gullies rattle away below the crest. Once in the basin, easy travel ensues through grassy hollows, until the main ridge is gained and we can rest to focus on the route ahead. Two kilometres of undulating ridgeline, a hanging basin and the final summit ridge lie before us. Though relatively easy, they are a test of endurance. Yet help lies at hand and is revealed in the stunning post-glacial landscape opening before us, a spectacle that takes away much of the difficulty of climbing.

There's no wind to drive away the leaden sky, which brings out a sombre, almost foreboding nature to the landscape, subtleties that always lend a note of caution when traversing ridgelines far above the valley floor. The way ahead is clear and we make the hanging basin below the summit and pause for a quick snack.

Tony has decided he does not want to continue on, so Fr Antoine and I clamber on to the summit ridge, but there's a sting in the tale at the top – the final 100m to the summit cairn is along narrow, exposed and broken rock. Care and a slow, steady approach see us through to the peak, where we are for a few moments, lords of the mountain. Our gaze from this rocky promontory encompasses Lake Brunner and the forests and valleys of the Taramakau, upper Otira and Rolleston rivers. These last two catchments are backed by Mts Rolleston and Philistine, two of the region's highest summits, though for now they are partially hidden in cloud.

Summits are but a perennial moment in time, as there is always the descent to consider, and we have a surfeit of metres to lose to access the valley floor, now over 1300m below. We are lords no longer; merely slaves to gravity.

32. Rolleston River and Waimakariri Col
2 days. **Hard+**

The Rolleston River route to Waimakariri Col (1780m) is a very difficult transalpine route, involving route finding in steep country and requiring an ice axe and crampons to cross the col all year round.

A rough route and track exist up the Rolleston River, river right, to the scrub line. Here the upper river is crossed to a high bench on the west side of the valley and the track then climbs upstream high above the incised riverbed to reach a knoll at around 1400m. From here climb southwest into a snow gully directly beneath Mt Armstrong. Do not head for the col itself, which is badly bluffed on its northern flanks. The true col lies 700m west of the marked Waimakariri Col.

Descend on the south side over snow, and sometimes ice slopes, to the upper Waimakariri River. There is one small hut, Waimakariri Falls Hut, on the southern side of the pass in Arthur's Pass National Park.

This route is suitable for well-equipped, experienced parties only.

Access is from the railway overpass on SH73, south of Otira. Head along a gravel road beside the railway line to the railway bridge over the Rolleston River. Then head upstream and cross to the river right bank to pick up the track, which climbs above the gorge. This is about 1.6km from the railway bridge.

33. Deception River
Highway footbridge to Goat Pass Hut: 7–8 hours. **Moderate**

This is the route for the popular Coast to Coast multi-sport event and is also a well-used tramper's route in the park.

The route up to Goat Pass, a Main Divide crossing, is not marked and involves steady boulder hopping and multiple river crossings to access the hut and pass. While there are some short sections of track, especially in the upper valley below Goat Pass, the route is mostly untracked. The valley should not be entered during or after heavy rain – it is easy to become stranded.

The Upper Deception Hut (6 bunks) lies about an hour below Goat Pass, on a bush terrace on the river right – it is easy to miss.

Access is via a large footbridge crossing the Otira River, 6km north of Otira on SH73.

Carroll Hut with Arthur's Pass in the background

34. Carroll Hut and Kellys Creek

SH73 to Carroll Hut: 2–3 hours. **Hard**

Carroll Hut to Seven Mile Creek: 4–5 hours.

Kellys Creek carpark to Hunts Creek Hut: 4–5 hours. **Hard**

Carroll Hut (10 bunks) is one of the most easily accessed tops huts in the Southern Alps. It lies in a large basin beneath Kellys Hill (1394m) and can be readily picked out by keen observers from above the Otira Gorge Viaduct.

A very steep track climbs from the creek directly to the hut, providing a grand view of the Arthur's Pass region. Above the hut a poled route climbs through Kelly Saddle, where there is a cluster of sparkling tarns, and heads southwest along the Kelly Range, past larger tarns, to link with the marked track down to Seven Mile Creek in the Taipo River. The Kelly tops can carry a large amount of snow during the winter months, with deep drifts present.

Kellys Creek has a marked track climbing to Hunt Saddle and sidling into Hunts Creek and Hut (4 bunks) – a remote and beautiful valley.

Access is off SH73 at Kellys Creek, 3km north of Otira. A short side-road leads to marked tracks to Hunt Saddle and Hut and Carroll Hut and tops.

KELLY CAPERS – KELLY RANGE, ARTHUR'S PASS NATIONAL PARK

From where I sat, in the warmth and comfort of our vehicle with a hot drink to hand, there seemed little incentive to venture onto the tops for our planned winter camp. Although it was a beautifully fine August day, with thick snow providing a tantalising spectacle for would-be adventurers above the dark forests of Westland, the wind raised a hand of warning. A steady southeast gale had been blowing for several days, bringing rain and snow to the eastern side of the Divide and fine, though bitterly cold and windy, conditions to western areas. The sun was shining brightly, yet providing only token warmth, while strong wind gusts funnelled through the valleys and airborne snow plumed from the ridges above. Thoughts of a peaceful high camp among the peaks had vanished as I recalled other times when we had braved the lash of the wind on high exposed ridges, later to retreat, thankful that we had not been blown from the tops. We therefore chose a valley tramp into Hunts Creek and its attractively sited hut to grant us a little time to consider a return route back to the car stationed at Kellys Creek.

As we tramped along the excellent track through Kellys Creek to Hunt Saddle we spied various options for our return but decided to continue on to Hunts Creek Hut for a comfortable night, hoping for the wind to abate so we could access the tops on the morrow.

At Hunt Saddle, a large park-like clearing filled with magnificent tall red tussock straddles the pass, beyond which the dark gulch of Hunts Creek drops away to the Taipo Valley. Here the track sidles up along the hillside and soon descends into the sub-alpine basin, which contains the hut.

This is a special place, where peaks rim the horizon in all directions and the tiny hut clings to the edge of a spacious tussock flat, a small stream runs nearby, and civilisation, though barely half a day's walk away, seems as remote as ancient history. It is a place to savour, and we did so, lighting the small log stove, resting and gazing hopefully at the high tops, where fingers of cloud and a haze of spindrift blurred their ragged outlines.

Before dawn next day we were on our way, returning to Hunt Saddle, to gain the southwestern extremity of the Kelly Range and complete a relatively easy loop route via Carroll Hut to the road-end. It was another cold, clear day, and though there was little wind in the valley we could see from the snow plumes that still issued from the ridges that the wind was unabated at higher levels. The sun was out, the day was superb, the snow looked (and proved to be) firm and packed, and we reasoned that we would perhaps find some shelter along the lee side of the ridgeline.

There is no track onto the southern end of the Kelly Range, but a rough route exists up a small stream east of Hunt Saddle into a large, swampy clearing. From there we made our way laboriously via a series of scrubby faces and small fault scarps into the tussock zone and finally the snow at 1200m.

Until now we had been enjoying pleasant conditions as we gazed out over the broadening swathe of the magnificent Taipo Valley to the great white tooth of Tara Tama (1854m), a major peak in the lower valley. But as we gained the crest of the broad ridge the wind slammed us like a hammer blow, sending us reeling for a moment as we struggled to find shelter and hastily 'gear-up' for the conditions ahead along 5km of open ridgeline.

The full force of the wind was intimidating, but as we ventured forth, fully protected under various windproofs and thermal layers, our destination, Carroll Hut, seemed possible. Acres of crisp, firm snow covered the low summits of the Kelly Range, which reaches a modest 1411m at its highest point, and this considerably aided our progress along the crest, where we were occasionally able to rest out of the sting of the wind. It was an exhilarating traverse and once we had the measure of the gale we were able to proceed with confidence through delightfully sculptured snow basins, over narrow ridge crests and past frozen tarns. The Taipo arced away below our boots, in its green and blue home where steep mountains crowded in, before disgorging its turbulent waters into the greater flood of the Taramakau. Out to the east and south, clawing fingers of wind-tossed cloud covered the Main Divide, leaving the outlying ranges clear.

At mid-point along the ridge our route intersected with the poled route over to Seven Mile Creek in the Taipo, where a plateau, littered with large frozen tarns, presented a spectacular winter scene. Beyond the plateau an easy and sheltered descent on softening snow led us first into the wide bowl of Kelly Saddle and finally to Carroll Hut.

We had made good time on the crossing and so there was a moment to pause in the hut for a rest from the gale and to survey the frigid winterscape across the Otira Valley, before committing mind and body to the final steep descent through Westland forest to the road below.

35. Lake Kaurapataka and Upper Taramakau River
Aickens on SH73: 2–3 hours one way to lake. **Moderate**
Townsend Hut from SH73: 5–6 hours. **Hard**
Harper Pass from SH73: 2 days. **Hard**

Nestled in the dense forests of the West Coast lies a secluded gem: Lake Kaurapataka. Its name is derived from kōura: crayfish and pātaka: a raised storehouse. This bush-fringed, large lake lies well above the valley floors of the Otehake and Taramakau rivers, and drains into the Taramakau via Lake Stream and Pfeifer Creek.

On the fringe of the Otehake Wilderness Area, the first of its kind, gazetted in 1955, the lake environs support a wide variety of forest trees, including red, silver and mountain beech, rimu, miro, tōtara, kahikatea and rātā, as well as numerous lowland bird species, including kākā, tūī, bellbird, parakeet (kākāriki), fantail, brown creepers, wren, kiwi and tomtit. It is also a sanctuary for grey duck and black teal.

The 2km-long by 0.5km-wide lake is bordered by steep, forested hillsides to the north and south, with the eastern end forming a low saddle above the shingle flats of the lower Otehake. This sheltered aspect and high rainfall, up to 7000mm a year, no doubt account for the profusion of forest trees and ferns found in the lake basin.

It is a delightful place to visit at any season, and the round trip to the lake from the highway, returning via the Otehake and Taramakau flats, can easily be made in a day. The major difficulty presented on the tramp is the ford of the Otira River, and possibly the Otehake (if you choose the round trip). However, in low to normal flows the Otira will present few problems.

Once across the Otira River, a gentle stroll up the open grassy expanse of the Taramakau, with its spectacular vistas of high snowy peaks and dense forested slopes, will take you to Pfeifer Creek. Here the marked track begins on the river left bank, later crossing to the river right. This easy track winds through impressive stands of tall red beech and pockets of leafy ferns as it gradually climbs to the lake.

At the lake the track continues along the south side, climbing to the saddle with the Otehake. There are several side-tracks that lead out to the lake itself, and depending on the water level, some small beaches. There are numerous campsites, though you need a good insect-proof tent if you intend to stay.

From the lake-shore a grand view is obtained of Mt Pfeifer, rearing 1300m above, its rock and tussock summit a challenge for those who want to explore further. In winter the lake reflects the peaks, and ice often rims the shore. This is a place to linger on a long summer afternoon, as sunlight filters in through the forest canopy and reflects off the lake into the depths of the forest gloom.

As you leave the lake and begin the return trip via the Otehake, the tranquility is replaced by the roar of the river as it surges past stony banks, leading you to the Taramakau (the meaning is uncertain but probably means 'to flow in a curve') and its open spaces, which provide a marked contrast to the dark, quiet interior of the lake basin.

Beyond the lake other routes are possible into the upper Taramakau Valley:

(i) Koropuku Tops and Hut
6–7 hours. **Hard**

A steep, lightly marked route to the open tops, from where an unmarked route continues over to Koropuku Hut. This route can be linked to Townsend Hut via the ridge and high basins to the east.

(ii) Otehake River
2–3 days. **Hard+**

Follow the old track and route south, into the Otehake Wilderness Area. This is a difficult route on an overgrown track.

(iii) Townsend Hut and Tops
3–4 hours from Otehake confluence. **Moderate/Hard**

On the main Taipo Valley route, 3.5km upstream from the Otehake River confluence, a signpost on the river left bank indicates the start of the steep track to Townsend Hut (6 bunks). Spectacularly set on a tussock bench high above the Taramakau River at 1100m, this snug little hut offers a wonderful vista over the valley and mountains to the north.

Above the hut an unmarked route to the upper Poulter River in Arthur's Pass National Park is possible over a high col west of Mt Koeti. Alternatively, sidle through high basins south and west of Townsend Hut to Koropuku Hut.

(iv) **Harper Pass to Lake Sumner**
3–4 days. **Moderate**

This is a popular, low-level trans-alpine route over Harper Pass to the Hurunui River and Lake Sumner. It is a well-facilitated route, with good huts and a marked track in the upper Taramakau and Hurunui valleys.

Access to the Taramakau is signposted on SH73 at Aickens, 8km north of Otira. Cross the fence stile to a marked route leading over flats to the Otira River. Take care with fording the Otira River.

36. Pfeifer Bivvy Route
5–6 hours from Morrison footbridge at SH73. **Hard**

A new bivvy (2 bunks) now resides in the high, remote basin below Mt Pfeifer (1704m), above the Taramakau Valley. Though reasonably difficult to reach, it makes an excellent 2-day trip or, in summer, a challenging 1-day excursion, climbing from the river flats of the lower Deception, through bush, scrub and tussock to reach a series of high basins and rock ridges.

Pfeifer Bivvy

The route from the footbridge heads into Parutu Stream, over easy farm flats, climbs the streambed steeply up to Waharoa Saddle (this section is marked here and there with tape), and then climbs south from the saddle up the ridge on a roughly cut trail to reach the open tops.

From here the ridgeline is followed until near Point 1592m, from where you can either continue on along the ridge to the basin containing the bivvy or descend into the basin below Point 1592m and traverse around to the bivvy on the 1300m contour.

Routes out from here include:

(i) Traversing Mt Pfeifer to the east and the long open spur that runs down over Point 1394m to reach the bush and the broad ridge that runs down to the eastern edge of Lake Kaurapataka. This is a challenging route requiring good fitness, navigation and favourable weather.

(ii) Descending to the Lake Creek/Pfeifer Creek confluence via a steep spur, scree and bush, east and north of the bivvy. Good visibility and navigational skills are required for this route to avoid bluffs and waterfalls. If you are unsure of the route or your ability, return via Waharoa Saddle.

TOPPED OUT IN THE TARAMAKAU

Evening is falling. The light is fading and tendrils of cloud are spreading out into the Taramakau Valley on the western flanks of the Main Divide, near Arthur's Pass National Park. A sudden breeze brings with it the call of kiwi, fossicking somewhere in the half-light on the steep forested gullies below Pfeifer Biv, where I am camped with a couple of friends. But mine is a solo journey, out to explore the rim of the large basin in which the bivvy lies, where undulating tussock mounds give way, suddenly, to sharp little gullies and scree slopes. There are routes to the valley floor here, but they need to be chosen carefully, as bluffs and waterfalls await the hasty.

I'm in no hurry, the day's work is done, our climb to the biv via the ridgeline from Waharoa Saddle, and now there's time to enjoy the fruits of our labours. Such freedom to wander is one of the great joys of tramping, exploring in magnificent surroundings with no particular goal other than the very act of exploration.

Mt Alexander, the undisputed lord of the Taramakau, hoves into view, its muscular bulk solidifying from behind the clouds. It's a majestic summit, which I have climbed on only one occasion, a subsequent attempt in winter failed due to too much ice on the western ridge. Now it's snow free, yet no less intimidating, its 1958m summit standing 1700m above the valley floor and seemingly impregnable. I can savour it from my perch and recall the rigours of the climb, safe in the knowledge that I don't have to face it again, at least not now, for a comfortable night awaits back at the bivvy, with good company amid mountains of silence.

Taramakau Valley and Mt Alexander at dusk

37. Taipo Valley

SH73 to Dillons Hut: 3 hours. **Easy**
Dillons Hut to Mid Taipo Hut: 2–3 hours. **Moderate**
Mid Taipo Hut to Julia Hut: 3 hours. **Moderate**
Kelly Range and Carroll Hut from Seven Mile Creek (Dillons Hut): 5–6 hours. **Hard**
Dunns Creek Hut from Dillons Hut: 3–4 hours. **Moderate**
Tara Tama from Seven Mile Creek: 8–10 hours. **Hard+**

The Taipo Valley has for many generations been a popular access point to and from the mountains west of Arthur's Pass National Park. Taipo means taniwha or 'monster' in Māori, so-named because it claimed the lives of many native greenstone hunters. Therefore beware: this is a huge catchment and all river crossings should be treated with care.

The valley is well served with huts, and has a formed track running much of its length, from Dillons Hut to the bushline in Mary Creek en route to the Harman Pass crossing to the upper Waimakariri River. The upper valley is very scenic and has the added attraction of hot pools in the riverbed, just downstream of Julia Hut.

Access to the Taipo is signposted on SH73, approximately 2km east of the Taipo River highway bridge. A small carpark lies just inside the treeline. The access road beyond here is rough and muddy and passable for 4WD only. It can be driven as far as Seven Mile Creek.

Where the 4WD access road reaches the Taipo River flats, easy travel on the river right continues, mostly on vehicle tracks, as far as the old Dillons Homestead (10 bunks) on a large flat south of the creek, and the new DOC hut (10 bunks) sited approximately 800m south of Dillons beside a stand of matai trees. The old hut is quite serviceable and provides rustic accommodation for those who enjoy the simpler pleasures in life.

There are several options for exploring further into the valley from here:

(i) Kelly Range

Boulder-hop for 500m up the river left bank of Seven Mile Creek to reach the marked track leading up a moderately steep spur to the open tops. A poled route then continues across these easy tops, along the Kelly Range, to Kelly Saddle and Carroll Hut (10 bunks). Good visibility is required to follow the open tops to Carroll Hut. (See notes for 'Carroll Hut and Kellys Creek'.)

CANTERBURY FOOTHILLS & FORESTS

(ii) Mid Taipo and Julia Hut

Continue up the Taipo River on a marked route on the river right, along scrubby terraces and rough riverbed, to reach Scotty's cableway. Cross the cableway and follow the riverbed and a short section of track to reach Mid Taipo Hut (6 bunks).

Above Mid Taipo Hut the track crosses the river flat to reach a swing-bridge over the Taipo and then travels upvalley over Tumbledown Creek (walk-wire) to Julia Hut.

At Hura Creek, 300m downstream of Mid Taipo Hut, a lightly marked route climbs over a bush saddle to Dunns Creek Hut (4 bunks). An unmarked crossing is possible from this hut over Newton Saddle to Newton Creek and Arahura River. It is also possible to reach Dunns Creek Hut by travelling directly up Dunns Creek from the Taipo to gain the old track cut above the gorge on the river left. This begins by travelling up a large slip from the river, at about 480m altitude, to the marked track.

(iii) Scottys Bivvy and Tara Tama (1854m)

This is a very strenuous option for reaching the open tops, and involves fording the Taipo River, climbing up a steep, partly overgrown track, and negotiating 9km of high, open ridge-top to reach the summit of Tara Tama. Though a challenging route, the rewards for fit, experienced parties are outstanding.

The route commences about 600m downstream of Seven Mile Creek, where the Taipo River is forded, when low, to reach the track near the mouth of a small stream. The stream is crossed just inside the bush and then a lightly marked trail is followed south onto the terrace above. Continue on up the broad, steep ridge (some care will be required to stay on the marked track) to the open tops and traverse the ridge southwest over several small knobs to Scottys Saddle. Scottys Bivvy lies 1km east of the saddle, and 300m lower, on a small bench.

Beyond the saddle continue south along the ridge to Point 2751m and then east to the summit.

It is also possible to descend to, or climb from, upper Dunns Creek via the northwestern feeder stream of this creek to a low point on the ridge north of Dunn Saddle. A sidle, to the north on scree, grants access to the main ridge via a gully just north of Point 1751m.

Ice axe and crampons will be essential on this route in winter conditions.

TOUGH TIMES ON TARA TAMA

My altimeter registers 1050m as Fr Antoine and I clear the bush edge on Scotty's Ridge in the Taipo Valley in central Westland. We are on my third attempt to climb Tara Tama (1854m), a remote outlier of the Main Divide. Although 1800m is not high by Southern Alps' standards, considering the starting altitude is 200m and the summit lies over 10km away along a tortuous ridge, it's a reasonable challenge for a 2-day trip.

Beyond the bushline we are faced with 6km of ridge-top, all the way to Scottys Saddle and its tiny two-bunk bivvy, sited 200m below in Scottys Creek. At times the crest is narrow and rocky, bluffed and rent by faults; at others it's wide and spacious, pitted with small tarns. However you cut it, travel is slow but never tedious, there's too much variety for that; and for inspiration, at the end of the ridge stands the great rocky wedge of Tara Tama, rising on clouds of noon.

Scottys Bivvy is a marvellous sight – rough, wind scorched, dented, yet weatherproof and offering two bunks. The hut book reveals we

Scottys Bivvy, Tara Tama, Taipo Valley

are the first party in almost a year to unlatch the bolt and crouch inside – the simple pleasure of a restful night in the hills after a good meal cooked in the moonlight is not lost on either of us. Tomorrow the adventure begins anew.

Early morning finds us on the upper slopes, which are steeper than they appear from below, and some brief moments of scratching through shallow gullies ensue until we cast ourselves up onto the summit ridge. 'Whoa – what a view', we gasp. It's Westland, arrayed below – inexpressibly magnificent. It's taken us almost 15 hours to reach the top and unbeknown to us a further 10 hours will pass, and an unplanned night, to reach my ute. For now, it's time to celebrate. Fr Antoine offers Mass, right on the summit, no doubt the first ever to do so in all of history. It's a poignant moment assisting him amid the overwhelming beauty of the Westland alps revealed in all their glory on this faultless day. Our descent begins at a broad scree on the south side of the mountain. Lower down it constricts into a deep, rock-walled, Z-shaped defile beyond which there is – space. Bluffed,

Fr Antoine Thomas approaching the summit of Tara Tama

we traverse out, enter another gully system of bluffs and traverse again over a sharp spur, scrub bashing to a rocky rib, and below – voila! It's the way down, rough, but possible. There's still a lot of riverbed travel between us and the road-end, but with four usable hours of daylight left we are keen to get out.

On nightfall we reach Dillons Hut, sited on a terrace in the lower valley. There are several groups inside, bedded down for the night, so our late arrival creates some disturbance. We have been walking 14 hours since leaving Scottys Bivvy and we're done. The bunks look good.

We're on the go before sun-up next morning for the final dash down the Taipo to reach my ute. It's been an exhausting climb, yet I wouldn't have thought so from the ear-to-ear grin Fr Antoine is wearing. 'They look like some good summits to try over there next time', he remarks, indicating towards the Taramakau Valley. Shaking my head, I sigh, 'It's time to head home'.

Fr Antoine Thomas on the summit ridge of Tara Tama

Speargrass on Dumblane

Lewis Pass Region

Introduction

This beautiful forest and alpine region lies only 2.5 hours' drive northwest of Christchurch on SH7, the Lewis Pass highway. The reserve, in general, covers the immediate areas to the east and west of the highway, from where the Doubtful River joins the Boyle River, through to the pass itself, and beyond to Maruia Springs. On approach to the reserve, via the highway, the first and most lasting impression is of a mountain, valley, river and bush setting that could not be more complete or more restful on the eye. Though it has none of the dramatic nature of parks further to the south, and the mountains are generally of a modest height, the scenes viewed from the sweeping bends of the highway are of outstanding beauty. Dense carpets of forest cover much of the valley floor and ramp up the steep mountainsides to open grassy basins, ridges and short, craggy summits. Along the forest floor, clear sparkling rivers dash past overhanging beech trees and wind through grassy river flats. Braided rivers and extensive shingle river terraces are rare here. The highway passes through some magnificent stands of red beech, reminding you of the spectacular Milford Road highway away to the south.

Just below the summit of the Lewis Pass highway, the bush drops back to reveal a grand scene along the upper Maruia Valley to the distant

Boyle River, Lewis Pass

peaks of Gloriana and Faerie Queene. In winter this valley and its many high ridges are swathed in snow, with numerous avalanche paths running onto the valley floor.

It is a region of much activity, both today and in the past.

Landscape and Climate

The altitude of the region ranges from approximately 500m on the highway to 2235m at the summit of Faerie Queene, the highest peak adjacent to the St James walkway. (There are other higher peaks immediately to the north and east, along the Spenser Mountains.) The mountainous backdrop of the Main Divide contains many features of heavy glaciation, which is the major force that has shaped the region, leaving behind cirques and U-shaped valleys, sculpting rocks and bluffs, and depositing tiny meltwater tarns in many of the high basins. Four major faults, running parallel to one another, cross the region from the northeast coast of the South Island to Westland.

Summit tarn, Lewis Pass

Displacement caused by these faults is evident above the highway. The Awatere Fault runs through the Ada Pass region, the Great Alpine Fault runs near Springs Junction, the Hope Fault runs through the lower Hope River to the Waiau, and the Clarence Fault traverses the upper Hope to Pussy Stream, Doubtful River and Magdalen Valley. There are numerous minor fault lines associated with these features.

The entire region is subject to frequent, heavy snowfalls during the winter months, and it is not uncommon to find up to a metre of snow on the flats and highway after severe winter storms. This is a fact commonly overlooked by those attempting the St James Walkway during winter, as well as the generally high elevation of the track throughout the length of the route.

Vegetation

Vegetation in the area is particularly diverse. The most dominant feature is the extensive beech forest, with red, silver and mountain beech being

A track-side stream, St James Walkway

luxuriant to an altitude of 1400m. On the lower slopes the sub-canopy consists of a complex mixture of shrubs and ground ferns. The high rainfall in the area, over 4000mm a year decreasing to 1000mm further east, sustains an unusual variety and richness of undergrowth, and many of the shrubs, ferns and mosses are rare and sometimes absent in other Canterbury forests. With increasing altitude, the undergrowth thins, giving way to stunted shrubs,

BEECH HONEYDEW

Beech honeydew is an unusual and distinctive feature found throughout the foothill beech forests and is readily identified as tiny droplets of sugary liquid suspended on silvery threads that hang from black fungus covering the beech trees. In some places the fungus is entirely absent, while in others it liberally coats the lower trunks and branches of large sections of the forest.

Bernadette Barrett getting honeydew in beech forest

The honeydew is produced by tiny scale insects, which inhabit the fungus, feeding on the sap of the tree and excreting the droplets of liquid. Honeybees collect the 'dew' and produce a rich, dark honey. This honey is sold on both the local and overseas markets, especially in Europe.

An unfortunate consequence of honeydew's widespread occurrence in our beech forests is the increasing wasp infestation of these areas, where they compete with bees and native birds, which feed off the 'dew'.

Special care should be taken when entering beech forests during late summer and autumn, when wasp numbers are normally high. A first-aid kit containing remedies for wasp stings should be carried.

including a range of coprosmas, snowberry, koromiko, alpine hardfern, snow tussock, red and blue tussocks, and native grasses.

The display of alpine flowers is particularly beautiful in early summer. These include mountain daisies, Mt Cook lily, gentians, ourisias, carrot plants and speargrasses.

Bird and Animal Life

Birdlife is abundant in the area, with all of the common forest birds present: bellbird, tomtit, fantail, warbler and bush robin. Kea, rifleman, kākā, tūī, skylark and pipit are also present. Yellow-crowned parakeet (kākāriki) and yellowhead are also found in the large undisturbed forests. The great spotted kiwi is found in the major river headwaters, as is the South Island weka. Of special interest are the occasional sightings of white heron, New Zealand falcon and southern crested grebe. Red deer are found in the bush, and chamois are in moderate numbers above the bushline. Possum are common.

All of the main rivers provide good trout fishing. Long-finned eel are present under riverbanks, and the common and alpine galaxias, native fish, are found in rocky and shingly streams.

History

Although only recently established as a walkway, the St James utilises historic access routes between Canterbury, Nelson and Westland. Before the arrival of Europeans, the route up the Maruia Gorge (Rumbling Current) was well travelled and popular with Māori because of its rich wildlife and easy access to other areas. Dispute over the area arose between the Ngāti Tūmatakōkiri and Ngāi Tahu tribes, ending in grisly fashion when a party of Ngāi Tahu were ambushed in the gorge by the opposing tribe and later furnished the substance of a celebratory meal for the victorious Ngāti Tūmatakōkiri. Hence the name Cannibal Gorge at the northern end of the St James Walkway.

The arrival of Europeans and the need for a viable route to Westland and Canterbury prompted exploration on the part of the Nelson provincial government, and between 1860 and 1870 several parties explored the area now covered by the walkway. Prominent among these explorers were Christopher Maling, Henry Lewis, W. T. L. Travers and D. Stuart. It is from Henry Lewis that the pass and region take their names.

Travers, a wild and eccentric Irishman, was companion to Maling on an extended foray, which first explored the headwaters of the Waiau (meaning 'water of the mist'). On their crossings to the Clarence and Waiau, Travers filled the empty landscape he found with names of his favourite poets and their verses. A lake became Tennyson and the mountains above it became Princess, Guinevere and Dora. The great range blocking their way to the west became Spenser and its major peaks Faerie Queene, Gloriana and Una. They crossed Maling's pass and explored the western tributaries of the Waiau, naming them after family: Ada, Henry and Anne. On reaching the saddle at the head of the Henry, they thought the river below, the Maruia, was the Grey. Here they turned for home, but Maling returned later with Henry Lewis to investigate further. They dropped off the pass into the Maruia and on down to the hot springs. Here they discovered that the river swung north and was the Maruia and not the Grey. Returning east in dismay they unknowingly made the first European crossing of the Lewis Pass.

Maling made several other trips to the area with Lewis and later Stuart, with a view to establishing a stock route due to the proximity of the new gold rushes opening up in the upper Grey and Inangahua.

By 1869 all the land in the Waiau and Clarence catchments had been leased for grazing. Travers established Lake Guyon Station in 1864, which took in the upper Waiau, Ada and Henry, from where he supplied food to the West Coast gold miners by driving cattle down the Maruia Gorge to the workings.

Numerous other stations became established in the watersheds of the Waiau and Ada, one of the more enduring of which was the Stanley Vale, not far from Traver's Lake Guyon. It was farmed by Walter Fowler and his wife from 1863 to 1892. All 14 of their children were born there, though not all survived the trauma of birth. Everything for Stanley Vale had to come in over Fowlers Pass (nearly1300m), and it was this and the harsh winters and huge stock losses that finally drove them out.

St James Station incorporated all of these smaller holdings and was established in 1859 by John McArthur, a Scottish shepherd. He established the Ada Homestead at the junction of the Ada and Waiau rivers as an outpost. Later it became a base for musterers, as it still is today. In early days the St James Station stocked sheep, but later turned to cattle, as the winters were too severe for sheep. Today it is famous for the superb horses that are raised, and the annual horse sale, in January, is a major attraction for horse breeders.

St James Walkway near Boyle Village

In recent years most of the St James has passed into the hands of DOC and is now classed as a Conservation Park.

The Lewis Pass Highway

The Lewis Pass highway was nothing more than a pack-track for over 70 years, up until the late 1920s, when pressure from runholders, the AA, and others brought about the start of construction. It was completed in 1937 and is said to have been the last major pick-and-shovel highway project in New Zealand.

The highest point on the highway is 907m, but the actual Lewis Pass (886m) is a little further southeast, at the carpark of the St James Walkway.

With the advent of the road link, this once isolated region was opened up for recreation and is now a major area of interest for outdoor enthusiasts.

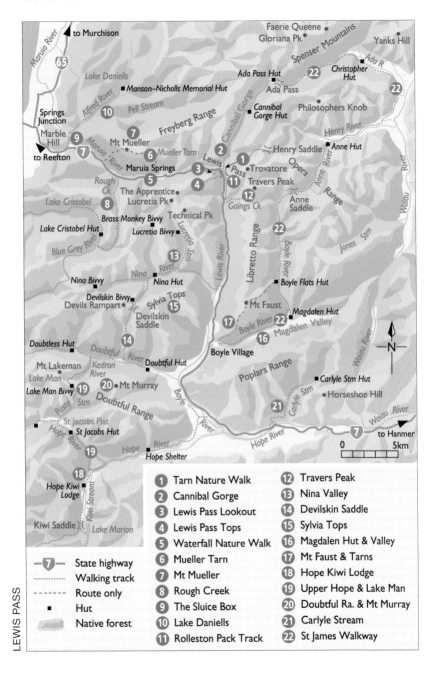

1	Tarn Nature Walk	**12**	Travers Peak
2	Cannibal Gorge	**13**	Nina Valley
3	Lewis Pass Lookout	**14**	Devilskin Saddle
4	Lewis Pass Tops	**15**	Sylvia Tops
5	Waterfall Nature Walk	**16**	Magdalen Hut & Valley
6	Mueller Tarn	**17**	Mt Faust & Tarns
7	Mt Mueller	**18**	Hope Kiwi Lodge
8	Rough Creek	**19**	Upper Hope & Lake Man
9	The Sluice Box	**20**	Doubtful Ra. & Mt Murray
10	Lake Daniells	**21**	Carlyle Stream
11	Rolleston Pack Track	**22**	St James Walkway

- –**7**– State highway
- .... Walking track
- - - - - Route only
- ■ Hut
- Native forest

LEWIS PASS

Lewis Pass – Western Side

1. Tarn Nature Walk
20–30 minutes round trip. **Easy**

On Lewis Pass, at the northern end of the St James Walkway, the Tarn Nature Walk takes its name from the still, dark pool (kettlehole) that resides amidst the sphagnum bog just east of the carpark. The tarn is a legacy of the once huge glaciers that covered this region; a block of ice left behind to melt by the retreating glacier.

A short trail and boardwalk skirt the southern end of the tarn to a photographic and viewing platform. From here a beautiful reflection of Gloriana Peak (2218m), on the Spenser Mountains, can be observed on still days. Even on misty days, the dark ridges and bush faces mirrored in the waters of the tarn can captivate the visitor, especially if you muse on the trials and tribulations of Travers, Maling, Lewis and Stuart, who passed this way beset by rain and cloud in their hunt for a route to the west during the 1860s, with no map, guide or experience of the region.

Returning from the tarn, a loop trail can be followed out to the north and west through the alpine wetland, which straddles the summit of Lewis Pass.

Good views of the Spenser Mountains and valleys, amidst the stunted, windswept trees, bog plants and lichen, are obtained as you complete the circuit back to the carpark.

2. Cannibal Gorge
To swingbridge: 30 minutes down, 50 minutes up. **Moderate**

Also at the northern end of the St James Walkway, a short excursion is possible along this track, descending to the Cannibal Gorge and swingbridge 170m below.

This well-graded track (St James Walkway) leaves the carpark and crosses a section of boardwalk before winding down into a small, shaded streamlet, which drains to the Maruia. This is a very attractive part of the walk, where the stream flows beneath the forest canopy and rich, soft mosses cover the floor. If the light is good, it is an excellent place for photography. Further on the track climbs away from the stream and contours around the hillside, before dropping steeply in a zigzag into the gorge and the swingbridge.

It is possible to descend from the bridge onto the rocky river flats (left side of the swingbridge facing north); there is no track and a short scramble is necessary.

Cannibal Gorge is a legacy of the days when this was a major route for Māori travelling from east to west in search of greenstone. During a dispute over territory and game rights the Ngāti-Tūmatakōkiri are reputed to have trapped the Ngāi-Tahu chief, Pareke, and his followers in the gorge, killed them, and then eaten them in a feast. In European times it became a route for gold and pastoral exploration and cattle were once driven through the gorge itself.

Beyond the swingbridge, the St James Walkway continues upriver.

3. Lewis Pass Lookout
Round trip: 30–45 minutes. **Moderate**

At the summit of SH7, just west of the Lewis Pass, a small layby above the road level can be seen as you flash past the trees. It is easy to miss on this busy road. (Note that this is 1km west of the St James Walkway carpark.)

From here a benched track runs up through the bush on a nature walk, which first heads west, granting walkers superb views of the steep Maruia River Gorge and highway below the track. There are several viewpoints along the trail, some with seats. Alpine flowers are also present here. Views out over the St James Walkway and Spenser Mountains are gained from the highpoint, before the trail descends more steeply down through forest and tussock to the road.

4. Lewis Pass Tops
Bush edge from road: 90 minutes. **Moderate**
Bush edge to ridge crest: 90 minutes.

At the upper limit of the Lewis Pass Lookout walk, a rough, through well-marked, track continues up the forested ridge, onto what is known as the Lewis Pass tops. (Note that a new track has been marked up the hillside, west of the St James Walkway carpark, to access the Lewis Pass tops.)

This moderately steep trail winds up through delightful silver and mountain beech forest, on a well-formed route with alternating flat and climbing sections. As you gain altitude you will notice a coolness in the forest interior

Lewis Pass tops

and the stunted nature of the beech trees now festooned with the epiphyte, Irish moss, which grows in profusion over the trunks and branches of these alpine forests.

The bush edge will be reached in only an hour and a half from the road, and here awaits a magnificent view of the mountains and valleys of the Lewis Pass National Reserve. Although even at the bush edge the view is spectacular, if the day is fine and there is not too much wind, you will want to climb higher up the ridge. The route onwards is again well defined and there are also poles (metal standards) to mark the way.

In early summer you will discover a multitude of alpine flowers growing among the golden tussocks that cover the ridge-top and basins. Another 1–2 hours will take you onto the ridge crest, at around 1500m, where a couple of minor peaks jut above the ridge. Now you are truly on the top of the Main Divide, though you have been following the Divide since you left the road. Here there is a panoramic vista of the region. Northeastwards in the deep

Brass Monkey Bivvy

glacial trench of the Maruia Valley runs the St James Walkway, above which stands a range of impressive summits. These are the highest peaks in the region: the Spenser Mountains. Gloriana and Faerie Queene are the highest visible, at 2218m and 2236m respectively. Directly across the valley to the north, through which the Lewis Pass highway is routed, stand the peaks of the Freyberg Range, and westwards a clutter of peaks and valleys is visible toward the distant sea.

Along the ridge, among undulating tops, can be found tiny alpine tarns residing in the sheltered hollows, and these provide a welcome stop for lunch. Further on, the easy ridge gives way to the craggy tops of Lucretia and Technical peaks, the latter summit presenting a challenge to the aspiring mountain climber. It is possible to traverse the entire Divide ridge westwards, passing a small alpine hut, known as the Brass Monkey Bivvy (2 bunks), and descend to the road again via the Rough Creek Track. However, this is an overnight excursion, requiring navigational skills on open tops and is not for the inexperienced.

On your return from the ridge back to the bush track, you will notice the thick, carpet-like appearance of the beech forest, which fills the gentle sweep of the Nina River to the south and ramps up the walls of the Libretto Range, which lies to the east of the Lewis Pass highway. It is this largely undisturbed forest that provides a home for the rich birdlife of the region, and you may well have been accompanied by tomtit, bellbird or fantail on your hike. If you are lucky you may also have been visited by that clown of the mountains, the kea, our alpine parrot.

Soon the swish of traffic can be heard, as you emerge again onto the shoulder of the highway.

VISUAL SYMPHONY ON LEWIS PASS TOPS

With the promise of a fine day and a good walk ahead, plus a new camera to try out, I head for one of my all-time favourite locations – the Lewis Pass tops. This area of the Main Divide lies to the southwest of the Lewis Pass, where SH7 cuts through the pass itself before climbing a shoulder to access the Maruia Valley. A track here climbs the hillside to the west, through silver and mountain beech, festooned with old man's beard moss on the higher slopes, to reach the bushline in a small hollow below the main ridge. Beyond here the route upwards is poled for some distance, until the crest is gained and the visual symphony of the Lewis Pass tops is revealed.

This is an unutterably beautiful landscape – subtle, nuanced and sublime. To walk it on a fine day, at any and all seasons, is pure pleasure and richly rewarding, especially for camera buffs. When snow is not lying thickly on the tops, there is the added dimension of a richly patterned landscape, thickly vegetated with luxuriant tussock, cushion plants, flowers (in spring) and carpet grasses.

This collage of plant life is set beside a random collection of glittering tarns punctuating the verses of the landscape, comprising hollows, ridges, valleys, peaks and sky. The tarns are exquisite and provide superb foregrounds for photos of the many-faceted peaks of the alps, from the tawny Freyberg Range to the north, all the way along to the spires and turrets of the Spenser Mountains, which march northeastwards into Nelson Lakes National Park. Between the Lewis tops and these ranges lies the shadowy defile of the Maruia Valley, 1000m below the ridge, through which the road passes to reach the Buller District.

Lewis Pass tops and Libretto Range

South of the tops is the more spacious and less oppressive Lewis Valley, its upper region formed by the hanging basins of Deer Valley beneath the citadel of Mt Technical – the highest summit south of the Spenser Mountains.

Roving the ridge-top I poke my lens into numerous watery hollows, trying to capture at least an excerpt of this poetic landform, so beautiful and yet so fleeting, highlighted for the moment by season and light, cloud and shade, only to vanish as the day advances.

A thread of a route, unmarked, continues along the crest all the way to Brass Monkey Bivvy, a full day's journey, and beyond into the Victoria Ranges. The ridge requires skill and care in places, but the reward for the challenge is ever present in the unfolding landscape. My time does not allow for such an extended trek on this occasion, and in any case I have come for another reason and I'm enjoying the different perspective I'm gaining up here on this manifestly beautiful mountaintop.

Descending the way I have come offers more opportunities to savour the nature of the terrain as it dips below my feet into a vale of shadows.

5. Waterfall Nature Walk
Waterfall from SH7: 10 minutes. **Easy**

Just 6.5km from Maruia Springs Hotel, on the left heading west, a small layby and sign indicate the Waterfall Nature Walk. (Be careful leaving cars unattended here.)

This short walk enters the mature red beech lowland forest and winds past many very large trees before crossing a small stream (bridged) and ascending a flight of steps and a well-benched track into a short gorge.

The sound of the waterfall grows louder as you sidle around the hillside and find your way barred by the 40m rock and bush face, down which tumbles a narrow ribbon of water. In high flows the ribbon turns to a torrent and you will be unable to approach too closely. The waterfall face towers above, requiring onlookers to crane their heads back to fully appreciate the height and angle. It is an impressive spectacle and a pleasant interlude on the drive through the Lewis Pass.

6. Mueller Tarn
2.5 hours from highway. **Hard**
2 hours return.

This is a short, very steep and strenuous tramp up to a hidden tarn, set on the bush edge above the Maruia River.

The track begins 500m west of the Maruia Springs Hotel, where cars can be left. A large wooden signpost indicates the track, which starts across the river on the true right bank. There is no bridge and you have to get your feet wet right at the start! Be wary here if the river is high; in normal conditions it should present no problem. Cross directly from the road sign to the far grass terrace just before the bush. Follow the bush edge back (east) toward the hotel for about 150m. You should easily pick up the large, faded, white-and-orange standard that marks the track entrance.

The track climbs for 600m directly up the bush face above you to the tarn, which lies on the bush edge at 1200m. It is very steep and will be slippery after rain. There is little respite until about 100m below the tarn, where the track sidles into a streambed, before climbing again to the lip of the basin. It is definitely not a track for the unfit; though short, it is very demanding.

The views and setting of the tarn are, however, ample reward for the grind up the hill, and a pleasant afternoon could be spent here exploring the tarn environs or even climbing onto the tussock shoulder to the northeast for a grand panorama of the Lewis Pass and mountains.

The tarn itself is a small green bowl of water, punctuated by large, grey, granite boulders, set amidst a sea of yellow tussocks on the southern aspect of the Freyberg Range, with deep green forest crowding in from the south.

There are some limited campsites here, notably right at the track entrance beside the lake.

Forest birds are common, as well as alpine flowers and plants.

7. Mt Mueller

Mt Mueller from SH7: 4–5 hours; return time to road: 3–4 hours. **Hard**
Mt Mueller to Mueller Tarn: 3 hours. **Hard**

It is a full day's walk to the summit of Mt Mueller (1630m), which grants extensive panoramas of the Lewis Pass region and Maruia Valley. The Maruia River must be crossed to reach the track, which is approximately 7km west of Maruia Springs Hotel.

The track is not signposted on the highway, so the best option for finding it is as follows. Locate the small grassy roadside layby on the northern side of SH7, which is about 200m east of the Bluffs picnic area. From here a rough gravel road will be seen extending out onto the riverbed. Follow this and cross the river to the far bank, directly opposite the layby. Walk upstream (east) for about 90m along the riverbed until you find the track, which is marked by red-and-white markers on a tree on a small bank above the river. Care must be exercised on this river-crossing as it may be impassable during and after wet weather. Also beware if setting off across the river in threatening weather; you may not be able to return.

Once safely over the river, the track is at first rather difficult to follow, though careful searching will pick it up. It crosses the bush terraces and then climbs very steeply to just above a bush saddle northwest of Mt Mueller. Gaining the ridge-top, the track continues climbing, though less steeply, until the tussock is reached. Here the first views of the Maruia Valley are gained as the ridge flattens off before the final steep pinch to the summit trig and a magnificent panorama of the Southern Alps and valleys.

There is no water on this route after leaving the stream, and the summit is a fine place for a well-deserved lunch stop. Far below, the highway can be seen snaking along the side of the Maruia Valley. Unfortunately Lake Daniells is not visible from here.

You can descend via the same route, or for experienced trampers there is a ridge-top route east along the range to above Mueller Tarn, from where the track descends to the hotel. This requires fine weather and careful navigation.

8. Rough Creek

Bushline from SH7: 2.5 hours; bush edge to ridgeline and viewpoint: 90 minutes. **Hard**

Ridge-top to Brass Monkey Bivvy: 3 hours. **Hard**

A very steep, though well-marked, trail leaves SH7 4.5 km west of Maruia Springs Hotel (signposted) and climbs through dense rainforest, crossing and re-crossing Rough Creek and side-streams higher up. It then ascends a bush spur into a large tussock basin, where alpine flowers grow in profusion.

This is an idyllic setting on a fine summer's day. Beyond the bushline, metal standards mark the route (no track) to the ridgeline. Beware if there is snow on the route above the bushline, especially if icy or slushy. Suitable equipment and experience are needed for these conditions.

The upper basin beyond the bush is a place to linger in summer amidst the flowers and seclusion of a high-alpine environment.

Those with the energy and time would be well advised to continue further, in summer, if the weather is clear, to the ridge crest, where there is an unsurpassed view out over Lake Cristobel and the peaks and valleys of the Upper Grey River and Maruia Valley. It is a stunning spectacle.

A poled route and track continues on from the ridge, down into the Upper Blue Grey River and Lake Cristobel Hut, but this is outside the limits of this guide.

Brass Monkey Bivvy and the Lewis Pass tops can be reached by heading east along the ridge over Point 1490m and into a saddle at Point 1390. From here sidle the north face of Peak 1674m at around the 1360m contour (the head of One Mile Creek) to reach the bivvy and saddle.

The Lewis Pass Tops Track can be reached in a day's walk by continuing on over Lucretia and The Apprentice to gain the easier, tarn-studded ridge.

9. The Sluice Box
5 minutes. **Easy**

This is accessed from the Marble Hill rest area and carpark for Lake Daniells (5km east of Springs Junction). The Lake Daniells Track is followed for 5 minutes through the forest to the large steel swingbridge that spans an attractive little gorge in the Maruia River: the Sluicebox. This narrow slot through which the river funnels has been gouged out of the marble by glacial action. It is an interesting subject for photography.

10. Lake Daniells
Hut from carpark: 3 hours. **Easy**
Lakehead from hut: 30–40 minutes.

This is an easy walk through mature red beech forest to an attractive bush-fringed lake and large hut. Lake Daniells is arguably the most popular tramp in the region, with good access, a large, comfortable hut, and a tranquil setting beside the lake.

The track begins at the Marble Hill picnic area, 18km west of Lewis Pass and 5km east of Springs Junction. Here cars can be left well off the road, though there have been some incidents of break-ins. From the carpark the trail enters the bush, crosses the river (Maruia) at the 'Sluicebox' and follows the Alfred River on a bush terrace above the river. Some signs of old gold workings (sluicing) can be sighted in the streambed along the way.

The track then enters an area of magnificent red beech forest on terraces above and away from the main river, though occasional glimpses of the stream (Frazer Stream) are seen below. This is a most attractive walk, through beautiful lowland forest, and often parakeet (kākāriki) and kākā are heard here.

The track climbs gently to the lake and skirts the shore in the forest, before ending at the small clearing that contains the Manson–Nicholls Memorial Hut (24 bunks). The hut is named in memory of three trampers who died in a mud-slide at an earlier hut, on the western shore of the lake.

The lake is beautifully set amidst high, steep, bush-covered hills and is a delightful place to spend the night and enjoy the peace of the bush. You can swim in the shallow water immediately in front of the hut, where a small jetty

Lake Daniells Hut

protrudes into the lake, however beware of submerged trees. There is better swimming along the lakeside and at the lakehead.

From the hut a track follows the eastern shore to the lakehead. There are excellent and much quieter campsites along the way, as well as at the head of the lake in the northwestern corner, where an old 4WD track disappears into the forest and later emerges at the extensive grassy clearing of Thompson's Flat and another, smaller hut.

The lake-shore track also provides opportunity to fish the lake, which is well stocked with trout.

The best views of the lake and environs are obtained from the northern end, opposite the hut.

SPECIAL ENDEAVOUR, LAKE DANIELLS

Lake Daniells, lying in the heart of the magnificent Lewis Pass region, is popular with tramping groups, especially families, so we chose it for a 3-day trip for our girls. Significantly, this is our middle daughter, Dominique's, first overnight tramp – she has Down syndrome, and walking over rough terrain presents many problems for her. Proprioception, that ability to judge distance and levels around us and particularly where to walk, is a major challenge. That and sensory integration dysfunction, a difficulty with filtering noise and activity, and her sometimes low muscle tone, has made tramping over long distances an impossibility for many years. But now, at 11 years, we think she is ready. So with some trepidation, we set out, our family of five (my wife, Christine, and I, Dominique, and her two sisters, Bernadette 9 and Anna-Marie 15), plus Brian Hall, an American friend who is keen to sample the New Zealand outdoors.

The trail to the lake is 8km long and climbs just over 100m, passing through heavy bush and alongside the picturesque Alfred River. Everyone is in high spirits, especially Dominique, who is wearing an ear-to-ear smile, excited that she is finally on her first big tramp with the family. She carries a small backpack, with wet weather gear and a few snacks, plus walking poles. We are not the only ones heading to the lake this day; several other groups are in front of us, and another family pulled into the carpark just as we left. They provide a great incentive for Dominique to get there first and claim some bunks in the Manson–Nicholls Memorial Hut.

After just 30 minutes' walking she states loudly, 'No more!' But that is not to be, and we continue to wend our way through the forested valley over the remainder of the day, taking four and half hours to reach the lake margins. At this point I go ahead to claim whatever bunks are left, otherwise we will have to camp.

On my return, about 20 minutes later, I am greeted with a sorry sight – Dominique dissolved in tears at trackside, with Christine and Brian attempting to cajole her along. Not only is the terrain here rough, boggy and slippery, but the other family whom we have been keeping

Dominique on the jetty at Lake Daniells

at bay have passed us, and Dominique sees little prospect of a comfy bunk. I tell her that I have already saved her a bed, but she's not convinced, her energy levels and confidence have run out, and there's nothing else for it but to hoist her onto my back and carry her the final 10 minutes to the hut.

There are quite a few already here, families, couples, fishermen and campers, and they add a social element to the trip and fun for the girls watching all the movements through the hut. That and exploring outside, swimming off the small jetty, and hiking to the lakehead fill the days with great variety. At night there's a bonfire beneath a night sky resplendent with stars, toasted marshmallows, and deep, peaceful sleeps. Dominique is very contented, chats with all comers and takes it all in her stride, as she does the walk out 2 days later, arriving at the road-end tired but full of her achievements. With an even bigger smile than before she gasps, 'I did it!'

Summit ridge of Travers Peak

Lewis Pass – Eastern Side

11. Rolleston Pack Track
90 minutes one way. **Easy**

This old trail formed in the 1800s can be walked in either direction, contouring around the hillside through the forest above the highway. This short track begins at the Lewis Pass carpark and heads south through beech forest above the highway to reach Goings Creek. It is described here from the south as it climbs from Goings Creek. Occasionally the road is glimpsed down a steep bank or shingle face, but mostly the track is well back on the terrace, where only the sighing of the wind and birdsong break the silence.

It is a wonderful, easy introduction to walking in the forest amongst some quite large beech trees and an array of forest ferns and mosses. If the day is sunny, sunlight filters down through the canopy, lighting the sometimes gloomy forest interior and exaggerating the greens, browns and greys of the understorey plants. This is the quiet hidden world of the forest, so take the time to observe carefully as the trail climbs gently to the pass summit.

Near the pass the track turns west and follows down a long corridor of trees to the open tussock and wetland of the pass proper. A toilet is located here, just inside the trees.

The track continues on for another 100m to the alpine tarn and carpark.

12. Travers Peak
Bushline from carpark: 2 hours; summit from bushline: 2 hours. **Moderate/ Hard**
About 1 hour less on the return.
Allow a full day for this climb, and carry water.

Travers Peak (1724m) is one of the best day trips in the pass region, albeit strenuous, as the track climbs a moderately steep ridge to the bushline from where an open tussock and rock ridge leads onto the summit. Care should be taken on this route in winter and in adverse weather.

The track leads up through silver and mountain beech, which progressively thins and becomes more stunted as the bush edge nears; this appears suddenly with little or no sub-alpine scrub zone. This means that you are quickly thrust into a very exposed alpine environment, which is much cooler and windier than the bush through which you have been climbing. Be prepared if you intend to continue to the summit of Travers Peak, which is approximately 1–2 hours from the bush edge. A warm hat, parka, gloves and extra clothing may be required, even on a sunny day. The upper part of the ridge onto the peak is steep and rocky and care is needed.

There is a wonderful 360-degree panorama of the entire Lewis Pass region and more-distant peaks from Travers Peak, which takes its name from W. L. Travers, an early explorer and surveyor in the region during the 1860s.

Extended ridge traverses are possible from the top for experienced trampers, particularly to Trovatore, about 1.7km to the north. This involves a very steep descent from Travers Peak and some sidling around rocky sections on the ridge to Trovatore. The southwest spur of Trovatore provides an excellent descent route back to the highway.

Foleys Creek Track and access to Travers Peak start opposite Deer Valley picnic area, where cars can be left out of sight.

13. Nina Valley
Nina Hut from SH7: 2.5 hours. **Moderate**

Described as the most beautiful valley in the Lewis Pass region, the Nina contains all of the most outstanding natural features of the region. Viewed from the highway as you drive west, the Nina presents a profile of densely forested valley floor and sides, with scattered grassy clearings and high open tussock ridges backed by rocky summits. It is a grand spectacle and completely devoid of any large gravel flats, as are found in many of the other valleys.

Vehicles can be left near the New Zealand Deer Stalkers' Association Palmer Lodge, from where the track starts across a swingbridge at the northern end of the flat beside the highway, where the road enters the bush. It is signposted, but the sign is not easy to see.

Beyond the footbridge, which is over the Lewis River, the track skirts the river and enters the forest, climbing onto a terrace that crosses through stunted lichen forest, emerging later beside the rushing blue water of the Nina.

It is a delightful walk upvalley, passing near some small rock gorges with beautiful blue pools. The track undulates beside and above the river,

Camp in Nina Valley

sometimes in dense forest on terraces where small streams bubble out through the bush, and other times on grassy flats where the spectacle of forest, river and mountain can be fully appreciated. An airy swingbridge is crossed at the top of the last gorge and then the south bank of the Nina is followed through forest and grassy flats before climbing to the terrace where the hut is sited (10 bunks).

There are various options for continuing further, either upvalley to the Nina Bivvy or onto Devilskin Saddle and Bivvy. Both of these are harder and rougher tracks.

14. Devilskin Saddle
Nina Hut to Devilskin Bivvy: 3 hours; saddle to Doubtful Hut: 3.5 hours.
Moderate
Doubtful Hut to SH7: 2 hours.

This is a moderate tramp through a spectacular tussock pass where the new Devilskin Bivvy (2 bunks) is located. The route is described from the Nina to the Doubtful, with the first section of the walk already described under 'Nina Valley'.

As you drive through the Lewis Pass toward the Nina you should carefully observe the level and condition of the Doubtful/Boyle confluence and whether it is crossable. The crossing is directly opposite the highway where it climbs onto a high shoulder above the river. If heavy rain is forecast, the trip should be postponed.

From the Nina Hut, the route up soon becomes very steep and quite rough in places, though the track is well formed, marked and easy to follow. It sidles around and up the hillside and descends into Blind Stream. Once in the stream, the track continues up the river right, crossing several small creeks and climbing higher through the valley. This section is quite spectacular, though rough going, finally culminating in a near-vertical ascent through the bush to bypass a large waterfall that cascades unseen through the forest below. Care is required here. Above the waterfall the valley falls back to an easy angle, which is followed through the last of the bush to the open upper valley and its magnificent red tussock fields beneath the Devils Rampart (1740m) and onto Devilskin Saddle (1234m). This route is poled. A good,

Tramper arriving at Devilskin Bivvy

though limited, view is obtained from the pass of the Nina and Doubtful valleys.

There is a long descent of Devilskin Stream, which lies to the south of the pass, first through tussock and then through dense forest. The track is picked up again at the bush edge and provides good travel as it sidles across the mountainside, staying well above the river.

Eventually, the track drops steeply down a broad spur and crosses a small terrace to Doubtful River, which is crossed to the river right bank and the somewhat dilapidated Doubtful Hut (3 bunks).

With the hard part of the trip now behind you, it is an easy wander down the Doubtful terraces, passing the small gorge, to the highway. There are some good views of the upper valley as you leave Doubtful Hut. The track stays on the river right all the way to the Boyle/Doubtful confluence, where a moderately deep crossing of the Boyle is made to SH7. This ford should be treated with care, especially if the river is high. An emergency (flood) route is possible by walking the Tui Track, part of Te Araroa Trail, southeast along the Boyle riverbank (marked by orange standards) to Windy Point swingbridge and back to SH7. This will add an extra 90 minutes.

Upper Doubtful Valley

Tarn on Sylvia Tops

15. Sylvia Tops
Devilskin Bivvy to SH7 via Sylvia Tops: 5–6 hours. **Hard**

For experienced trampers, and in good weather, the Sylvia Tops offers an exciting and rewarding high-level ridge trip to return to SH7 and the lower Nina Valley.

This unmarked route begins at Devilskin Saddle and heads east directly up the steep face onto the ridgeline just north of Point 1625m. This short, steep climb is the hardest part of the route. From here head north and east over Points 1484m, 1524m, 1561m and 1624m, sidling and climbing as necessary. There are some spectacular views along the ridgeline and several small tarns, with generally easy travel. However, this same ridge would prove difficult to navigate in cloud or mist.

From Point 1624m head down into some shallow basins and then to the bush edge at the top of the spur that heads directly east down to the lower Nina opposite SH7. Ford the Nina and Lewis rivers to reach Palmer Lodge. Other spurs, farther to the north, have many bluffs on the lower bush faces.

16. Magdalen Hut and Valley
Magdalen Hut from highway: 3 hours. **Easy**

This is a beautiful walk that begins at the southern entrance to the St James Walkway and traverses an easy, open river valley to a swingbridge and small, secluded hut. This trip forms part of the last day on the 5-day St James Walkway and begins at the Boyle Outdoor Eductaion Centre on SH7. Cars can be left here, either at the public carpark, or with the lodge warden for a small fee.

A marked track begins from the public carpark and heads into the Boyle River Gorge and later onto its swingbridge. This is a particularly attractive part of the walk, especially near the swingbridge, which spans the narrow rock-walled gorge. If the river is high it creates a dramatic spectacle as it surges through the canyon beneath the bridge. Beyond the swingbridge the track continues upvalley on the river right, passing first through forest and small flats, until the extensive grassy river flats of the mid-valley are reached.

Magdalen Hut

Faust tops and Magdalen Valley

Here the formed track continues in the forest, undulating along and just above the flats. This is tramping at its best: an easy track with wide, open views of valley, forest and mountain.

Unfortunately, the grassy flats no longer form part of the marked track: it has been realigned in the bush as part of an agreement between DOC and the runholder. However, it is still an easy and well-marked trail, which leads to the second swingbridge over the Boyle River, above its junction with the Magdalen Valley.

This bridge is set in another scenic part of the catchment and links two large grassy terraces. There is a trap here for the unwary! If you are planning to go to Magdalen Hut (6 bunks), turn sharp right when descending the far side (eastern) of the swingbridge. Do not follow the well-marked and signposted St James Walkway: this leads onto the Boyle Flats Hut, which is a further hour upvalley.

A rough little trail leads from the bridge down along the terrace and through some scattered forest to the Magdalen Hut, which should be reached in about 10–15 minutes. The hut is set in a large, grassy clearing, bordered by leafy beech trees, and provides a quiet, secluded setting away from the main track, with magnificent views of the Poplars Range, particularly in winter and spring.

If you are staying overnight, a good excursion is up to the Boyle Flats Hut (1 hour), through the beautiful Boyle Gorge. Trips into the upper Magdalen Valley require permission from Glenhope Station (phone 03 315 7697).

17. Mt Faust and Tarns
Boyle River carpark to bushline: 2 hours; tarns from bushline: 30–40 minutes. **Hard**
Mt Faust summit from tarns: 1 hour; return to Boyle River from summit: 3 hours. **Hard**
Boyle Flats Hut from Mt Faust: 3 hours. **Hard**

This is a steep climb onto easy tops, providing extensive views of the Lewis Pass region and access to a number of attractive tarns above the bushline.

The Mt Faust Track, which is not signposted, begins on the river right of the Boyle River highway bridge, which is opposite the Boyle River Outdoor Education Centre, at the southern entrance to the St James Walkway. Immediately after crossing the bridge, going north, an old road beyond a fenceline will be seen. Cross the fence and head up the road, which soon becomes a track, onto the terrace and into the bush. A signpost and track-marker indicate the Mt Faust loop track. Inside the bush, a rope and climbing skills course will be encountered; cut through this and head left toward the hillside, where a zigzag trail will be seen heading up onto a higher terrace where the track continues. This will take you to a small clearing on the shoulder of the hill, where some careful observation will be needed to relocate the onward track as it moves back into the bush and up a steep, broad spur toward the tops. Not far along here, there is another signpost; head right here.

The track is now easy to follow and steadily gains height toward the bushline, with the bush opening out as it does so. The forest gives way to tussock and open tops at a small step in the ridge, from where poles continue onto the tarn basin. This is an easy section of ridge but very exposed to the wind.

It climbs a small knoll, where the first of the tarns is encountered. There are more tarns a little higher to the northeast and these make superb lunch spots, or even high-level campsites in fine weather. From here extensive views of the Boyle and Magdalen valleys and Poplars Range are obtained.

If time and weather allow, it is worth continuing along the ridge above the tarns to the summit of Mt Faust (1711m). This is an easy climb along the gravel and rock ridge, however there is no marked route. There are outstanding views of the Main Divide as well as the Nina, Doubtful and upper Boyle valleys from here. On your return to the tarns, pick up the poles again and circle out to the southeast, where the poled and marked track descends a steep spur to the lower Boyle Valley and St James Walkway. The views of mountain and valley as you descend are spectacular. Note that this track becomes indistinct lower down and involves some steep bush-bashing and rough riverbed, and is longer. If you are not experienced with this type of travel, it is best to return via the main track.

Ridge-top Route to Boyle Flats
Keener walkers might consider traversing the sub-range northeast to the Boyle Flats Hut. This is a spectacular route over easy open tops.

In fine weather the ridge crest northeast of Mt Faust can be followed over Points 1712m, 1661m and 1627m to reach the bush edge on a moderately angled spur that drops to the Boyle Flats Hut. The ridge is easily followed, but a compass or GPS reading will help you to stay on the bush spur and arrive directly behind the hut. Follow the St James Walkway out from here.

RANGE ROVER – MT FAUST, LEWIS PASS

If there is one thing I especially enjoy when it comes to the outdoors, it's to walk the open tops – the ridges – where the world is at your feet and the sky runs forever. To be able to trek up through the cool dark of the early morning forest and then break out into the open tussock-lands, freshly sprinkled with dew, is sublime. The Mt Faust tops are one such place, located near the Lewis Pass National Reserve above the southern entrance to the St James Walkway – these tops just beg to be explored.

I've cruised these ridges several times over the years and always found them to be a spectacular environment of rolling, tussock-clad tops, majestic forests, high peaks and numerous black-eyed tarns pock-marking the landscape. The terrain is moderate, and with only one access track near the range's southwestern end there are ample opportunities to create your own route and stretch out the legs for a range rove.

The route up is moderately steep and begins on the river right of the Boyle River, opposite the outdoor lodge. It's only lightly marked, so make sure you have a good map and know what you are about.

Once at the bush edge there's around 3km of open going to climb to the summit of Faust. There are numerous tarns along this section and some shelter off to the south if the nor'wester is up. The tarns make great lunch spots where you can rest awhile on a grassy bench high above the Boyle River surveying the Lewis Pass region.

The summit of Faust will be reached at 1710m and from here you have a choice – drop back to the Boyle via the southeastern ridges (one of these has a rough track), or continue into the wild, blue yonder over the ridge and through a few dales to reach Boyle Flats Hut in the mid Boyle. This is my choice on the day I go. With a good day and a few tops tramping trips under your belt it should be a cinch, albeit a little strenuous, to get there and back in a day. Some might choose to camp out on the tops (there are lots of options here), or stay at the hut, or as I did, just go for it in a long day. I had my plan, had left written routes' notes at home, and there is no one else to consider now that I'm here. With a benign day and time up my sleeve it was the best choice – to complete the ridge, descend through open beech forest on deer trails and arrive right behind the hut before exiting the valley on the St James Walkway.

Such is the freedom to roam the ridges, it's a singular pleasure that pits mind, body and soul into the mix and brings great rewards – particularly at the end of the day when you can finally sit down! But enough of such talk, there's a day to capture, a route to follow, and an adventure to be had.

18. Hope Kiwi Lodge

Windy Point to Hope Kiwi Lodge: 4–5 hours. **Moderate**

This is a moderate walk into a major catchment with a large hut. The Hope Kiwi Lodge (24 bunks) is a popular destination for tramping clubs and youth groups. It is comfortable and well located on a flat beside the river and has good views of mountain and valley.

From the carpark at Windy Point the Hope Valley, which is part of the 4–5-day trek through Lake Sumner to Arthur's Pass, is followed. Beyond the bridge the poled track continues over farmland to the bush edge, where the track proper starts. This travels through dense beech forest over several terraces and small streams to the Halfway Hut (6 bunks). The track continues through the mixed red and mountain beech forest, passing a small bluff beside the river, and eventually exiting the bush onto the extensive upper flats of the Hope. This is a particularly attractive part of the walk, where the route leads across easy flats toward the junction of the Hope and Kiwi rivers. Here another swingbridge spans the short Hope Gorge, where the blue-grey river swirls against bluffs. Over the bridge the track crosses more flats and through a bush tongue to reach Hope Kiwi Lodge.

From the hut a side-trip can be taken to Lake Marion and Kiwi Saddle in the upper Kiwi Stream, about 90 minutes each way.

19. Upper Hope and Lake Man

Hope Kiwi Lodge to St Jacobs Hut: 1 hour. **Easy**
St Jacobs Hut to Lake Man Bivvy: 4–5 hours; bivvy to Lake Man: 1 hour. **Hard**
Bivvy to Doubtful River (Kedron confluence): 2–3 hours. **Moderate**
Kedron confluence to Doubtless Hut: 1 hour. **Easy**
Doubtful River/Kedron confluence to SH7: 3 hours. **Easy**

Continuing up the main Hope Valley from the Hope Gorge swingbridge, the route follows a 4WD track well into the Hope River headwaters, passing through the small gorge and into the forest, before emerging on a small flat beside the river where St Jacobs Hut (8 bunks) is located. It has a sense of remoteness, with fine views of mountain and forest.

From the hut the 4WD track passes through forest and out onto the St Jacobs Flat, where there are sweeping vistas of the Doubtful Range, Main

Divide and Upper Hope curving away to the west. It is one of the best and least obstructed views of peaks and valleys in the region and a magnificent high-country setting. From about mid-way along St Jacobs Flat, Pussy Stream valley will be seen entering from the north on the river left; this is the route to Lake Man Bivvy and Lake Man. Cross the Hope and head up Pussy Stream, where careful searching will locate the track in the bush edge on the river right. Mostly, though, the river-bed is followed along the bouldery bed of the stream to where a very steep and narrow spur enters the valley above the second major forks. The bottom edge of the spur has been badly eroded by floods, making it necessary to scramble up some loose rock and through forest to reach the track.

From here the track climbs the spur (this spur has Point 1005m marked) to the bush edge and a poled route in the tussock zone, which sidles well out to the

Tramper fording Pussy Stream

right (east) before dropping into the saddle on the Doubtful Range. This is an exhilarating trip over the open tops, with extensive views of the Lewis Pass mountains as you move around and through the pass.

From the saddle the route sidles again, this time to the left (west) and drops steeply down a scrubby face to Lake Man Bivvy (2 bunks). The bivvy has an attractive setting in the bush edge above the river and good views toward Mt Lakeman (1780m) at the head of the valley. Unfortunately, there is not much in the way of camping near the bivvy, perhaps one or two rather lumpy sites, so if the bivvy is full you would need to head some distance downvalley to locate more sites.

There is a spectacular side-trip to Lake Man, which lies in a small cirque beneath Mt Lakeman. This unmarked route scrambles up the streambed from the bivvy, thus avoiding scrub-bashing, and then threads through bluffs on the river left of the waterfall that drains the lake, which is the largest alpine lake in the region. The setting is magnificent, beneath the bluffs of Mt Lakeman. There is a campsite here, suitable in fine weather only.

From the bivvy the marked route descends down the valley, traversing out above the stream through sub-alpine forest. This section is initially quite easy travel, however the valley soon steepens and drops away in a series of cataracts in the Kedron River. The track sidles away from the stream and descends a bush spur to the Doubtful Valley. Notice the changing forest as you lose altitude. Soon the roar of the river is heard again as the track exits onto the riverside just upstream of the Kedron River. From here the track continues downstream on the river right to Doubtful Hut and on out to SH7. (See notes for 'Nina Valley' and 'Devilskin Saddle' for details.)

Note: Side-streams and the main valley stream can become impassable during and after heavy rain.

20. Doubtful Range and Mt Murray
Lake Man Bivvy to Mt Murray: 3 hours. **Hard**
Mt Murray to lower Doubtful River track: 2–3 hours. **Moderate**

A high route along the open tops east of Lake Man Bivvy is another option for returning to SH7. To reach these tops it is necessary to climb back to the broad saddle leading to Pussy Stream and then up the wide face onto the Doubtful Range and Point 1693m. Continue northeast along the range to Mt Murray (1611m). There are fantastic views over the Lewis Pass region en route. Descend from here to Point 1510m and then down farther to the bush-edge clearing at Point 1258m, where an old metal standard will be found. This is the start of the unmarked route down through steepening forest to the valley floor. The best place to exit the forest in the valley is the large grassy terrace above the Doubtful, just north of the stream draining the south side of Mt Murray. Avoid the cliffs on the terrace by descending to the Doubtful River to the west.

This is a route for experienced parties only.

HOPEFUL HEADING, LEWIS PASS

The rush of wind and flap of powerful wings at head-height gives me a start. Instinctively, I duck and raise my arms to fend off the unknown attacker, which soars away. Magpie! I'm tramping with companion Mike Latty in the upper Hope Valley of Lake Sumner Conservation Park, it's dusk and we are not far from St Jacobs Hut. The second attack by the piebald fiend is lower and closer. I shout at the gliding bird in anger and alarm and search quickly for a stick to raise above my head. It doesn't work, the avian attacks twice more, skimming in from behind, to spread more terror in this tramper's camp.

Fortunately, the hut is not far off and I am pleased to retreat there. Mike arrives later, having been buzzed several times, but by now I have the fire lit and thoughts quickly turn to dinner. Outside, cloud dogs the tops, and as dinner is served the first heavy drops of rain begin to fall on the hut roof.

By morning the rain has ceased, dense fog clings to the hillsides, ribbons of water streak the hillsides and the dull roar of the river dominates. Mike and I stride upvalley, bound for Pussy Stream, our route to Lake Man Bivvy, which entails a ford of the Hope. A sturdy link-up is required for the moderately deep crossing to Pussy Stream and its broad lower valley, but as we ascend the ravine through which the stream runs, its nature rapidly transforms; the pussy appears to have a lion's heart.

Major storm events have trashed the valley, felling trees into the stream, undermining banks and scouring the riverbed, making progress slow and cold.

Eventually, we locate the track to climb the narrow spur towards Kedron Saddle. Up here the weather looks promising, so we lunch on the track and later climb snow-covered tussock to reach the saddle, before dropping into the dramatic head of the Kedron River, a tributary of the Doubtful. Lake Man Bivvy sits on the bush edge in a remarkable setting beneath the ancient ice-steepened flanks of Mt Lakeman. Intermittent rain falls throughout the afternoon, with snow higher up, so we chat, read, sleep and sup on another brew as day ebbs into dusk.

Mike Latty above Kedron Saddle

Just a dusting of new snow covers the tops next morning, enough to scuff our boots through to bite into the firm snowpack below, ideal conditions for walking. Cutting back to the pass we gain the ridge, topping out at an unnamed high point of 1693m. Snowy summits march away towards the Boyle Valley, our destination, just five clicks of ridge travel before descending. We set down for lunch on Mt Murray, and pass over tussock and frozen tarns near ridge's end, before entering the bush to glide, in a measured fall, through trees, ferns and vines, to the valley floor.

Hastening on down the flats we reach the Boyle River. It's high. The ford is one I know, so we push on out, linked-up. Cold, waist-deep water swirls powerfully around us, but the bottom is flat and we manage the passage with relative ease, traffic flashing past on the highway, oblivious to our adventure among the valleys and ridges of the Hope.

21. Carlyle Stream
Highway to hut: 3 hours. **Moderate**

Carlyle Stream is mostly of interest for hunters, however its old-style hut and pleasant bush track also hold attraction for trampers, provided access can be secured. The only public access to the valley involves a ford of the Hope from the Lewis Pass highway to the mouth of Carlyle Stream. However, this is seldom possible, usually only in late autumn and winter, and so is not recommended. Alternatively, if permission from Glenhope Station can be obtained (phone 03 315 7697), then driving, or at least an easy walk in, is possible from west of the Hope River highway bridge, where a gravel road leads to a locked gate. Once through the gate, the road leads on for a couple of kilometres to the Carlyle Stream ford, where cars can be left on the flats.

Follow up a rough track on the river right of the Carlyle Stream gorge, climbing steeply onto a high terrace, which is then followed back to the bush edge and the track proper. The track is easily followed into the valley, first sidling and dropping through some deep ravines and fording side-streams, before flattening off as it enters the valley floor. This is a delightful walk beside the rushing stream and along small grassy flats. Later the track crosses the stream (normally an easy crossing) and re-enters the bush, before climbing to a large, grassy clearing in which Carlyle Hut (8 bunks) is set. The hut is an older-style Forest Service construction, and was probably an ex-roading hut. It has a fire and is a comfortable base from which to explore the untracked upper valley.

22. St James Walkway
Lewis Pass to Cannibal Gorge Hut: 3 hours. **Moderate for entire track**
Cannibal Gorge Hut to Ada Pass Hut: 2 hours; Ada Pass Hut to Christopher hut: 4 hours.
Christopher Hut to Anne Hut: 5 hours; Anne Hut to Boyle Flats Hut: 5–6 hours.
Boyle Flats Hut to SH7: 3–4 hours.

The St James Walkway was constructed as the first long-distance walkway in the South Island, and was officially opened in 1981. The walkway is approximately 65km long and can be started from either end: Lewis Pass or Boyle Lodge. The former is more popular as it involves less climbing and a greater

Bernadette Barrett crossing the Boyle River

appreciation of the dramatic views of the Southern Alps, particularly on the early part of the route. The total average time for covering the distance is about 24 hours, so that a fit, experienced tramper might complete the trip in only 2–3 days. In fact, the walkway has been run in a day of 10 hours! However, as the walkway is well supplied with good, comfortable huts, set in some beautiful locations, and the nature of the changing scenery en route is something to be savoured and enjoyed, a more reasonable timeframe is 5 days (4 nights). I have walked the route several times, both as a trip in itself and as an access route to other, more distant mountain areas, and it has become a favourite tramp.

Beginning at Lewis Pass, the track descends to the Maruia swingbridge and then climbs steadily beside the rushing torrent of the Maruia en route to Ada Pass. This section of the walk is my favourite, especially from the Cannibal Gorge Hut onwards. Here the valley changes into a more alpine setting, with open, grassy flats beneath a spectacular mountain backdrop of craggy,

Crossing a footbridge in the Boyle River Gorge

snow-covered summits and high basins. This section can be covered in 2 short days of approximately 3 hours each, overnighting at the large Cannibal Gorge Hut (20 bunks), or a longer day of 5–6 hours if going all the way to Ada Pass Hut (14 bunks). The walkway climbs steadily over this distance, though it is not steep.

Onwards from the pass the terrain changes abruptly, as the bush falls back on the sides of the open expanses of the upper Ada Valley, below the towering summits of Gloriana and Faerie Queene. (Both of these peaks can be climbed off the walkway; they are not technical summits but require experience with route-finding and weather/snow conditions.) Here there is ample reason to pause and consider the spectacle that surrounds you as the trail descends gently to Christopher Hut (14 bunks) and the valley changes again in nature as it merges into the rounded lower hills of the mid-Waiau. This is cattle and horse country, and you will pass numerous small herds throughout the day. Christopher Hut has probably the best setting of any on the walkway, and a feeling of space and isolation that encourages you to linger. A longer day takes you out down the open expanse of the Ada Valley to the Waiau River. The track then climbs gently back into the Henry Valley, where it forks with the Anne. On a terrace above the river, beneath the Opera Range, sits the new Anne Hut (20 bunks).

The remaining 2 days take you over the Anne Saddle, a short, sharp climb out of the Anne River, and a long descent into the Boyle Valley, to the very comfortable Boyle Flats Hut (12 bunks). This section of the walkway again retains your interest in this relatively drier region away from the Main Divide. The peaks are lower and of an easier nature, but the pervading sense of beauty remains, as you pass through endless beech glades and open river flats.

The final day's route re-crosses the Boyle River on a swingbridge and sidles and descends through the short Boyle Gorge to its junction with the Magdalen Valley and Magdalen Hut (5 bunks).

The track follows the bush/river fringe above the river all the way to the final swingbridge set in the lower Boyle Gorge, before climbing around the gorge and out to the road-end at the Boyle Outdoor Education Centre on SH7.

Note: The St James Walkway should not be attempted by the inexperienced during winter or early spring as avalanches are a major hazard at this time.

Hanmer Springs Region

The Hanmer Springs region has long been a popular destination for Cantabrians, who find the hot pools, general ambiance of the town and numerous short walks an agreeable distraction from their busy lives in the city. While there are a huge number of short walks available on the town boundary, I have only included here the large foothill summits immediately north and west of Hanmer Springs.

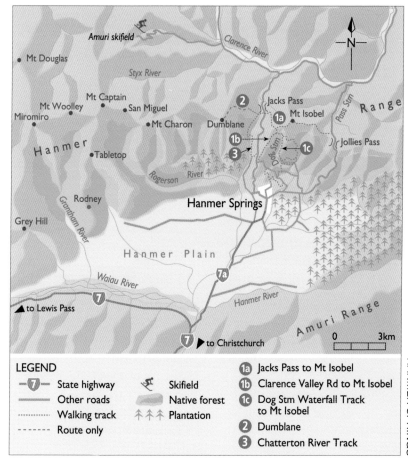

LEGEND

-7- State highway
——— Other roads
············ Walking track
- - - - - Route only

Skifield
Native forest
Plantation

1a Jacks Pass to Mt Isobel
1b Clarence Valley Rd to Mt Isobel
1c Dog Stm Waterfall Track to Mt Isobel
2 Dumblane
3 Chatterton River Track

Mt Isobel summit in winter

1. Mt Isobel

Jacks Pass to summit: 2 hours. **Moderate**
Clarence Valley road to summit: 3 hours. **Moderate**
Dog Stream Waterfall Track to summit: 3.5 hours. **Moderate/Hard**

Mt Isobel (1319m) rises directly behind the township and is possibly the most-climbed mountain in Canterbury, maybe even in the South Island. It is accessible via one of three tracks to the summit, with the easiest and shortest (but most exposed) being along its northern and western ridges from Jacks Pass summit. This marked track has spectacular views throughout its length and is recommended if time is short and the weather is fine. It can also be extended by traversing the mountain to Jollies Pass to the east, but this will necessitate additional transport arrangements to return to your car. The summit view covers the Hanmer Plain, Waiau Valley, parts of the distant Lewis Pass region, and north into the St James Conservation Area, and is especially attractive in early winter, with a dusting of new snow.

Hanmer Plain from Mt Charon

The best return option is to descend via the southern faces from Point 1145m, to the Clarence Valley road carpark.

An alternative, though longer and steeper, route to the summit is via the Dog Stream Waterfall Track, which is accessed from the forestry plantation roads east of Hanmer off the Jollies Pass Road. These roads grant access to the Jollies Saddle tracks, which connect to the Dog Stream Waterfall Track.

All tracks are well marked and signposted.

2. Dumblane
Jacks Pass to summit: 1.5 hours. **Moderate**

West of Jacks Pass rises the great bare mound of Dumblane (1303m), another summit on the Hanmer Range. It also offers excellent views over the Hanmer region, especially into the upper Clarence Valley – a view that is somewhat blocked by Mt Isobel. The route begins along a 4WD trail on the crest of the pass, later turning into a good ground trail that is marked by cairns and further on by poles. It climbs to Point 1057m and then more steeply to the ridge crest north of Dumblane. From here turn south (left) and on along to the summit, which is about 1km away over the broad ridge. The view is outstanding. It is possible to continue along the Hanmer Range all the way to Miromiro (1875m), the highest summit on the range, via several sub-summits – Mt Charon, San Miguel, Mt Captain and Mt Woolley. This is a long journey, however, requiring good fitness, fine weather, and at least one high camp. Mt Charon is possible in a day from Jacks Pass. Do not descend into Styx River as much of the riverbed is choked with broom.

3. Chatterton River Track
Jacks Pass to Hanmer: 1.5 hours. **Easy**

This track descends from Jacks Saddle into the Chatterton River and follows it out to Chatterton Road and the AA camp. Alternatively, it can be followed across to the line of the original Jacks Pass Road and down this to the new road or the camp.

Trip Planner

Rangitata Region

Easy Walks
Orari Gorge

Moderate Walks
Peel Forest Walks
Deer Spur and Little Mt Peel
Access Easements off Rangitata Gorge Road (Mackenzie Stream, Lynn Stream, Raules Gully, Coal Hill)
Forest Creek
Bush Stream to Crooked Spur Hut
Havelock River
Te Araroa Trail
Macaulay Valley

Hard and Hard+ Walks
Middle and Big Mt Peel
The Thumbs
Mt Alma
Range Crossings (Alma Col, Tom Thumb Col, Cassandra Col)
Mt Tripp from Hinds Gorge Access Easement

Ashburton Lakes and Rakaia Valley

Easy Walks
Woolshed Creek Short Walks
Sharplin Falls
Lake Camp to Lake Emma
Mt Sunday
Lake Heron Walks
Mt Hutt Forest and Awa Awa Rata Reserve
Rakaia Gorge Walkway
Dry Acheron Stream Access to Big Ben

Moderate Walks
Mt Somers Walkway
Mt Somers Ascent
Mt Alford Scenic Reserve

Mt Barossa
Mt Guy and Lake Clearwater Tracks
Potts River and Hut
Te Araroa Trail
Lawrence and Clyde Valleys
Cameron Valley, Arrowsmith Range
South Branch Ashburton
Pudding Hill Stream Track and Scott's Saddle to Alder Track
Redcliffe Saddle and Tribb Hut
Turtons Saddle
Double Hill
Banfield Hut, Rakaia River
Peak Hill
Avoca and Harper Valleys
Upper Wilberforce Valley
Flagpole

Hard and Hard+ Walks
South Face Route (Mt Somers)
Mt Winterslow
Mt Harper, Erewhon
Mt Potts, Erewhon
Mt Taylor
Mt Catherine, Lake Heron Basin
Pudding Hill Range
Mt Hutt Summit
Steepface Hill
Palmer Range and Godley Peak
Mt Ida
Mt Oakden
The Spurs
Gargarus

Waimakariri Plains Region

Easy Walks
Kowai Hut
Broken River
Ryde Falls
Wharfedale Track
Mt Thomas Loop Tracks
Glentui Loop Tracks
Lake Janet Picnic Area and Track
Grey River Nature Trail

Moderate Walks
13 Mile Bush and Hut
Coach Stream and Trig M
Ben More
Red Hill
Mt Lyndon
Mt Oxford
Black Hill Hut and Salmon Creek
Ashley Gorge Waterfall Track
Bob's Bivvy
Wooded Gully Track and Mt Thomas
Pinchgut Hut
The Richardson and Blowhard Tracks
Mt Grey Summit and Tracks
Scout Road Track
Mt Karetu
Townshend River

Hard and Hard+ Walks
The Gap
Mt Torlesse and Range
Foggy Peak to Castle Hill Peak
Whistler River and Chest Peak

Waimakariri Basin and Arthur's Pass National Park

Easy Walks
Craigieburn Valley Walking Track
Lyndon Saddle to Helicopter Hill
Jacks Pass to Dracophyllum Flat
Hut Creek Track
Castle Hill Nature and Scenic Reserve
Devil's Punchbowl Falls and Bridal Veil Falls
Bealey Chasm and Valley
Dobson Nature Walk and Lake Misery Track

Moderate Walks
Lyndon Saddle–Camp Saddle Traverse
Cass to Lagoon Saddle Circuit
Mt Bruce
Avoca River
Cave Stream Scenic Reserve
Temple Basin Skifield

Mingha and Edwards Valleys
Mingha River and Hut
Edwards Valley
Upper Waimakariri Valley and Huts
Bealey Spur and Hut
Hawdon Valley
East Hawdon
Woolshed Hill
Sudden Valley
Casey–Binser and Lake Minchin
Lower Poulter
Deception River
Lake Kaurapataka and Upper Taramakau River
Taipo Valley

Hard and Hard+ Walks
Half Moon Saddle
Mt Enys, Craigieburn Range
Purple Hill and Lake Pearson
Otira Valley Track and Mt Rolleston
Avalanche Peak Tracks
Avalanche Peak to Crow River
Mt Bealey
Kelly Range
Scottys Bivvy and Tara Tama
Mt Bealey
Con's Track to Mt Cassidy
Mt Aicken
Rome Ridge
Lake Mavis and Taruahuna Pass
Dome Peak
High Crossings from Sudden Valley
The Pyramid
Upper Poulter and Poulter Bivvy
Mt Binser
Mt Barron
Goat Hill
Rolleston River and Waimakariri Col
Carroll Hut and Kellys Creek
Pfeifer Bivvy Route

Lewis Pass Region

Easy Walks
Tarn Nature Walk
Waterfall Nature Walk
The Sluice Box
Lake Daniells
Rolleston Pack Track
Magdalen Hut and Valley
Chatterton River Track

Moderate Walks
Cannibal Gorge
Lewis Pass Lookout
Lewis Pass Tops
Travers Peak
Nina Valley
Devilskin Saddle
Hope Kiwi Lodge
Upper Hope and Lake Man
Carlyle Stream
St James Walkway
Mt Isobel
Dumblane

Hard and Hard+ Walks
Mueller Tarn
Mt Mueller
Rough Creek
Sylvia Tops
Mt Faust and Tarns
Doubtful Range and Mt Murray

Further Reading

The author wishes to acknowledge the use of the following books and publications for information on history, geography, flora and fauna, weather and access details. These are also recommended for further reading.

Brabyn, S. (1995) *Tramping in the South Island: Nelson Lakes to Arthur's Pass.* Brabyn Publishing

Brabyn, S. (2004) *Arthur's Pass to Mount Cook: A Tramping Guide.* Brabyn Publishing

Cook, Y. & Spearpoint, G. (2010) *The Canterbury Westland Alps.* New Zealand Alpine Club

Dennis, A. (1986) *The Story of Arthur's Pass National Park.* Department of Lands and Survey

Malcolm, B. & Malcolm, N. (1998) *New Zealand's Alpine Plants Inside and Out.* Craig Potton Publishing

Various DOC information leaflets are available from local DOC area offices and the Information Centre in the Botanical Gardens, Hagley Park. They include:

Hakatere Conservation Park
St James Conservation Area
Lake Sumner & Lewis Pass
Te Kahui Kaupeka Conservation Park
Korowai/Torlesse Tussocklands Park 2001 DOC
Lake Sumner Forest Park Infomap

Further information can be found at the following websites:
www.doc.govt.nz
www.remotehuts.co.nz

About the Author

Pat is a keen outdoorsman, with 40 years' experience, who began his forays into the hills in the Tararuas, north of Wellington. He has competed in three Coast to Coast events, as well as the inaugural Southern Traverse multi-sport event, together with numerous triathlons and mountain runs. For 10 years he has guided for his own adventure-travel company, Karavan Adventure Treks.

Pat has been a regular contributor to *NZ Wilderness* magazine since 1993, as well as *The Press* (Christchurch), *The Dominion Post*, and several other periodicals. He is the author of six other titles, most of which are available from his website: www.patbarrettimages.co.nz.

Pat lives in Christchurch with his wife Christine and their three children, Anna-Marie, Dominique and Bernadette, who get regular trips to the outdoors.

Other Titles by Pat Barrett

Wilderness Walks: Lewis Pass (2002) Lifestyle Publishing
Canterbury Foothills & Forests (2002) Shoal Bay Press
True South: Tramping Experiences of the South Island Hinterland (2003) Reed
Westland Foothills & Forests (2004) Shoal Bay Press
Nelson/Marlborough Foothills & Coastal Regions (2007) Longacre Press
Southern Lakes Tracks & Trails (2012) Otago University Press

Author's website:
www.patbarrettimages.co.nz

Bless the Lord, mountains and hills, praise and glorify Him forever!
Daniel 3:75

Climber approaches low peak of Steepface Hill, Rakaia Valley